THE ASSAULT ON AMERICAN LABOR LAW

THE
ASSAULT
ON AMERICAN
LABOR LAW

UNIONS BEFORE
THE SUPREME COURT,
1965–2025

ROGER C. HARTLEY

UNIVERSITY OF MASSACHUSETTS PRESS

Amherst and Boston

ISBN 978-1-62534-915-6 (paper); 916-3 (hardcover)

Designed by Deste Relyea
Set in Adobe Garamond Pro and Scala Sans Pro
Printed and bound by Books International, Inc.

Cover design by adam b. bohannon

Library of Congress Cataloging-in-Publication Data
Names: Hartley, Roger C., author.
Title: The assault on American labor law : unions before the Supreme Court,
1965-2025 / Roger C. Hartley.
Description: Amherst : University of Massachusetts Press, 2026. | Includes
bibliographical references and index. |
Identifiers: LCCN 2025012377 (print) | LCCN 2025012378 (ebook) | ISBN
9781625349156 (paperback) | ISBN 9781625349163 (hardcover) | ISBN
9781685751968 (ebook) | ISBN 9781685751975 (epub)
Subjects: LCSH: Labor unions—Law and legislation—United States—History.
| Collective bargaining—Law and legislation—United States—History. |
Labor laws and legislation—United States—History. | United States.
National Labor Relations Act. | Industrial relations.
Classification: LCC KF3389 .H37 2026 (print) | LCC KF3389 (ebook) | DDC
344.7301/88—dc23/eng/20250320
LC record available at https://lccn.loc.gov/2025012377
LC ebook record available at https://lccn.loc.gov/2025012378

British Library Cataloguing-in-Publication Data
A catalog record for this book is available from the British Library.

The authorized representative in the EU for product safety and compliance is
Mare-Nostrum Group.
Email: gpsr@mare-nostrum.co.uk
Physical address: Mare-Nostrum Group B.V., Mauritskade 21D,
1091 GC Amsterdam, The Netherlands

To my father, Thomas Hartley

CONTENTS

PREFACE

I graduated from Cornell University's New York State School of Industrial and Labor Relations (the ILR School) in 1965. It was a momentous year. The Vietnam War was escalating, the United States had invaded and occupied the Dominican Republic, the space race was in full swing, the Rolling Stones' world tour was underway, and the bravery of those marching to Selma, Alabama, had come to the attention of a broad audience and was leading to the passage of the Voting Rights Act. Malcolm X was assassinated in 1965; the Los Angeles neighborhood of Watts erupted in race riots; Great Britain's wartime prime minister Winston Churchill died; and Lew Alcindor (later known as Kareem Abdul-Jabbar) was a seventeen-year-old, seven-foot-one-inch New York City basketball wonder who seemed to have a promising future in the NBA. Oh, yes, and the twist turned out to be a dance.[1]

Moreover, in 1965, nearly one-third of American workers belonged to a union. That was close to the 1954 peak union density rate of almost 35 percent. Fifteen states had union density rates of 35 percent or higher in 1965. Today, no state other than Alaska, Hawaii, and New York has a union density even as high as 20 percent. Overall, private sector union density currently hovers at about 6 percent.[2] To be clear, unions' impact is greater than their membership numbers suggest because many hundreds of thousands of American workers who are not union members are covered by collective bargaining agreements. This is because unions must represent all bargaining unit members equally, union members or not. But the union membership decline in the United States since 1954, especially since 1965, is stunning.

As union density rates fell during the sixty years after 1965, the U.S. economy experienced a yawning wealth gap that continues to pose serious economic and political challenges. A well-documented consensus among economists substantiates the following:

- From the mid-1940s until the early 1970s, the substantial economic growth in the American economy was broadly shared, benefiting Americans at roughly the same rate. Income disparities continued but remained relatively constant during this period.[3]

- As economic growth slowed beginning in the 1970s, the income gap widened, and today income disparities are the highest they've been in one hundred years. Not since the 1920s has the share of income and wealth going to the top 1 percent been so great. At the dawn of the current decade, "nearly one-third of workers earn[ed] less than twelve dollars an hour, often with unpredictable schedules and poor working conditions."[4]

- The share of income going to the top earners has swelled. The wealthiest among us (the top 1 percent) net roughly 25 percent of our national income and possess 40 percent of the nation's wealth.[5] Ten percent of families hold almost three quarters (74 percent) of all of the household wealth in America.[6] This change has been described as "the birth of a new economic divide."[7]

- Conditions worsened as American workers' real wages stagnated. Those at the bottom increasingly are locked in; and especially since the Covid pandemic, those in the middle have lost ground.[8] Only beginning in 2023 did wages begin (marginally) to outpace the rate of inflation. "Nonetheless, a gap between household buying power and inflation remains. At its current pace, workers' wages aren't set to recover their loss of total purchasing power [which began in 2021] until at some point in the fourth quarter of 2024."[9]

- Political equality also is threatened as a small number of large corporations and wealthy political donors wield disproportionate influence over many facets of governance.[10]

- In his best-selling *Who Stole the American Dream?* Hedrick Smith concluded that "getting nowhere and slipping backward . . . has provoked popular discontent[, with] two-thirds of Americans . . . say[ing] they see 'strong' conflicts between rich and poor, and they see economics [as] more divisive than race, age, or ethnic grouping."[11]

There are multiple causes for the continuing wage and wealth gap, but one statistic stands out: "U.S. income inequality has varied inversely with union density over the past hundred years."[12] The three most respected recent studies to date agree that, since the early 1980s, especially among males, as union membership declines, income inequality rises proportionately.[13]

Many are surprised to learn that there is a substantial unsatisfied desire for union representation among nonunion workers—what industrial sociologists refer to as the "representation gap."[14] Several studies have concluded that nearly 50 percent (or more) of nonunion workers surveyed state that they would vote for a union if given the opportunity.[15] And, consistently, a supermajority of workers currently represented by unions (83 percent) state that they would vote for a union again.[16]

And there is more. Now, as nonunion workers grapple with an unmet desire in gaining a workplace voice through unionization, public approval of unions is soaring and is at nearly an all-time high. Gallup polling shows that 70 percent of Americans now approve of labor unions. These current approval levels are up from 64 percent before the pandemic, marking the fifth straight year this reading has exceeded its long-term average of 62 percent.[17] This same polling shows a steep decline in those who disapprove of unions, a nearly 21-percent decline in the disapproval rate in just one year and the lowest disapproval rate in fifty years. In addition, this Gallup polling documents an unprecedented uptick since the prior measure, in 2018, in perceptions that unions in the country will become stronger than they are today. A third of Americans (34 percent) believe this today, compared with 19 percent in 2018 and no more than 25 percent at any time since 1999, when this question was first asked.

When I discuss the current state of union density with friends and colleagues, even those who are well educated and generally politically progressive, their initial response is often "But what about globalization, technological developments, and changes in the labor market? Don't these factors account for the precipitous decline in unionization and workers' increasingly precarious economic condition?" In previous work, I rigorously examined that question. The answer is yes, partly, but not mostly.[18] Structural economic forces are contributing factors in the decline in union density. These forces include deindustrialization, increasingly global and competitive product markets, technological change such as flexible specialization production methods, and the advent of computerized technologies that place a premium on higher-skilled, more educated workers and a lower demand for less-skilled, undereducated workers.[19] Unions' own complacency and lack of commitment to organizing for several crucial decades also should not be overlooked.[20] But as I have previously explained:

> The crisis in union representation is primarily the result of corporate America's self-conscious determination to free itself of the constraints on managerial discretion imposed by collective

bargaining. Corporate managers developed the view that labor unions and collective bargaining are incompatible with the new job structures that increasingly began to dominate American business at the dawn of the digital era, sometime after the mid-1980s. In other words, technology and globalization did not themselves account for the decline in collective bargaining, but they caused profits to be squeezed, thereby motivating employers to . . . double-down on their opposition to unions. And labor relations law provided no real hindrance to this employer counter-attack on unionism.[21]

I and others have taken a stand on the reforms that are needed to restore the efficacy of our core labor relations statute, the National Labor Relations Act (NLRA), if we are to begin to level the playing field and redress workers' unmet desire for unionization.[22] Absent from the academic literature is how all of this happened: how the current crisis in U.S. labor relations law evolved. Specifically, we need a thoroughgoing investigation of how the Supreme Court's decisions interpreting the NLRA during the post–World War II decades of the late twentieth- and early twenty-first centuries led to today's situation, when the NLRA seldom poses any real hindrance to employers who are determined to remain union-free or rid themselves of their existing unions in the private sector.[23]

This book fills that gap. In many of the approximately one hundred Supreme Court decisions that have interpreted the NLRA during the past sixty years (1965–2025), the Court often has operated more like a legislative than a judicial body. Many of these decisions effectively amended the NLRA by abandoning its collectivist policy underpinnings in favor of interests of individuals and claims by business for greater managerial autonomy and protection of property rights. The NLRA hoped for more than simply improving returns to labor in economic bargaining. It also envisioned some democratic restructuring of the organization of work. These aspirations have been thwarted. Many of the one hundred decisions discussed in this book create staggering obstacles to American workers' ability to obtain the collective workplace representation that so many millions strongly desire. These judicial decisions are complicit in forcing workers to face globalization, deindustrialization, and technological change individually, without the negotiating leverage provided by union representation.

Any subject of study needs justification: its advocates must explain why it is worth attention. So why do the Supreme Court's labor law decisions rendered over the sixty-year period discussed in this book warrant attention? They are, after all, history. These holdings will not be reversed, no matter how eloquently one might demonstrate how any of them (or even many of them) rest on questionable legislative history and may have subverted our national labor policy first stated in section 1 of the 1935 NLRA and reaffirmed in the 1947 Taft-Hartley amendments: that is, "it is hereby declared to be the policy of the United States [of] encouraging the practice and procedure of collective bargaining and . . . protecting the exercise by workers of full freedom of association, self-organization, and designation of representatives of their own choosing, for the purpose of negotiating the terms and conditions of their employment or other mutual aid or protection."[24]

I argue that these Supreme Court labor law decisions are worth our attention for several reasons. First, studying the history of the Court's decisions offers the best evidence for understanding *how the Court functions.* By now we widely understand that legal problems (including the labor movement's legal problems) "are not simply legal in nature; they are inseparable from the economic and political matrix in which they . . . unfold[ed]." Because legal rules and decisions "take their meanings from the social contexts in which they are deeply embedded, . . . moral and political value judgments . . . are always a part of legal analysis."[25] Illuminating the political and value judgments animating the Court's post-1965 labor law decisions better equips us to maintain vigilance in an effort to keep the Court within accountable boundaries as an institution operating in a democratic system of government. In this sense, examining the Court's labor cases over the past sixty years fits well into a project that is currently underway, one that investigates whether there are such severe pathologies in the judicial process that there is a need for reforms that would limit the Supreme Court's power and increase congressional and presidential engagement in judicial oversight.[26] For example, the general counsel to the AFL-CIO has testified that "the labor movement—its leaders, its lawyers, and its members—no longer believe labor organizations and working people seeking to act together to improve their wages, hours and working conditions can obtain a fair hearing before the Court."[27] Testifying before the Presidential Commission on the Supreme Court, labor leaders have expressed concerns about ethics of Supreme Court justices, criticized the justices' entanglement with corporate interests, and urged court reform.[28] As Professor Kate Andrias has stated, "Ultimately, courts are political institutions embedded in the broader political economy. Their promise depends on the institutional structures that create them and the character of the judges who comprise them."[29] A careful analysis of the last sixty years of the Court's labor jurisprudence provides valuable insight into the institutional structures of the Court and the character of the justices who have decided cases that have had such a monumental impact in determining whether we have kept our pledge, made in 1935, to secure industrial democracy for American workers.

Second, carefully evaluating the Supreme Court's post-1965 labor law decisions is warranted to uncover and clarify the *interpretive mechanisms* deployed by Supreme Court majorities in these cases. My claim in this book is that, on the whole, the Court's interpretations of the NLRA over the past half-century or so have eroded the Act's commitment to protecting workers' collective rights. Suggesting that some of the Court's NLRA jurisprudence may have subverted the will of Congress over the course of six decades is serious business. Such an indictment should not be undertaken lightly. I am mindful that, as Learned Hand admonished, the judicial branch of government is "essential to prevent the defeat of the venture at hand."[30] A judicial system that earns the trust of the American people is essential for democracy to prosper. All of us, particularly we who are lawyers and thus officers of the Court, have the right to critically evaluate the work of the Court, but we are concomitantly dutybound to provide an authoritative account of its work that is grounded in fact. Illuminating the interpretive mechanisms that Supreme Court majorities relied on in its post-1965 labor cases helps to provide that factually grounded account.

Finally, a close examination of the Court's past sixty years of labor-and-management-relations rulings can *uncover otherwise invisible interpretive mistakes*, patterns of faulty normative assumptions, and sets of value preferences that have incrementally eroded the NLRA's power to protect workers' ability to act in an autonomous, collective fashion. This clarification can inform the challenges that will need to be overcome by those who strive to provide workers with a meaningful voice at their places of work. In this regard, Nelson Lichtenstein is onto something important. He argues that if the "dignity and value of work are to return to the top of the national agenda," we need to focus on a compelling set of ideas and values that "give labor's cause power and legitimacy."[31] One step in rekindling a national ideology that can sustain worker empowerment and legitimacy is exposing the values and assumptions in the Court's labor decisions that, on the whole, have undermined the institutionalization of collective employee voice and favored a sympathetic accommodation of greater managerial prerogatives and control.[32] By exposing the underlying but often unarticulated ideological tenets that have hijacked the Court labor cases for the past sixty years, we position ourselves to more intelligently propose and justify a counter-ideology that legitimizes worker empowerment.

One important point: as the following pages will show, the burden of my argument is not that *all* of the Court's post-1965 labor law decisions contravened congressional policy favoring workers' collective rights. Some have been faithful to the NLRA's commitment to encourage the practice and procedure of collective bargaining. The Court deserves commendation for decisions that are faithful to the promise of the NLRA, and these are clearly noted in the book. Moreover, subsequent labor laws, especially the 1947 Taft-Hartley amendments, strengthened the hand of management by restricting union activity. These amendments sometimes required the Court to issue rulings harmful to workers' freedom of collective action. Congress, not the Court, must answer for them.

My claim here is modest: that not always, but far too often, the Court has rejected worker representatives' compelling arguments in support of worker-friendly interpretations of the NLRA, arguments that were grounded in persuasive NLRA legislative history, that were in accord with the considered views of the National Labor Relations Board, and that reflected an understanding of congressional intent that other Supreme Court justices adopted. It is in these mostly five-to-four and six-to-three split decisions that the Court's majority incrementally dismantled much of the NLRA's collectivist foundations through reliance on strained and often clumsy renditions of NLRA legislative history and congressional intent. Adopting a truncated view of employee freedom of collective action, these decisions adopt an ideology that prioritizes the interests of individuals, claims for protection of management's contractual (or property) rights, and the need to afford business greater managerial autonomy. These are serious claims that require the careful demonstration I offer in the following pages.

THE ASSAULT ON AMERICAN LABOR LAW

PART I

Hindering Workers' Ability to Establish
Bargaining Relationships

CHAPTER 1

Curtailing Statutory Coverage

Employer Exclusions

Employers favor limiting NLRA coverage while workers and their representatives favor the opposite. Coverage matters, as evidenced by the fact that fourteen of the Supreme Court's one hundred post-1965 labor relations decisions analyzed in this book involve disputes related to statutory coverage. First, unions often are able to effectively organize workers only by petitioning the NLRB to conduct a union representation election. But the NLRB may conduct such an election only if the workers who would gain union representation rights are employees as defined by the NLRA. Second, while both union and nonunion workers receive NLRA protections from employer discrimination, coercion, and other interference with the right to engage in concerted activity for mutual aid and protection, that statutory protection applies only to those who are employees as defined by the NLRA.

Qualifying as a covered employee requires a two-step process.[15] First, a worker must be employed by an entity that section 2(2) of the NLRA defines as an employer. Most employing entities qualify, but section 2(2) contains several exclusions, the three most important being the U.S. government, state governments and their political subdivisions, and persons subject to the jurisdiction of the Railway Labor Act. As I will discuss, the Supreme Court on its own has fashioned an additional employer exclusion: certain religious entities.

Second, workers must meet the definition of employee in NLRA section 2(3), which contains four important exclusions: agricultural laborers, those who work in domestic service for any person in that person's home, independent contractors, and supervisors. As I will mention later, the Supreme Court has also devised two additional employee exclusions nowhere mentioned in the NLRA: managerial employees and confidential employees.

The NLRA provides little guidance with respect to the scope of its sections 2(2) and 2(3) exclusions. The resulting ambiguity creates fertile ground for the Supreme Court to introduce its own policy predilections as it fills the statute's interstices. Employers are highly motivated to score victories in these cases in order to expand the number of workers who are excluded from the NLRA's protections. Labor organizations fight hard to limit the number and scope of these exclusions. Much is at stake, as the parties and the Court know. Narrowing the scope of exclusions from the NLRA's coverage is understood in broad terms as "part of labor's broader project to extend fundamental labor rights to all workers and to end structural hierarchy and inequality within the labor market and economy, transforming conceptions of who counts as an equal member of 'we the people.'"[16]

Employer Exclusions
STATE POLITICAL SUBDIVISIONS

NLRB v. Natural Gas Utility District of Hawkins County, Tennessee was an early example of the Burger Court's shaping of the NLRA to favor management interests.[17] Decided in 1971 during the Court's second term under Chief Justice Warren Burger, the majority in *Hawkins County* adopted an expansive test that significantly increased the number of entities that are excluded from NLRA coverage because they are a political subdivision of the state.

Upon the petition of a local of the Plumbers and Steamfitters Union, the NLRB ordered that a representation election be held among the pipefitters employed by the Natural Gas Utility District of Hawkins County, Tennessee.[18] The utility district objected on the sole ground that it was exempt from NLRB jurisdiction because it was a political subdivision of the state. Rejecting the argument, the NLRB ordered an election, which the union won. The NLRB found that the utility district had committed an unfair labor practice when it refused to comply with an order to bargain with the union. In an enforcement action, the Court of Appeals for the Sixth Circuit denied enforcement on the ground that the utility district was correct in claiming that it was an exempt political subdivision of the state.[19]

The Supreme Court agreed that the utility district was exempt. Professing that it was applying the same test that the NLRB had found to be appropriate, the Court concluded that the NLRA excluded all entities "(1) created directly by the state, so as to constitute departments or administrative arms of the government, or (2) administered by individuals who are responsible to public officials or the general electorate." In the *Hawkins County* case, the outcome turned on application of the second part of this test for defining a political subdivision. The record made it plain that the commissioners who administered the utility district were appointed by an elected county official and thus were "responsible to public officials."

The NLRB had come to a different conclusion because the test that the Supreme Court adopted was not, in fact, the Board's test. As I have noted, the second part of the Court's test defined a political subdivision as including entities "administered by individuals responsible to public officials," whereas the second part of the Board's test excluded an employer as a political subdivision only if the entity was "administered by public officials themselves."[20]

The Court neither explained nor tried to justify its misrepresentation that it had simply adopted the Board's test. In truth, it had actually fashioned a modified, more employer-friendly, test.[21] It is implausible to conclude that the altered test that the Court majority adopted was the result of a mistake or an oversight because Justice Potter Stewart, dissenting, correctly understood and summarized the test that the Board had used. He argued that the NLRB had followed its settled policy of weighing all relevant factors, "with particular emphasis here on the circumstances that the District is neither 'created directly by the State' nor 'administered by State-appointed or elected officials.'"[22]

Many more entities are exempt from NLRA coverage when government control regarding the notion of political subdivision simply depends on whether administrators are *responsible* to public officials rather than whether the administration is *by* public officials themselves. This is apparent in subsequent cases in which the NLRB concluded that entities that were not "administered by public officials themselves" nevertheless were exempt from NLRA coverage under the political subdivision rationale because administrators had been appointed by public officials.[23]

RELIGIOUS ENTITIES

Another good example of how the Burger Court used statutory coverage litigation to impede workers' ability to organize was the five-to-four decision in the 1979 case *NLRB v. Catholic Bishop of Chicago*.[24] In this case, the Court forged an exemption that removed religious schools from the NLRA definition of employer, even though such an exemption lacks any foundation in the NLRA's text or legislative history

In *Catholic Bishop*, the NLRB concluded that church-operated schools had violated the NLRA by refusing to recognize or bargain with unions representing lay faculty members at the schools. The Court of Appeals for the Seventh Circuit denied enforcement of the Board's order.[25] In an opinion written by Chief Justice Burger, the Court fashioned what has come to be known as the clear statement rule. The Court reasoned that the Board's exercise of jurisdiction over teachers in church-operated schools might possibly implicate the guarantees of the religion clauses of the First Amendment. Accordingly, to avoid addressing those constitutional issues, the Court required that there be a "clear expression of an affirmative intention of Congress" before it would bring within the coverage of a broadly worded regulatory statute such as the NLRA certain persons whose coverage might raise constitutional questions.[26]

The majority's denial of NLRA protections to thousands of teachers at religious schools was based on a thin premise: that the majority was unable to find evidence that Congress had clearly expressed an intention to protect these teachers. It precipitated a vigorous dissent.[27] Justice William Brennan, joined by three others, charged that the majority had invented a novel, never previously applied canon of statutory construction to, in effect, amend the NLRA.[28] The dissent pointed out the well-known fact that Congress seldom adds explicit expressions of congressional intent in broadly inclusive statutes such as the NLRA. Accordingly, the dissent argued, with its new canon of statutory construction, the Court could virtually remake congressional enactments. This contravenes Supreme Court precedent that admonishes "that amendment may not be substituted for construction, and that a court may not exercise legislative functions to save [a] law from conflict with constitutional limitation."[29] Textualists who favor a plain reading of statutory text should be offended because the NLRA text covers "all employers" except those in certain specified categories. Moreover, in considering the 1947 Taft-Hartley amendments to the NLRA, Congress rejected an amendment to exempt religious employers, thus further substantiating its desire to protect the collective bargaining rights of parochial school teachers.

According to 2019 figures, 10 percent of all K–12 students in United States are educated in private schools (5.8 million students). Of that number, 75 percent are educated in religiously affiliated schools.[30] As of 2020, 288,000 teachers teach in parochial schools of all faiths in the United States, 115,000 of them in Roman Catholic schools.[31] These are estimates, but they show the likely adverse impact of *Catholic Bishop* in impeding a great many workers' ability to organize and benefit from the NLRA's protections. Of course, reasonable persons may well disagree about whether national labor policy should or should not be crafted to exempt a parochial schools' lay teaching faculty from the protections of the NLRA. But Congress never chose to exempt religious schools and, in fact, in 1947 declined the opportunity to do just that. Modifying labor policy to exclude parochial school teachers from NLRA coverage is a legislative judgment, and it is difficult to disagree with the dissent's charge in *Catholic Bishop* that the Court assumed that legislative role and amended the NLRA by adding an exemption, nowhere found in statutory text, that severed hundreds of thousands of parochial school teachers from the NLRA's protections. *Catholic Bishop* has generated some very harsh criticism over the years.[32]

Employee Exclusions
UNDOCUMENTED WORKERS

Sure-Tan, Inc. v. NLRB and *Hoffman Plastics Compounds, Inc. v. NLRB* represent a recurring category of Supreme Court cases that uniquely impede workers' ability to organize.[33] In this pattern, the Court first grants a group NLRA protection. Later, without overruling the first case, a more conservative Court majority saps from the earlier decision much of the benefit that it had provided to workers.

In *Sure-Tan*, the NLRB found that an employer had engaged in an unfair labor practice by reporting to the Immigration and Naturalization Service certain employees known to be undocumented aliens in retaliation for their engaging in union activities, thereby causing their immediate departure from the United States. The Board issued a remedial order. The Court of Appeals for the Seventh Circuit agreed that the employer had violated the NLRA but modified the Board's remedial order in several significant respects.[34]

Before the Supreme Court, the threshold issue was whether undocumented aliens were employees covered by the NLRA. Writing for the majority, Justice Sandra Day O'Connor reasoned that undocumented aliens are NLRA-covered employees because of the "striking" breadth of section 2(3)'s application to "any employee," subject to specific exemptions that do not include undocumented aliens. In addition, the Court reasoned that extending the coverage of the Act to undocumented aliens is consistent with its avowed purpose of encouraging and protecting the collective bargaining process. In this regard, the majority reasoned:

> If undocumented alien employees were excluded from participation in union activities and from protections against employer intimidation, there would be created a subclass of workers without a comparable stake in the collective goals of their legally resident co-workers, thereby eroding the unity of all the employees and impeding effective collective bargaining. . . . Thus, the Board's categorization of undocumented aliens as protected employees furthers the purposes of the NLRA.[35]

This is what a judicial decision sounds like from a Court that is committed to protecting the collective foundations of the NLRA. Note that, unlike in *Catholic Bishop*, decided five years earlier, there was no suggestion in *Sure-Tan* that undocumented aliens could be excluded, unless there was "clear expression of an affirmative intention of Congress" to bring them within the NLRA's coverage.

In *Sure-Tan*, what remained were questions regarding remedy.[36] The Court approved conditioning offers of reinstatement on employees' legal reentry into the United States and approved tolling backpay for periods when the employees were unavailable for work because they were not lawfully entitled to be present and employed in the United States.

Sure-Tan was the NLRA rule for eighteen years, until 2002, when the Rehnquist Court decided *Hoffman Plastic Compounds, Inc. v. NLRB* and withdrew the availability of any backpay for undocumented aliens whose NLRA rights had been violated. In *Hoffman*, an employer discharged an employee named José Castro for attempting to organize a union. That was a violation of the Act, and the NLRB issued its normal reinstatement and backpay remedial order. During compliance proceedings, it was discovered that Castro had been born in Mexico and was not legally authorized to work in the United States, and the NLRB concluded that he had misrepresented his immigration status to Hoffman when he was hired.[37] The Board responded to this newly acquired information by denying reinstatement and limiting backpay to the period between the date of Castro's unlawful termination to the date when Hoffman first learned of his undocumented status. The Board reasoned that this remedy appropriately accommodated the federal immigration laws that make it unlawful for employers knowingly to hire undocumented workers or for employees to use fraudulent documents to establish employment eligibility, with the policy goals of the NLRA to protect workers' right to organize. Specifically, this backpay remedy would have reduced employers' right to hire and exploit undocumented workers.

The Supreme Court disagreed. Ruling five to four in a decision written by Chief Justice William Rehnquist, the Court held that the NLRB may not order either reinstatement or backpay as a permissible remedy for the antiunion discharge of undocumented workers. The majority reasoned that proper regard for the nation's immigration laws demanded this result, a curious basis for the decision, given that the Department of Justice, which at that time administered the immigration statutes through the Immigration and Naturalization Service, argued in support of the Board's limited backpay order.[38]

Hoffman has been interpreted as barring any backpay to undocumented workers, even when, in violation of immigration laws, the employer initially hires the workers knowing they are undocumented.[39] The case significantly undermined the delicate balance built into Justice O'Connor's *Sure-Tan* decision, which reasoned that the efficacy of the collective bargaining process requires that employers not be given incentives to hire undocumented workers. Ironically, however, by barring reinstatement and eliminating all risk of backpay liability, *Hoffman* offered employers a reason to violate the immigration laws: they now can hire undocumented aliens with the assurance that they get one free pass to violate the labor laws with impunity should they choose to discharge any undocumented worker who might engage in union organizing.[40] The only consequence is to post a notice stating that the employer will not do so again.[41] Nothing in the immigration laws compels such a lopsided result, one that addresses the needs of the immigration laws but fails to incorporate any of the NLRA's underlying policy goals. Members of the NLRB have decried it, concluding that, as a result of *Hoffman*, "employees are chilled in the exercise of their Section 7 rights, the work force is fragmented, and a vital check on workplace abuses is removed." With nothing discouraging employers from violating the Act, "the foreseeable result will be widespread retaliation against undocumented workers brave . . . enough to assert their rights under the [NLRA]."[42]

EMPLOYEES PAID BY A UNION TO HELP ORGANIZE (SALTING)

In *NLRB v. Town and Country Electric, Inc.* union members filed a complaint with the NLRB claiming that Town and Country Electric and an employment agency had refused to interview them or retain them because of their union membership.[43] The NLRB found that the company had violated the NLRA by discriminating against two full-time union organizers and other union members who had interviewed for jobs. In a unanimous opinion written by Justice Stephen Breyer, the Supreme Court held that workers may be a company's employee, within the terms of the NLRA, even though they intend to try to organize the company's employees if they are hired and will be paid by the union while they conduct their organizing activities. The Court thus upheld the NLRB's salting doctrine, relying on the broad statutory language in section 2(3) that defines employee.[44] The significance of the *Town and Country* holding is best understood in the context of the Court's decisions broadly denying unions' access to an employer's property to engage in organizing (see chapter 2).

AGRICULTURAL LABORERS

The term *employee* in NLRA section 2(3) "[does] not include any individual employed as an agricultural laborer."[45] The term *agricultural laborer*, as used in that section, derives its meaning from the definition of agriculture supplied by section 3(f) of the Fair Labor Standards Act of 1938. This definition includes farming in both a primary sense, which includes "the raising . . . of [farm products]," and a secondary sense, which encompasses practices "performed by a farmer or on a farm as an incident to or in conjunction with such farming operations."[46]

In *Bayside Enterprises, Inc. v. NLRB*, the NLRB directed owners of a vertically integrated poultry business to negotiate with the union representing drivers who were employed to deliver feed from the employer's feed-mill operation to 119 separate farms owned by contract farmers who were raising chicks that would be returned to the employer for slaughtering and processing. The Board's order was enforced by the Court of Appeals. The issue before the Supreme Court was whether delivering feed constituted work "performed by a farmer . . . as an incident to or in conjunction with such farming operations."

The Court agreed with the Board that the employer's operation of the feed mill was a nonagricultural activity, so the work of the truck drivers to deliver feed was not work performed by a farmer.

The key contribution of *Bayside Enterprises* is the Court's observation that "this conclusion by the Board [that the drivers were not agricultural laborers] is one we must respect even if the issue might with nearly equal reason be resolved one way rather than another."[47] That standard of review, which is highly deferential to the judgment of the NLRB, masks value judgments embedded in the Court's labor law decisions. The obligation to defer to the NLRB's conclusions operates as a toggle switch that the Court turns on or off depending on its agreement or disagreement with the policy underpinnings of a Board decision. In *Bayside Enterprises*, there was no indication that the Court strongly disagreed with the policy preferences animating the NLRB's decision, so the Court held that it was bound to defer to the Board. Yet as we have seen in cases such as *Hoffman*, when the Court disagrees with the collectivist values underlying an NLRB decision, its conservative five-member majority exhibits no hesitation in choosing to impose its own value judgments and policy preferences by concluding that, for some reason, the Court is not bound to defer to the NLRB. In *Hoffman*, for example, the Court justified its freedom to reject the NLRB's construction of the NLRA by citing the exigencies of the federal immigration statutes, even though the Board's decision in *Hoffman* fully supported the policies of the immigration statutes, as the federal agency administering those laws readily agreed.

A subsequent agricultural exemption case nicely demonstrates the toggle-switch nature of the Court's invocation of its obligation to defer to the NLRB's judgments regarding statutory interpretation of the NLRA. Decided nearly twenty years after *Bayside Enterprises*, the decision in *Holly Farms Corporation v. NLRB* again addressed the agricultural laborer exemption in the context of drivers employed by a vertically integrated poultry producer. Here, three categories of workers were considered: (1) Holly Farms' chicken catchers, who manually rounded up, caught, and caged live chickens on farms owned by third-party contractors; (2) forklift operators, who loaded the caged chickens onto the beds of flatbed trucks; and (3) live-haul drivers, who drove the loaded trucks to Holly Farms' processing plants, where the chickens were slaughtered and prepared for market. The issue before the Supreme Court was whether catching, loading, and transporting chickens qualified for the agricultural exemption because the work was performed "on a farm as an incident to or in conjunction with" the independent contractors' farming operations. The Court concluded that "Holly Farms' position that this [is] work on a farm that is incident to the raising of poultry is a plausible, but not an inevitable, construction" of the NLRA agricultural laborer exemption.[48] The majority upheld the Board's view that the workers were employees because all of this work was integrally and primarily tied to Holly Farms' processing operations and thus was not work on a farm. The Court reasoned that the Board's view was a reasonable interpretation of the governing legislation and therefore was a view that the Court was bound to accept

Protecting worker's rights in *Holly Farms* was a close call, however. Justice O'Connor and three others members of the conservative wing of the Court— Chief Justice Rehnquist and Justices Antonin Scalia and Clarence Thomas— joined in a concurring and dissenting opinion. They agreed that transporting chickens to the processing plant *was not* exempted agricultural laborer work but concluded that those who caught the chickens and those who used forklifts to load them onto trucks *were* exempted agricultural laborers. The dissenting view was based on the reasoning that the "statute does not require [the result reached by the NLRB] that work be performed 'incident to or in conjunction with' [an] employer's farming operations, but only [that it is work that is] incident to or in conjunction with [some] farming operations."[49]

To appreciate how the agricultural laborer exemption cases have expanded the Court's capacity to undermine the NLRA's commitment to protecting workers' collective activity, it is important to focus not on the semantic debates and disparate approaches to statutory interpretation that divided the justices in *Holly Farms*. Rather, *Holly Farms* and *Bayside Enterprises* demonstrate the malleability and toggle-switch nature of the Court's oft-repeated incantation that it will defer to reasonable Board's interpretations of the statute. In *Holly Farms*, a group of justices, just one justice shy of a majority, concluded that they were not bound to defer to the Board because the Board's view of the NLRA was not required by any explicit statutory text and runs "contrary to common sense."[50] Given the open-texture nature of the language used in the NLRA, most NLRB decisions find no support in the explicit text of the NLRA. If that fact justifies using a contrary-to-common-sense canon of statutory construction to determine the appropriate degree of deference to the NLRB, justices are free to impose their own policy choices whenever they so fancy.

INDEPENDENT CONTRACTORS

In 1968, the last year of the Warren Court and just prior to the June 1969 inauguration of the Burger Court, the NLRB required United Insurance Company of America to bargain with a union that represented the company's debit agents, whose primary function was to collect premiums on existing policies for a commission. The company trained and supervised the debit agents and retained the right to discharge them. The Court of Appeals for the Seventh Circuit found that the debit agents were independent contractors and refused to enforce the Board's order. In an opinion written by Justice Hugo Black, the Supreme Court upheld the Board's decision that the insurance company's approximately 3,300 debit agents were NLRA-covered employees rather than exempt independent contractors. The Court concluded that this was "a choice between two fairly conflicting views" and that, under the circumstances, the Board order should have been enforced.[51]

All parties agreed that the proper standard of review was application of the common law agency test distinguishing an employee from an independent contractor. The Court's reasoning for upholding the Board's decision is instructive:

> This was not a purely factual finding by the Board, but involved the application of law to facts—what do the facts establish under the common law of agency: employee or independent contractor? It should also be pointed out that such a determination of pure agency law involved no special administrative expertise that a court does not possess. On the other hand, the Board's determination was a judgment made after a hearing with witnesses and oral argument had been held and on the basis of written briefs. Such a determination should not be set aside just because a court would, as an original matter, decide the case the other way. "[E]ven as to matters not requiring expertise a court may [not] displace the Board's choice between two fairly conflicting views, even though the court would justifiably have made a different choice had the matter been before it de novo." Here the least that can be said for the Board's decision is that it made a choice between two fairly conflicting views, and under these

circumstances the Court of Appeals should have enforced the Board's order. It was error to refuse to do so."

The somewhat over-the-top affirmation of deference to the NLRB in *United Insurance* might seem to assure the Board that it has extensive freedom to interpret and apply national labor policy, at least when two views are "fairly conflicting"—whatever that means to a particular Supreme Court justice. But as this book will repeatedly demonstrate, the Court's references to its supposed obligation to defer to the institutional competence of the NLRB are rhetorical maneuvers, not a mode of reasoning that determines specific results. The Supreme Court has adopted a myriad of analytical tools that give it ample opportunity to impose its own anticollectivist policy views when it so chooses, as increasingly became the case with the Burger, Rehnquist, and Roberts courts. The cases I discuss next are a good example. They repeatably reject the NLRB's interpretation of the NLRA and strengthen management's hand. They uphold management's insistence that tens of thousands of workers should be denied NLRA protection, thereby enhancing employers' ability to exercise control over these many thousands of excluded workers, with the goal of keeping them allied with management rather than with their co-workers. These cases illustrate how easily the Court is able to excuse itself from deferring to the NLRB when its policy preferences so dictate, resulting in denial of statutory rights for vast numbers of workers.

EMPLOYEES SUPPOSEDLY ALLIED WITH MANAGEMENT: SUPERVISORS, MANAGERIAL EMPLOYEES, AND CONFIDENTIAL EMPLOYEES

Other than exempting agricultural and domestic workers, Congress did not exclude workers from NLRA coverage in the 1935 Wagner Act. No employee lost protection in response to management claims that some workers should be understood to have a class alignment with management. That changed to a degree in the 1947 Taft-Hartley amendments. There, Congress added *supervisors* as an excluded category, on the theory that unionization among supervisors threatens to weaken management authority on the shop floor. Corporate managers argued that, in order to be able to control the workplace, they needed to maintain the legal vulnerability of supervisors who, without union protection, would feel threatened by orders from above. Only then could low-level supervisors serve as reliable agents of corporate power to maintain production and discipline among the rank-and-file workers. "Seniority rights, grievance procedures, and union representation by foremen were subversive," employers argued, as these protections made front-line supervisors less legally vulnerable and thus less threatened by orders from above.[52] In other words, in 1947, employers argued for the vision of a clear industrial relations divide—those who were management and those who were workers—and to some degree Congress reinforced that class-divide vision by placing supervisors on the management side of the line.[53] The Taft-Hartley amendments added no other exclusions grounded in management's yearning for additional vulnerable employees who could be recruited as reliable agents to enforce managerial control.

Beginning in the mid-1970s, however, as the Burger Court solidified control, the Supreme Court, on its own, began adding exclusions in the name of enhancing employers' ability to compel additional classes of workers to stand with management against the collective interests of co-workers. First, in 1974, in *NLRB v. Bell Aerospace Company, Division of Textron, Inc.* a five-to-four majority excluded a class of workers that the Court described as "managerial employees"—those who do not supervise other employees but are in a position to formulate or effectuate managerial policy.[54] Disagreeing with the NLRB, the Court concluded that, like supervisors, managerial employees are naturally aligned with management and must be excluded because unionization would deprive management of their undivided loyalty. Six years later, in *NLRB v. Yeshiva University*, in another five-to-four decision that rebuffed the NLRB, the Court expanded the boundaries of the managerial employee category to exclude faculty of a university.[55] A year later, in *NLRB v. Hendricks County Rural Electric Membership Corporation*, the Court created yet another exclusion category in another five-to-four split opinion, one excluding those who have access to confidential information relating to labor relations matters.[56] Here, too, the exclusion was based on the perception that such employees are aligned with management and their unionization creates a conflict of interest. In another five-to-four decision, the Court in 1994 again disagreed with the NLRB, this time in *NLRB v. Health Care and Retirement Corporation of America*.[57] In this case, the Court held that a group of ordinary workers, licensed practical nurses, were excluded as supervisors because, as is true of millions of professional employees, they sometimes "responsibly direct[ed]" the work of others. Finally, in 2001, again refusing to defer to the NLRB, the Court, in *NLRB v. Kentucky River Community Care, Inc.* split five to four in concluding that a nurse's exercise of "ordinary professional or technical judgment in directing less-skilled employees to deliver services" was sufficient to characterize a nurse as an excluded supervisor.[58]

In short, in a series of five-to-four split decisions that mostly set aside NLRB decisions, the Court over the course of roughly twenty-five years—from 1974 to 2001—in effect amended the NLRA to exclude millions of American workers from the Act's protection. The logic behind these decisions was the Court's view that the fundamental tenet of the NLRA—the right of workers to unionize and thereby exercise power collectively—must be contained because it unduly threatens managerial control of the workplace.[59]

Impact of the Judicially Created Managerial Employee Exclusion

In *NLRB v. Bell Aerospace*, the NLRB found that the employer was guilty of an unfair labor practice in refusing to bargain with the union that represented a group of its buyers. The NLRB disagreed with the employer's contention that the buyers were excluded managerial employees. On review, the Court of Appeals for the Second Circuit denied enforcement. At the Supreme Court, Justice Lewis Powell, writing for a five-member majority, agreed with the company that Congress intended to exclude from the protections of the NLRA all employees who are properly classified as managerial, defined as those who are in a position to formulate or effectuate managerial policy. The majority rejected the Board's more nuanced, more balanced, and more worker-protective policy of excluding only so-called "managerial employees," whose participation in a labor organization would create a conflict of interest with their job responsibilities. In other words, the Court rejected the Board's view that only those managerial employees in positions related to labor relations matters were excluded from the Act's coverage.

Prior to the 1947 Taft-Hartley amendments to the NLRA, the Board had identified a subgroup of workers called managerial employees, defined as "executive employees who are in a position to formulate, determine and effectuate management policies. These employees . . . express and make operative the decisions of management."[60] It excluded some managerial employees from bargaining units containing non-managerial employees, but it at no time completely excluded the broad category of all managerial employees from the class of employees protected by the Act.[61] By 1947, when Congress excluded supervisors from the NLRA's definition of employee, the legislative history of the supervisor exclusion shows that Congress understood that the NLRB had excluded, and would continue to exclude, employees engaged in labor relations. But the legislative history provides no support for finding congressional intent to exclude all managerial employees, defined broadly as any worker who is in a position to formulate or effectuate managerial policy, however unrelated that policy is to the admonition of labor relations.

Following the Taft-Hartley amendments, various NLRB majorities vacillated.[62] But in 1970, the Board returned to its long-held view, excluding from NLRA coverage only those managerial employees in positions susceptible to conflicts of interest in labor relations matters.[63] Perhaps the most convincing evidence that Congress did not intend the Taft-Hartley amendments to exclude all managerial employees was the inclusion of section 2(12) in the Taft-Hartley Act, which defined, as NLRA-covered professional employees, a special subclass of employees who had special skills and duties "involving the consistent exercise of discretion and judgment" in the performance of their work. These employees are obviously *employees* for the purposes of the Act, as the dissent in *Bell Aerospace* explained:

> It is apparent . . . that there are many professional employees who would qualify as managerial employees[, yet] the Act clearly treats them as employees for purposes of the Act[,] and Congress assumed they would have full organizational and bargaining rights unless it was provided otherwise in accordance with congressional desires. . . . Insofar as the face of the Act is concerned, . . . the present ruling of the Board, which excludes only those managerial employees whose work may involve them in a conflict of interest if they are permitted to bargain collectively, is a far narrower exclusion adhering much more closely to the rationale of the supervisory exclusion and to the apparent intent of Congress.[64]

The Supreme Court's implicit logic in rejecting the NLRB's statutory interpretation in *Bell Aerospace* was that once employees have attained any real ability to influence management policy, they no longer can be considered employees under the NLRA, even when such protection would not create any actual conflict of interest.[65] *Bell Aerospace* often is underappreciated as an early example of the post-1970s trajectory of Court decisions that incrementally but increasingly limited opportunities of workers to unionize and thereby exercise power collectively. These cases prioritize employer claims that workers' unionization unduly endangers managerial control of workplace.

The expansive definition of managerial employee adopted by the majority in *Bell Aerospace* threatened to nullify the Act's inclusion of professional employees as NLRA-covered employees because their special skills and duties "involving the consistent exercise of discretion and judgment" in the performance of their work often entails performing tasks bordering on the managerial.[66] To avoid this, the NLRB, in *General Dynamics Corporation*, ruled that a professional employee is not vested with managerial authority merely "because work performed may have a bearing on company direction. [Managerial employees are those whose job functions are] aligned with managerial authority rather than with work performance of a routine, technical, or consultative nature."[67]

EXCLUDING UNIVERSITY FACULTY

The decision in *General Dynamics* solved one problem: it preserved NLRA coverage for many professional employees. However, the opinion created an opening for colleges and universities to attempt to expand the definition of managerial employee to cover faculty members. The theory was that faculty often participate in determining policy such as admission standards, grading policy, academic standards, and so on. Accordingly, they might in this sense be viewed as "aligned with managerial authority" and therefore be excluded. In 1980, colleges and universities successfully advanced that argument to a conservative Supreme Court majority in *NLRB v. Yeshiva University*.[68]

The NLRB first asserted jurisdiction over university faculty in the early 1970s, when it rejected employer claims that university faculty were excluded managerial employees.[69] Relying on shifting rationales, the Board adhered to this view throughout the decade.[70] When the issue reached the Supreme Court in the *Yeshiva* case, the NLRB argued that, although faculty members sometimes possess decision-making authority with respect to certain academic matters, such collective decision making represents independent professional judgment that is exercised in the faculty's own interest rather than in the interest of the university. Accordingly, the normal collegial governing authority of university faculty in academic matters does not convert faculty into excluded managerial employees.[71]

The Supreme Court disagreed, concluding that the Yeshiva faculty, acting as a collegial body, exercised "absolute" authority by implementing management policies in academic matters, authority that "in any other context unquestionably would be managerial."[72] The Court's logic was that, in order to manage the university effectively, a faculty's aspirations for a degree of self-determination through unionization must yield to university officials' insistence on control unhindered by faculty possessing legally enforceable collective rights.[73]

It has been suggested that *NLRB v. Yeshiva University* may soon stand beside other highly criticized landmark Supreme Court decisions such as *Loewe v. Lawlor* and *United States v. Hutcheson* "both in terms of controversy provoked and the number of [mostly critical] resulting learned articles written by labor relations scholars and practitioners."[74] There is no point repeating here the wide-ranging criticisms spawned by the *Yeshiva* decision. Two observations seem warranted, however.

First, Risa L. Lieberwitz has written persuasively that the collective authority that university faculties often exercise over academic matters has a genesis that is far different from the authority at issue in other managerial employee cases such as *Bell Aerospace*. In the typical industrial setting, management determines that it is in an enterprise's self-interest to vest some workers with discretionary authority in order to implement managerial policies. In such cases, it is management that unilaterally moves the class lines shifting an employee from worker to manager. University faculties' discretionary authority over academic matters has a far different provenance. Faculties gradually gained academic freedom that gave them independence from their university employer following years of struggle to secure individual and collective faculty autonomy over their work—in part by insisting on a degree of autonomy to set certain aspects of academic policy. Lieberwitz explains:

> Developed outside the legislative and judicial context, professional norms of academic freedom were built on the foundation of collective faculty demands in the early 20th century for independence from university administration, trustees, and financial

supporters. Prior to 1980, the legal identity of university faculty under the . . . NLRA was consistent with these professional norms, as the . . . NLRB defined faculty as employees with rights to unionize, through which they could [continue to] promote employment-related interests independent from their university employer. . . .

The [Supreme Court's] decision in [*Yeshiva*] represent[s] [an] opposing vision of university faculty identity. While the professional norms of academic freedom stress the faculty's autonomy as central to their distinctive role in the university, the legal norms of *Yeshiva* ignore academic freedom, emphasizing only the alignment of interests between university administrators and faculty as part of management.[75]

In short, Lieberwitz shows that the wide-ranging acceptance of academic freedom today, which was "born out of years of conflict [and faculty activism and this history,] is central to locating faculty within the ranks of labor—[on] the opposing side of the class line from the university administration and Board of trustees. . . . [A]cademic freedom distinguish[es] individual and collective interests [of university faculty] from those of the administration, trustees, and third party financial donors."[76] In *Yeshiva*, the Court was made aware of this far different genesis of faculty collective authority compared to the managerial authority that employers bestow on some workers in an industrial setting. But that information made no difference.[77]

Second, it is stunning that the *Yeshiva* majority omitted to address this history of class struggle among faculty to achieve academic freedom, given the self-evident relevance of that history to the question of whether the NLRB was correct in concluding that faculty collective decision making in some academic matters represents independent professional judgment exercised in the faculty's own interest rather than in the university's. This omission seems more understandable when *Yeshiva* is understood as another installment in the Court's self-appointed role to redefine the NLRA's class lines that determine who is a worker and who is management. Others have argued that the Court's post-1970s labor law decisions address the question of "to what degree can the industrial relations system accept the exercise of [empowerment] by unionized workers[, with the Court responding by crafting] doctrines that limit unions' ability to exert their economic power to expand employee participation in running the enterprise."[78] The *Yeshiva* decision supports that thesis. A Court committed to enhancing managerial control of the workplace will interpret the NLRA as constraining employee access to collective bargaining without tarrying over whether, as with university professors, the collective power that makes a worker a manager was achieved through years of struggle and faculty activism.[79]

The NLRB decision in *College of Osteopathic Medicine and Surgery (COMS)* provides strong evidence that the *Yeshiva* decision was primarily rooted in thwarting workers' collective power to insist on a degree of workplace participation with management and was only marginally rooted in protecting employers' legitimate interests in the undivided loyalty of those who truly are management.[80] In *COMS*, the NLRB held that members of a university faculty lost their NLRA protection due to their status as managerial employees, notwithstanding the fact that the faculty's managerial authority had resulted from gains achieved through success in the collective bargaining process.[81] The jaded logic of *COMS* and *Yeshiva* is that employees become more vulnerable to losing their NLRA protection as they are more successful in gaining workplace control through their collective struggle and activism.

EXCLUSION OF SUPERVISORS

The supervisor cases also illuminate how, via its post-1970s cases, the Supreme Court redefined the industrial hierarchy in favor of employers by moving the class lines that delineate who is management and who is a worker. As I have mentioned, in a 1994 split decision, the Court, in *NLRB v. Health Care and Retirement Corporation of America*, reversed the NLRB's interpretation of the NLRA by extending the Act's supervisory exclusion to include licensed practical nurses (LPNs).[82] Then, in 2001, again refusing to defer to the NLRB's statutory interpretation in *NLRB v. Kentucky River Community Care, Inc.* the Court ruled that nurses are excluded supervisors when they direct less-skilled employees to deliver healthcare services, even though such direction is integral to their exercise of "ordinary professional or technical judgment . . . in accordance with employer-specified standards."[83] These two decisions have resulted in the exclusion of many thousands of this nation's nurses from NLRA protection and contain the potential to exclude tens of thousands of other healthcare and non-healthcare professional employees.[84]

Section 2(11) of the NLRA defines the term *supervisor*. Three elements must be proved: a supervisor must (1) "hav[e] authority, in the interest of the employer," to (2) "hire, transfer, suspend, lay off, recall, promote, discharge, assign, reward, discipline other employees, or responsibly to direct them, or to adjust their grievances, or effectively to recommend such action," and (3) "the exercise of such authority [must] not [be] of a merely routine or clerical nature, but requires the use of independent judgment."[85] In early cases, the NLRB attempted to distinguish those registered nurses (RNs) who truly are part of management—"nurse supervisors"—from other rank-and-file nurses who are not supervisors in any real sense. The Board's initial effort allowed nurses to retain their status as NLRA-covered employees (not supervisors) if they primarily performed nursing functions. This conclusion held, even though such nurses occasionally implement patient care decisions that require them to make assignments or otherwise direct less skilled workers, such as nurses' aides. The NLRB reasoned that these incidental patient care assignments directed to less-skilled employees do not convert rank-and-file nurses into supervisors because these directions to other employees are in the interest of patient care, not "in the interest of the employer," as required by 2(11) if one is to be classified as a supervisor.

In *Health Care and Retirement Corporation*, the management of a nursing home discharged four LPNs for engaging in union activities. Finding that they were employees, not supervisors, the NLRB ordered the nurses' reinstatement. The Court of Appeals vacated NLRB's decision, and *certiorari* was granted. The Supreme Court, in an opinion authored by Justice Anthony Kennedy, declared that the LPNs were excluded supervisors because their duties included directing nurses' aides in administering patient care in a nursing home. It did not matter that this occasional direction of lesser-skilled employees was incidental to a nurse's provision of patient care. In the Court's view, all on-the-job professional decisions that direct other employees are made "in the interest of the employer."[86] As the dissent pointed out, the majority was unwilling to accept that by assigning and directing some tasks to other employees, nurses are bound by professional nursing standards rather than by an employer's interest in profits.[87] Both the NLRB and the dissent in *Health Care and Retirement Corporation* warned that if exercising independent judgment to assign tasks to others or to direct their work qualifies a person as a supervisor, few professionals will receive the NLRA's protections.[88]

The majority seemed to invite the NLRB to find ways to avoid having the Court's decision result in the wholesale conversion of most American nurses and many other professional employees into supervisors. Specifically, the Court seemed to leave open the possibility that the incidental directing of lower-skilled employees as part of normal patient care would not qualify as exercising "independent judgment" within the meaning of NLRA section 2(11). In the years immediately following the decision in *Health Care and Retirement Corporation*, the NLRB developed the view that a nurse's incidental assigning of tasks or otherwise directing others as part of routine patient care is not the exercise of "independent judgment" as defined in section 2(11) and thus does not place nurses in the category of a supervisor. Rather, such assigning or directing is "informed by professional or technical training and experience."[89]

In *NLRB v. Kentucky River Community Care, Inc.* a 2001 Rehnquist Court decision written by Justice Scalia, the Supreme Court refused to defer to the NLRB's statutory interpretation with respect to the meaning of *independent judgment*. A conservative majority of the Court accused the NLRB of defining the term one way when a nurse "assigns" or "otherwise directs" and another way for all of the other indicia of section 2(11) supervisory status such as hiring, firing, disciplining, promoting, and so on. The Court advanced no policy basis for its decision assigning supervisory status to thousands of professional employees, such as nurses, whose incidental responsibilities include minor oversight of others. But in so doing, the Court thwarted the NLRB's effort to harmonize the language of section 2(11) with NLRA section 2(12), which defines professional employees as NLRA-covered employees, even though section 2(12) confirms that professional employees also periodically make assignments and direct lower-skilled workers incidental to their exercise of ordinary professional judgment.

In *Oakwood Healthcare, Inc.* the NLRB considered whether charge nurses met NLRA criteria for supervisors and in the process gave the *Kentucky River* decision an expansive interpretation.[90] Regarding the "authority to assign" factor, the NLRB focused on the authority to direct employees regarding when, where, or for how long they performed their duties. The Board found that the charge nurses at Oakwood Healthcare had demonstrated the "authority to assign" by designating staff nurses to particular care units or to care for particular patients. Regarding the alternative indicia of supervisory status—

authority to responsibly direct—such authority was found to be exercised by any person who has authority over other employees to determine what job or task shall be undertaken next, or who shall do that job, provided that the one giving the direction is responsible to perform oversight of the other employees and is held accountable for their performance.

The nurse supervisor cases create a "barrier to unionization," making it, "as a practical matter, . . . impossible for [many] nurses to form bargaining units," thus leaving them helpless if healthcare industry employers, for example, discipline those who fight for improved nursing ratios and patient care.[91] Since *Kentucky River,* "employers have been emboldened to seek to exclude from NLRB rights entire existing as well as proposed bargaining units of staff nurses . . . on grounds of their . . . task delegation of nursing aides or technicians. [In addition,] manufactur[ing] [employers] ha[ve] challenged as supervisory the team leaders of its self-directed production teams."[92] These cases further reduce the number of workers who qualify for the NLRA's protection, gradually hollowing out the right to freedom of association first promised in 1935. "In the modern workplace, with flattened managerial hierarchies, and with managerial authority pushed downward to the lowest possible level and distributed as widely as possible, a broad construction of the section 2(11) factors could render nearly everyone a supervisor."[93]

EXCLUSION OF CONFIDENTIAL EMPLOYEES

In another split decision, this time in an opinion written by Justice Brennan, the Court, in *NLRB v. Hendricks County Rural Electric Membership Corporation,* backed away from finding implied broad exclusions from the NLRA after the liberal bloc on the Burger Court mustered a fifth vote. Instead, the Court held that there is a reasonable basis in law for the Board's practice of excluding from collective bargaining units only those confidential employees with access to confidential labor relations information and rejected the claim that all employees with access to confidential business information that is not associated with labor relations are beyond the reach of the Act's definition of employee. Three issues were critical to the outcome: (1) at the time of the Taft-Hartley amendments, the NLRB had excluded only those employees whose confidential information had a labor nexus; (2) the Taft-Hartley amendments included professional employees, many of whom possess confidential business information that is not associated with labor relations; and (3) Congress expressly rejected a provision in a House bill that would have excluded confidential secretaries, whether or not they had access to labor-related confidential information.

The dissent, composed of the Court's conservative wing at that time— Chief Justice Burger and Justices Powell, Rehnquist, and O'Connor—adhered to the theme of the Court's post-1970s cases that expanded the number of workers excluded from NLRA protection. Wanting more workers to fall "on the management side of the line and [thus] be excluded from the Act," the dissent rejected "the labor nexus which the Board insists . . . must be viewed as part of this larger effort to keep the line between management and labor distinct."[94] Adopting a broad view of "allied with management," the dissent insisted on excluding all "confidential employees, who are privy to the daily affairs of management, who have access to confidential information, and who are essential to management's operation [because unionization] may . . . subject [them] to conflicts of loyalty when the essence of their working relationship requires undivided loyalty."[95] In short, the conservative dissenters in *Hendricks* would have delegated to the NLRB, and ultimately to the federal judiciary, the authority to decide on a case-by-case basis when, because of access to confidential business information, "the essence of [one's] working relationship requires undivided loyalty," thus disqualifying the worker from access to unionization with co-workers. That certainly would have opened many opportunities for conservative courts of appeal judges to move the class lines even further in favor of employers.

The Sociopolitical Implications of Excluding Workers Who Are "Allied with Management"

As I have noted, in 1947 business leaders persuaded Congress that they needed to exert unhindered authority over frontline supervisors in order to control them and thus the workforce. To use a military analogy: these frontline supervisors were seen as equivalent to the noncommissioned officers who unquestionably obey the orders of their superior officers and enforce those directives among the rank-and-file troops. The argument was, and is, that supervisor unions inhibit the creation of this necessary degree of management control over supervisors. Think of it as the authoritarian, hierarchical justification for the supervisor exclusion. But excluding supervisors from NLRA coverage, and then over time adding additional judicially created layers of exclusion, has had far-reaching, society-wide implications that go beyond the production concerns of an individual enterprise.

According to Nelson Lichtenstein, "Taft-Hartley's debilitating exclusion of foremen and supervisors from labor law coverage" has proven to be "the single most powerful weapon crafted by labor's opponents under the new statute."[96] Given the many other very potent antiunion provisions added in 1947, this is a startling statement. Lichtenstein's argument, in sum, is that, together, these exclusions have created a "blue-collar-job ghetto" for unions. In his view, supervisor unionism does not "just threaten to weaken management authority at the point of production. It also erode[s] the vitality of corporate ideology . . . by shattering the unitary façade of management and open[ing] the door to a much larger definition of what constitute[s] a self-conscious working-class identity." For with the advent of the supervisor union, not only does a supervisor align her own class allegiance more closely with the workers, but supervisor unionism also creates the risk that other "lower middle class clerical workers, salesmen, store managers, bank tellers, engineers, and draftsmen would also abandon their identification with the corporate order." The Taft-Hartley Act's "forced draft conscription" of workers back into the ranks of management was necessary to create the "reghettoization of the union movement and the victory of management all along the white-collar frontier." Over time, the Supreme Court piggy-backed onto the supervisor exclusion more and more judicially created statutory exclusions, based on its agreement with business's claimed need to shift class lines by defining more workers as management. "The magnitude of labor's defeat on the issue of supervisory unionism [became] clearer with each passing year. [Now] the unionization of finance, engineering, insurance, banking, and other private-sector service industries [has] prove[n to be] virtually impossible. . . . The ranks of these white-collar and service sector workers swell[ed, but] the evolving labor law [as shaped by the Court] failed to take the new sociology of work into account," leaving hundreds of thousands unable to obtain union representation. "The legal straightjacket imposed by Taft-Hartley ensured that the unions reborn in the New Deal would now be consigned to a roughly static geographic and demographic terrain, an archipelago that skipped from one blue-collar community to another in the Northeast, the Midwest, and on the Pacific Coast." From this critique, it is not difficult to understand Lichtenstein's conclusion that the availability of the NLRA's framework of representation is being whittled down substantially, though not yet entirely, to those whose jobs have been reduced to "mindless routine" and "simple drudgery." In our Information Age, these are not the jobs of the future. [97]

THE CASES

CHAPTER 2

Impeding the Ability
to Create a Duty to Bargain

Adopting a Voluntarist View

Unions sometimes possess sufficient leverage to be able to negotiate what are commonly referred to as *neutrality and card check agreements*.[15] In these agreements, unions and employers "establish varied sets of ground rules governing unions' and employers' conduct during organizing campaigns, procedures for registering workers' preferences on the question of collective representation, and mechanisms for resolving disputes."[16] Per these private agreements, an employer will often voluntarily recognize the union based on a showing of majority support through union authorization cards.[17] When unions lack the leverage needed to obtain such private agreements, U.S. labor law permits "an employer's reasonless insistence on an election-certification as a precondition for its duty to bargain."[18] This was not always so.

The NLRA provides that it is unlawful for an employer "to refuse to bargain collectively with the representatives of his employees, subject to the provisions of Section 9(a)," which states that "representatives designated or selected for the purpose of collective bargaining by the majority of the employees in an appropriate unit for such purposes, shall be the exclusive representatives of all the employees in such unit for the purposes of collective bargaining."[19] Section 9(a) does not specify any particular method by which this exclusive representative is to be "designated or selected" by a majority of the employees. From the earliest years following the enactment of the NLRA, the NLRB and the courts recognized that a union does not need to have been certified as the winner of an NLRB-conducted election to invoke the section 8(a)(5) bargaining obligation. Unions could obtain the majority status needed to create an employer's duty to bargain by other means, such as by authorization cards, through which employees authorize a union to represent them for collective bargaining. In *United Mine Workers v. Arkansas Oak Flooring Company*, the Supreme Court could not have been clearer when it explained that section 9(a), "which deals expressly with employee representation, says nothing as to how the employees' representative shall be chosen [and that a] Board election is not the only method by which an employer may satisfy itself as to the union's majority status."[20]

THE JOY SILK DOCTRINE AND THE GISSEL PACKING DECISION

Two years after enactment of the 1947 Taft-Hartley amendments to the NLRA, the NLRB, in *Joy Silk Mills, Inc.*, held that if an employer has a "good faith" doubt as to a union's majority based on authorization cards, that employer could lawfully refuse to bargain and instead require the union to prove its majority through an NLRB election.[21] In the absence of such a doubt, employers were obligated to recognize and bargain with a union that represented a majority of the bargaining unit employees. For many years, the NLRB applied the *Joy Silk* doctrine without its having been tested in the Supreme Court.

Finally, *NLRB v. Gissel Packing Company* adjudicated whether the NLRA permitted the NLRB to order bargaining based on union authorization cards and, if so, when.[22] In its brief to the Supreme Court in *Gissel*, the NLRB equivocated in its explanation of its current practice of applying the Board's *Joy silk* doctrine.[23] One could read the Board's *Gissel* brief literally, when it stated that "whether in a particular case an employer is acting in good or bad faith is . . . a question which . . . must be determined in the light of all the relevant facts in the case, [and] the presence of employer unfair labor practices [has] an important [but not essential?] bearing." NLRB precedent supported the conclusion that a duty to bargain sometimes can arise based on authorization cards, even when an employer does not misbehave by engaging in conduct constituting an unfair labor practice.[24] Or one could read the NLRB's *Gissel* brief more narrowly: that a finding of "the absence of good faith doubt as to majority [requires evidence of] contemporaneous employer unfair labor practices which tended to dissipate the union's majority and to preclude a fair Board election."[25]

Gissel was a consolidated case involving four unrelated cases. In each, the NLRB had ordered the employer to bargain with a union that had never won a representation election among the employer's employees but had obtained union authorization cards from a majority of the bargaining unit employees. In each case, the employer had committed unfair labor practices. They were of varying severity, but in each the unfair labor practices had interfered with the holding of a fair election.

At oral argument in *Gissel*, the Court requested clarification of the Board's position with respect to whether the NLRB would issue a bargaining order when an employer had committed no unfair labor practices and the employer insisted that the union establish its a majority status through a representation election. As Laura Cooper and Dennis Nolan state in their thoroughly researched evaluation of the *Gissel* cases, "the attorney for the National Labor Relations Board advance[d] a position that contradicted Board precedent and the Board's own brief [and] then den[ied] to the Court that his position represented any change."[26] Counsel for the NLRB incorrectly represented to the Court that the NLRB had abandoned good faith/bad faith alone as a test of an employer's duty to bargain based on cards. Counsel stated that the Board now limited the issuance of a bargaining order entirely to the fact that the employer had committed serous unfair labor practices.

In a unanimous opinion, the Court in *Gissel* accepted this representation by NLRB counsel and in its opinion stated that "the Board announced at oral argument that it had virtually abandoned the *Joy Silk* doctrine altogether [with the result that] an employer can insist that a union go to an election, regardless of his subjective motivation, so long as he is not guilty of misconduct."[27] The Court in *Gissel* held that the NLRB may issue a bargaining order when the union once had majority support (normally manifested by authorization cards) and the employer engages in serious unfair labor practices that interfere with the holding of a fair union representation election. The nature of the unfair labor practices is highly relevant.[28] The Court declined to express a view with respect to the NLRB's right to issue a bargaining order when an employer had not engaged in unfair labor practice conduct.

Gissel appeared to be a solid victory for the NLRB and the NLRA's commitment to encouraging the practice and procedure of collective bargaining. It affirmed the reliability of authorization cards as a legitimate means of ascertaining union majority support and confirmed the authority of the NLRB in some circumstances to remedy employer misconduct by means of a bargaining order.[29] The reality, however, was much different. A close examination of *Gissel's* several triumphs for extending workers' access to collective bargaining "reveal[s] many of the features of Jonah's triumph over the whale" (to paraphrase John Kenneth Galbraith).[30] First, *Gissel* was a Pyrrhic victory—one hardly worth winning because so much was lost to achieve it. Second, following *Gissel*, the lower courts remained hostile to NLRB bargaining orders, seldom upholding them. Finally, unions that do obtain a bargaining order seldom ever achieve a stable bargaining relationship—or even a first contract.

PYRRHIC VICTORY: THE DEMISE OF THE JOY SILK DOCTRINE

In *Gissel*, the Court concluded that, because all of the employers in the *Gissel* cases had committed unfair labor practices, it "need not decide whether a bargaining order is ever appropriate in cases where there is no [employer] interference with the election processes."[31] Five years after its *Gissel* decision, the Court decided *Linden Lumber Division, Summer and Company, v. NLRB*.[32] In a five-to-four decision, the now well-entrenched Burger Court agreed that it was a permissible construction of the NLRA for the three Republican members of the Nixon NLRB to conclude that, in the absence of serious unfair labor practices, an employer may insist that a union petition for and win a representation election as a precondition to finding a duty to bargain.[33] The majority in the Court's *Linden Lumber* decision rejected the reasoning of the two dissenting Democratic Board members in the case, who had argued that a bargaining order was warranted, based on undisputed evidence that the employer "had knowledge, independently of the authorization cards, that a majority of its employees supported the Union."[34]

The Washington, D.C., Court of Appeals disagreed with the three-member Republican majority in *Linden Lumber* but did not adopt the "independent knowledge" test advanced by the dissenting Board members.[35] The Court of Appeals held that an employer may act in total disregard of convincing evidence of a union's majority status, based on union authorization cards, but that such convincing evidence of the union's support among the bargaining unit employees

> create[s] a sufficient probability of majority support as to require an employer asserting a doubt of majority status to resolve the possibility through a petition for an election, if he is to avoid both any duty to bargain and any inquiry into the actuality of

his doubt. . . . [I]f "independent knowledge" is [insufficient alone to create a duty to bargain], some alternative must be put in its place to prevent an employer's deliberate flouting and disregard of union cards without rhyme or reason. The complete lack of such an alternative would not be consistent with the Act.[36]

In its *Linden Lumber* decision, the Supreme Court rejected the Court of Appeals' balanced approach and held that the NLRA does not require, but permits, the outcome mandated by the three-person NLRB majority in *Linden Lumber*. As the Court stated, "in light of the [Act's] statutory scheme and the practical administrative procedural questions involved, we cannot say that the Board's decision that the union should go forward and ask for an election on the employer's refusal to recognize the authorization cards was arbitrary and capricious or an abuse of discretion."[37]

The Court's four-justice dissent in *Linden Lumber* mostly adopted, but refined, the view of the D.C. Court of Appeals. Had the Court chosen to adopt the approach advanced in the *Linden Lumber* dissenting opinion, the subsequent course of American labor relations law would have been significantly altered. The dissent focused on the addition of section 9(c)(1)(B) in the 1947 Taft-Hartley amendments to the NLRA, which "provides an alternative to immediate union recognition for an employer faced with a union demand to bargain on behalf of his employees" by permitting an employer confronted with a demand for recognition to file a petition for a Board-supervised representation election.[38] This 1947 addition to the Act, the dissent argued, showed congressional intent that employers presented with convincing proof of a union's majority support could not sit idly by. Under the *Gissel* dissent's approach, employers presented with a demand to bargain supported by evidence of a union's majority support would have four choices: (1) agree to bargain, (2) file their own request for an NLRB-conducted representation election, (3) agree to be bound by the results of an expedited consent election ordered after the union had filed a representation election petition, or (4) refuse to recognize the union, despite convincing evidence of the union's majority support, at which point the union could charge the employer with a section 8(a)(5) refusal-to-bargain unfair labor practice. If the NLRB general counsel chose to issue a complaint about the union's refusal-to-bargain charge, the Board would determine if the union in fact represented a majority of the employees, in which case the Board must issue an order directing the employer to bargain with the union.[39] One way or another, the question of representation would have been resolved expeditiously with a minimum of opportunity for employer delay, intimidation, or interference. "When an employer petitions for or consents to an election, the election process is expedited."[40] And when the NLRB determines the union's majority status in a section 8(a)(5) refusal-to-bargain unfair labor practice adjudication, the employer is ordered to bargain, thereby hindering the employer's ability to avoid the duty to bargain through interference and coercion, as is typical during the conduct of union representation elections. By just one vote, the Court in *Linden Lumber* rejected this sensible, practical approach, which balanced employer interests, employee free choice, and the NLRA's policy of encouraging the practice and procedure of collective bargaining.

HOLLOWING OUT THE GISSEL BARGAINING ORDER REMEDY

Some persons of good will may have believed that the *Gissel* bargaining order would become an efficacious alternative to the bargaining order previously provided by the *Joy Silk* doctrine. But following *Gissel*, the courts so attenuated the right to a *Gissel* bargaining order that today it is effectively useless as a means to deter the often-present employer restraint and coercion that interferes with the representation election process.[41] This is because the *Gissel* standard for issuing a bargaining order is highly indeterminate: "*Gissel* [typically] asks whether an employer's ULPs [unfair labor practices] have made the conduct of a fair election unlikely . . . , even after the application of traditional remedies. Because this inquiry asks a question about future events, courts have struggled with the speculative nature of the doctrine, demanding increasingly strict proof from NLRB's General Counsel before affirming bargaining orders."[42] Almost immediately after the Court decided *Gissel*, the circuit courts demanded "specific findings" and "detailed analysis" with respect to the following:

> 1) the immediate and residual impact of the unfair labor practices
> on the election process; 2) the possibility of holding a fair election
> in terms of any continuing effect of misconduct; 3) the likelihood
> of recurring misconduct; and, 4) the potential effectiveness of
> ordinary remedies [and later] hard-to-address categories such as
> the likelihood of future recurrence of ULPs and the impact of
> events that occurred *following* the administrative hearing from
> which the bargaining order first issued.[43]

In most cases today, a bargaining order will issue only if the employer has engaged in the hallmark unfair labor practices of discriminatory discharge or layoff of union activists and threats to close unionized facilities.[44] Because a majority of the circuit courts of appeal characterize the *Gissel* bargaining order as an "extraordinary remedy," it is rarely entered and thus provides little deterrence to employers' illegal conduct.[45] The D.C. circuit, which hears a disproportionately large percentage of *Gissel* bargaining order cases, has acknowledged that it has "long viewed them with suspicion," and some circuits "greet the Board's bargaining order with [such] 'overt hostility,'" that they deny enforcement of most bargaining order cases.[46] Perhaps the meager enforcement rates in bargaining order cases explain the paucity of bargaining orders that the NLRB now issues.[47]

Bargaining orders seldom result in a stable bargaining relationship. Studies demonstrate that even when unions are able to surmount the many obstacles to obtaining a bargaining order, those that receive *Gissel* bargaining orders are seldom able to create productive bargaining relationships. Indeed, a union "will have just a one chance in five of actually obtaining [even] an initial bargaining agreement."[48]

Still, there has been a possible reprieve for authorization card–based duty to bargain. While the *Joy Silk* doctrine's creation of a duty to bargain (based on the absence of an employer's good-faith doubt as to a union's majority support) apparently had its final demise in *Linden Lumber*, that death may prove to be at least partially reversible. Charles Morris has argued persuasively that "the *Linden* rule is . . . only an agency's 'permissible' construction of the statute—as it was correctly and expressly so labeled by Supreme Court Justice Stewart in his [*Linden Lumber*] dissenting opinion, [and, therefore,] a Labor Board that is so inclined will have clear legal authority to change that regressive rule without further legislation."[49] The NLRB did just that on August 25, 2023, when it released its decision in *Cemex Construction Materials Pacific, LLC.*[50] *Cemex* avoids reentering the thicket of evaluating employer good or bad faith but overrules the NLRB's 1971 decision in *Linden Lumber* and could help workers establish representation rights more easily. Under the new standard, an employer violates section 8(a)(5) by refusing to recognize, upon request, a union that has been designated as a section 9(a) representative by the majority of employees in an appropriate unit unless the employer "promptly" (normally within two weeks) requests that the NLRB conduct an election. However, if the election process commences but the employer then commits an unfair labor practice that interferes with the conduct of a fair election, the election petition (whether filed by the employer or the union) will be dismissed, and the employer will be subject to a remedial bargaining order directing it to bargain with the union. The bargaining obligation would attach from the date of the union's demand for recognition. Thus, pursuant to longstanding Board precedent, employers act at their own peril in refusing to recognize and bargain and in making unilateral changes in employees' terms and conditions of employment after such a demand is made.[51]

Cemex could be a game changer by dramatically reducing opportunities for employer interference and coercion in employee free choice with respect to whether to choose unionization. For example, in April 2024, the NLRB announced that union election petitions increased by 35 percent in the first half of fiscal year 2024 (October 1, 2023, through March 31, 2024), the period almost immediately following the Board's *Cemex* decision.[52] Instead of delaying and creating opportunities to intimidate workers who were seeking unionization, employers reacted to *Cemex* by filing their own election petitions that expedite the election process.[53] Of course, whether *Cemex* becomes a staple in labor relations law doctrine will depend on how the courts of appeal respond in enforcement actions involving *Cemex*-like cases and perhaps ultimately the reception that the doctrine receives from the Supreme Court with it's a six-to-three conservative majority. It is noteworthy that the dissent in the Supreme Court's *Linden Lumber* case was written by Justice Potter Stewart and joined by Justices Byron White, Thurgood Marshall, and Lewis Powell. Certainly, Justices Stewart, White, and Powell were no liberals. Moreover, *Gissel* bargaining orders have not worked out as planned: they are not deterring employer interference with employee free choice. So some revision of the *Gissel* approach is needed. *Cemex* should receive a favorable reception from the courts because it assures a union election through the simple device of having the employer file an election request with the NLRB and not subsequently misbehave by engaging in conduct that interferes with holding a fair election. A significant hazard to the longevity of *Cemex*, however, is that the next Republican-controlled NLRB might (and probably will) choose to reverse *Cemex*, at which point we are back to having national labor policy be determined by the outcome of the most recent presidential election, with all of the uncertainty that this brings—hardly a wholesome outcome.

Denying Access to Employer Property

Unions typically fail in their efforts to access employer property to communicate with workers. Moreover, employers are able to suppress much discussion of unionization among coworkers when they are in the workplace. The Supreme Court has endorsed the legality of these employer impediments to the exchange of information. These decisions, which curtail important channels of communication through which workers can learn the merits of union representation, greatly hinder workers' ability to establish bargaining relationships—especially today, when widely dispersed housing patterns impede communication with workers away from the workplace.

Many commentators have plumbed the "tension between employees' right to act in concert with one another to advance mutual interests, enunciated in section 7 of the Act, and employers' traditional right to exclude others from their property under state trespass law."[54] Prior to the 1935 enactment of the NLRA, employers were able to advance broad-based claims that most labor activity was an unlawful invasion of property rights. The NLRA defeats that claim because it provides workers with federally guaranteed rights to promote their mutual interests—through strikes, if necessary—even if some economic harm to the employer results. To that degree, federal law "sacrificed . . . employer property rights to accommodate newly recognized rights of labor. [But] the traditional right of employers as private property owners to exclude others from their premises continued to exert a powerful constricting influence on . . . employee rights that the Act guaranteed."[55] The Court has decided many access cases. They arise in two related but analytically distinct contexts: (1) employee access to employer property to advance mutual interests and (2) access by nonemployees.

EMPLOYEE ACCESS TO ADVANCE MUTUAL INTERESTS

Employees are business invitees or licensees, not trespassers, when they enter an employer's private property with the employer's permission to perform services and, while there, conform their activities to the conditions of entry. Employers often place restrictions on union activity by its employees, even as they are invited to enter the employer's private property. A core issue that labor relations law has needed to address is which of these employer restrictions violate the NLRA's ban on interference with employees' exercise of rights as guaranteed by section 7 of the act.

The Supreme Court began to sort this out in its 1939 decision in *NLRB v. Fansteel Metallurgical Corporation*.[56] There, the Court held that the employer's property right to exclude includes the right to ban a prolonged sit-down strike at the employer's factory, even when it occurs in response to that employer's unlawful antiunion conduct. The Court held that the NLRA did not ban discharge of the sit-down strikers. But what about other restrictions that an employer might place on employees' activities while they are on the employer's property during the workday, such as bans on discussing the merits of unionization?

The 1945 decision in *Republic Aviation Corporation v. NLRB* remains a bedrock case regarding the accommodation of employer property rights and the NLRA's commitment to protecting workers' rights to engage in concerted activities for mutual aid and protection.[57] *Republic Aviation* concerned the lawfulness of an employer rule prohibiting employees from soliciting for any reason on the employer's premises. The Board struck a balance: employers presumptively may bar employee soliciting during working time but not during nonworking time, such as lunch and break periods. In *Republic Aviation*, the Court affirmed this accommodation of the NLRA's protection of section 7 rights and the employer's property rights.

Republic Aviation might best be understood as protecting a property interest that accrues to employers from the wage contract. The Supreme Court perceived the employer-employee relationship as one in which the employer has paid for working time; thus, working time belongs to the employer, to be used as the employer dictates. Conversely, nonworking time belongs to the employee, and the employer presumptively lacks any justification for restricting this time.

In the hands of a conservative Supreme Court, the *Republic Aviation* rule has proven to be highly flexible, resulting in decisions permitting considerable employer incursion into concerted activity during employees' nonwork time. The *Republic Aviation* rule states: "It is . . . not within the province of an employer to promulgate and enforce a rule prohibiting union solicitation by an employee outside of working hours, although on company property . . . in the absence of evidence that special circumstances make the rule necessary in order to maintain production or discipline."[58] But this "special circumstances" exception creates a giant loophole: "An employer with an interest to protect that is unrelated to union activities may place contractual limitations on break time as well. [For example, the] Board and court[s] [have held that] prohibitions against union solicitation during nonworking time on the selling floor of a commercial business is perfectly consistent with [the *Republic Aviation*] rationale."[59]

NLRB v. Baptist Hospital, Inc. is a good example of the flexibility that the *Republic Aviation* rule provides to employers who desire to regulate the nonworking time of their employees.[60] There, the Supreme Court held that a hospital could apply a no-solicitation rule, even during nonworking time, to "corridors and sitting rooms on patient floors" and to immediate patient-care areas, notwithstanding the hospital's failure to show any adverse effect on patient care from anything communicated in such discussions.[61] Think of two nurses during their break time having a quiet discussion in a hospital corridor about an upcoming meeting at a union hall and one asking the other to attend the meeting. Or consider one handing the other a union authorization card. Patients might overhear such a muted conversation, but quiet nurse discussion of union matters in the corridor is no more disruptive than quiet discussion of hot-button political issues.

Another implication of the *Republic Aviation* rationale that the employer has paid for working time and thus owns it is the Court's endorsement of the employer's use of working time to force antiunion messaging on employees during captive-audience speeches while denying unions an equal right to communicate with workers at the workplace. In *NLRB v. United Steelworkers of America (Nutone)*, the employer violated its own rule banning solicitation during work time by holding captive-audience antiunion gatherings during these hours.[62] The Court held that the NLRA gives the NLRB discretion to find (that is, does not require it to find) that employers may conduct such worktime captive-audience meetings while also prohibiting its employees from conducting pro-union solicitations during working hours. In late 2024, in *Amazon.com Services*, the NLRB reversed course and concluded that compelling employees to attend captive audience meetings, under threat of discipline or discharge, interferes with their right to freely decide whether to unionize, "including the right to decide whether, when, and how they will listen to and consider their employer's views concerning that choice."[63] Once the second Trump NLRB is in place, this *Amazon.com* precedent may well be on a priority list for reversal.

Occasionally, the liberal wing of the Court has been able to muster a slim majority in access cases to provide a rare win for workers. *Beth Israel Hospital v. NLRB* is one example.[64] There, the NLRB petitioned for enforcement of an order requiring a nonprofit hospital to rescind its rule prohibiting distribution of union literature and union solicitation in the hospital cafeteria. The First Circuit enforced the order in part, and on review a five-member majority of the Supreme Court held that (1) the freedom of employees to communicate with one another regarding self-organization on the jobsite is essential to their rights to self-organize and bargain collectively; (2) the NLRB may adopt the rule that, absent special circumstances, an employer's restriction on employee solicitation during nonworking time in nonworking areas is presumptively unreasonable; and (3) there was substantial evidence to support the Board's order requiring the hospital to rescind its rule prohibiting solicitation and distribution in its cafeteria, which was an area rarely visited by patients but a natural gathering place for employees during nonworking periods.

The presence or absence of the indeterminate "special circumstances" exception is a fragile reed for determining when employees have the right to engage in organizing activities during their break times, especially when the rule is applied by judges and justices who are not prone to supporting workers' rights. No better evidence can be found than the concurring opinions of the four conservative justices in *Beth Israel Hospital*.[65] One concurring opinion (Justice Harry Blackmun, joined by Chief Justice Burger and Justice Rehnquist) concurred only because the Beth Israel cafeteria operation was an "unusual case," very restricted and more akin to a manufacturing plant's employees' cafeteria. It suggested that a different result, based on "special circumstances," would have been warranted had "a more usual hospital case been the one first to come here."[66] A second concurring opinion, this from Justice Powell (joined by Chief Justice Burger and Justice Rehnquist), would have radically undercut the *Republic Aviation* rule by finding it per se inapplicable to retail establishments, including a hospital's cafeteria, settings that are entirely different from the industrial factory in which the *Republic Aviation* rule was formulated. But the justices concurred because "the Board's decision was based on substantial evidence even without the assistance of the *Republic Aviation* presumption" because the cafeteria was predominantly the employees' facility.[67]

In sum, the *Republic Aviation* rule holds that "no restriction may be placed on the employees' right to discuss self-organization among themselves [while lawfully on the employer's property], unless the employer can demonstrate that a restriction is necessary to maintain production or discipline."[68] Though appearing to be supportive of the law's protection of employee organizational rights, the rule has proved to be porous. In the hands of an antiunion NLRB or judiciary, it provides ample opportunities for employers to divest employees of the freedom to use the workplace during nonworking time to communicate with one another regarding their collective interests.[69]

PRIORITIZING EMPLOYER PROPERTY RIGHTS

Unlike employees who enter employer property to perform services, nonemployees are not business invitees or licensees when they enter an employer's property without permission. In the view of the courts, nonemployee union organizers do not exercise their own right of self-organization when they seek access to an employer's property to assist employees in the exercise of *their* section 7 rights by providing information regarding the merits of union representation. In other words, nonemployee access cases are factually distinct from employee access cases. In an early case, *NLRB v. Babcock and Wilcox Company*, the Supreme Court held that "th[is] distinction [between employees and nonemployees] is one of substance. [Nonemployees'] access to company property is governed by different considerations [from employee access]."[70] The Court has acknowledged that nonemployees advance solid policy and pragmatic grounds for insisting on some access to an employer's property because "the right of self-organization depends in some measure on the ability of employees to learn the advantages of self-organization from others." But in *Babcock*, the Court ruled that employers must allow the union to approach employees on the employers' property only if "the location of a plant and the living quarters of the employees place the employees beyond the reach of reasonable union efforts to communicate with them."[71] In *Babcock*, the Court found that the employer could ban the use of its company-owned parking lot for the distribution of pro-union leaflets because other communication means were readily available to the union.[72] Following the decision in *Babcock*, the NLRB typically found that the union had reasonable alternative means of reaching employees when employees were not isolated from normal contacts, and thus the Board routinely denied access. The courts of appeal refused enforcement in most of the few cases in which the NLRB had ordered nonemployee access.[73]

For a while, the public access that is typical of the modern shopping center seemed to foreshadow access opportunities for unions based on the free speech guarantees of the First Amendment. In 1968, near the end of the Warren Court years, the Court decided *Amalgamated Food Employees, Local 590, v. Logan Valley Plaza, Inc.*[74] In *Logan Valley*, the Court analogized a privately owned shopping center to public property, concluding that peaceful union picketing at the shopping center was protected by the First Amendment. Within four years, the Burger Court began its retreat from *Logan Valley*'s view that the First Amendment protects union access to private property that has been opened to the public. In 1972, in *Central Hardware Company v. NLRB*, a union entered a hardware company's parking lot that was open to the public in order to solicit union authorization cards.[75] Disagreeing with the NLRB, the Court ruled, six to three, that *Babcock*, not *Logan Valley*, controlled because the *Logan Valley* principle was limited to large commercial shopping centers, not the parking lot of a standalone retail store, as was the case in *Central Hardware*. Then, four years later, in *Hudgens v. NLRB*, the Court reversed *Logan Valley*, holding that a claim for access to private property "is dependent exclusively upon the National Labor Relations Act," not the Constitution.[76] In concluding that the *Babcock* criteria controlled, the Court described *Babcock* as "a case which held that union organizers may intrude on an employer's private property only if no alternative means exist for communicating with the employees."[77]

In *Hudgens*, the Court ended its flirtation with giving unions First Amendment rights to enter retail property open to the public but then added, in dicta, a curious new twist to the calculus for gauging the accommodation between section 7 rights and employer property rights in nonemployee access cases. The Court posited that the balance may vary according to the circumstances of the case: "The locus of that accommodation . . . may fall at different points along the spectrum depending on the nature and strength of the respective section 7 rights and private property rights asserted in any given context."[78] This dictum appeared to abandon a static test that applies mechanically in all settings, substituting a balancing test requiring "a careful weighing of the interests implicated in particular settings where nonemployees claim a need for access."[79]

Sears, Roebuck, and Company v. San Diego County District Council Carpenters, decided in 1978, two years after *Hudgens*, signaled not only the Burger Court's return to a single static test in nonemployee access cases but also a view that nonemployee access should be denied in almost all cases.[80] *Sears* was a preemption case deciding whether the NLRA preempted enforcement of a state trespass statute because a union's entry onto employer private property was protected (or even arguably protected) by the NLRA. The Court concluded that there was almost no chance that entry would be deemed as protected under existing law. The employer's right to bar nonemployee access, the Court concluded, is "the general rule." To gain access, the union has the "heavy burden" of showing that "no other reasonable means of communicating its organizational message to the employees exists [and] the balance struck by the Board and the courts under the *Babcock* accommodation principle has rarely been in favor of trespassory organizational activity." Access for organizational activity "has generally been denied except in cases involving unique obstacles to nontrespassory methods of communication with the employees."[81]

In 1988, when the Board consisted entirely of members appointed by Republican presidents Ronald Reagan and George H. W. Bush, a unanimous NLRB decided *Jean Country*.[82] Notwithstanding the Court's strong signal in *Sears* that it was not prepared to endorse nonemployee access in any but the rarest cases that entail "unique obstacles to nontrespassory methods of communication with the employees," *Jean Country* followed the guidance in *Hudgens* and adopted a multifactor balancing test for all access issues.

> In each case, the Board agreed to weigh "the extent of impairment of the Section 7 right if access should be denied, in balance with the extent of impairment of the private property right if access should be granted." Decisions under this *Jean Country* balancing test tended to turn chiefly on the existence of reasonable alternative means of communication that did not involve the employer's property. The Board deemed alternatives "reasonable," by and large, only when they did not significantly dilute the effectiveness of the union's message. . . . *Jean Country* [usually resulted in access and] garnered support from each of the circuit courts in which it was challenged.[83]

Jean Country lasted only four years. In 1992, in *Lechmere, Inc. v. NLRB*, the Supreme Court rejected the NLRB's balancing approach.[84] In a six-to-three opinion authored by Justice Thomas, the Rehnquist Court issued its most explicit renunciation yet of nonemployee access rights. Acknowledging that, in previous cases, the Court had recognized the need for accommodation between employees' and employers' rights, the majority opinion made it plain, that in cases in which nonemployee organizing is at issue, "so long as nonemployee union organizers have reasonable access to employees outside an employer's property, the requisite accommodation has taken place" and there is no need for balancing the strength or weakness of section 7 interests compared to the employer's property interests.[85] "*Access* to employees, not *success* in winning them over, is the critical issue—although success, or lack thereof, may be relevant in determining whether reasonable access exists." As a matter of law, access is "reasonable" in the absence of "unique obstacles," as when workers are housed at remote locations such as mountain resorts, mining camps, or lumber camps.[86]

Advancing on two fronts, Cynthia Estlund has developed a powerful criticism of *Lechmere*. First, she demonstrates that there is no support in the NLRA for the Court's assignment of an overarching priority to the employers' property right to exclude while disregarding the degree of dilution of the effectiveness of the union's message if access is denied. A test for access that undercuts the NLRA's commitment to encouraging employees' full freedom of association by depriving workers of critical information needed to make an informed decision about unionization cannot be assumed to be within Congress's intent when it enacted the NLRA. Yet *Lechmere* is grounded in a view of the NLRA that embraces a sweeping rejection of access in nearly all cases, coupled with a total disregard to how inefficacious alternative communication options might be.[87]

Second, Estlund demonstrates that *Lechmere* is out of touch with modern property law by endorsing a right to exclude that many states have rejected as overly broad. In this regard, "the last fifty years have seen the rise of a whole array of new [state law] statutory and constitutional limitations on the right to exclude, as well as a reinvigoration of common law limitations in some jurisdictions," especially in property generally open to the public.[88] To accommodate the modern view of the right to exclude with section 7 rights, property owners should be permitted to exclude only for a substantial business reason independent of a bare desire to inhibit communication.

Access Rights Grounded in State Law

The common denominator of the above Supreme Court nonemployee access cases is that they all operate by upholding states' right to enforce trespass bans. By holding that, in nearly all situations, the NLRA does not protect nonemployee access, the cases permit enforcement of a state's trespass statute—for example, against a union leafletting at a shopping center. These state trespass bans are not preempted by federal law, as the Court explicitly held in *Sears*.[89]

But what if a state or local jurisdiction *permits* members of the public to have access to employer property to discuss labor issues by exempting from its trespass laws access to engage in such speech? Nonemployee access then is available, not because the NLRA protects the claim of access but because local trespass law does not prohibit it. Claiming access rights grounded in state law "inhabit[s] a controversial legal space: the intersection of the federal regulatory state embodied by federal labor law, free speech concerns of the public seeking access and the businesses resisting access, and the role of state and local governments in defining what property rights an owner actually may exercise."[90]

States expand free speech access to private property primarily through three mechanisms: legislation, judicial redefinition of traditional common law property rights, and access rights grounded in provisions of state constitutions. State legislation permitting public access to certain types of property is a growing mechanism for expanding free speech public access.[91] Some states provide by statute for free speech access at property generally open to the public, such as shopping malls. California, for instance, tracking the precedent of federal anti-injunction legislation applicable to federal courts, legislatively protects unions from injunctions arising from their communications with employees on employer-owned property.[92] Likewise, a city might enact an ordinance that extends free speech rights to members of the public in parking lots of any retail store that leases city-owned property. Or a state might extend access rights in certain industries, such as agriculture. Courts in some jurisdictions have redefined common law notions of traditional property rights to limit the right to exclude.[93] New Jersey is a leading example. Oregon also has redefined traditional common law property rights to provide public access.

California's is perhaps the most widely discussed example of a state constitution that grants the public free speech access to private property. In *Robins v. Pruneyard Shopping Center*, the California Supreme Court ruled that the state constitution's free speech clause grants citizens the right to engage in nonviolent, orderly expression in the public spaces of a shopping mall.[94] California is not alone: other state courts have followed its lead, finding in the free speech provisions of their state constitutions access rights on private property open to the public. A pattern of use by the public is critical.[95] These various state and local initiatives have withstood challenges based on labor preemption, for as the Supreme Court stated in *Thunder Basin Coal Co. v. Reich*, "nothing in the NLRA expressly protects employer rights to exclude organizers from their property when other laws require such access."[96]

State laws that provide nonemployees with access to employer property protect employees' freedom of association in two ways. First, they insulate union organizers from liability under state trespass laws when, for example, these organizers enter to peacefully distribute literature. Second, they render unlawful under the NLRA employer efforts to expel nonemployees from the employer's property. For example, in *Bristol Farms*, the NLRB held that employers violated the NLRA by ejecting from its property persons distributing union literature when those ejected possessed a right of access under state law.[97] The principle is straightforward: *Lechmere* insulates employers from NLRA liability when the employer exercises a right to exclude provided by state property law. When, however, state property law provides employers with no such exclusion interest—by, for example, permitting speech access to the public—there is no property right to accommodate with the section 7 right to receive the union message. Therefore, the NLRA prohibits the employer's attempt to eject nonemployees who are engaged in lawful, peaceful, nondisruptive speech activities.

State Law Granting Access Rights as an Unconstitutional Regulatory Taking

In 2021, the Supreme Court decided *Cedar Point Nursery v. Hassid*.[98] In this case, *it* struck down a forty-year-old California administrative regulation giving union organizers a right to meet with agricultural workers at their worksite on private property. For up to four thirty-day periods each year, union organizers could meet with agricultural workers at their place of work for one hour before and after employee shifts and for one hour during lunchbreaks. The Court concluded that this law physically "appropriated" property and thus constituted a per se physical taking. In the Court's view, the regulation "appropriate[d] a right to invade the growers' property," or "appropriate[d] for the enjoyment of third parties the owners' right to exclude," or "appropriate[d] an easement."[99] A commentator has described this six-to-three opinion as a "bellwether case," one that "was eye-opening in its breadth, its divergence from precedent, its implications for longstanding regulatory practices, and its provocative rhetoric . . . . After *Cedar Point*, it is now clear that nearly all recurring physical invasions imposed or authorized by the government—at least as to property closed to the public—are per se takings, however minimal the impact on the use and value of the property."[100] It remains to be determined how far-reaching the implications of *Cedar Point* will be—and scholars disagree. According to the most chilling view:

> *Cedar Point* marks a new path for narrowing . . . union activity . . . that necessarily burdens employer property interests. For example, under existing law, workers have Section 7 rights to use employer property to engage in union activity and pro-union speech while on nonworking time in a host of different ways. But *Cedar Point* could be marshalled to argue that those statutory rights also present "takings," and the government must compensate employers for all of those longstanding rights.[101]

Cases such as *Pruneyard*, which involve state law providing public speech access to commercial property that is generally open to the public, may survive *Cedar Point*'s expansive definition of Fifth Amendment taking. As the *Cedar Point* majority observed, "limitations on how a business generally open to the public may treat individuals on the premises are readily distinguishable from regulations granting a right to invade property closed to the public."[102] Time will tell.

THE CASES

CHAPTER 3

Limiting the Duty to Bargain in Response to Asset Restructuring

Business Transfers and Acquisitions: Successorship Issues

Over the course of roughly a quarter-century, in five cases spanning the years 1964 to 1987, the Supreme Court reshaped labor relations law by gradually permitting successor employers to avoid being bound by the collective bargaining agreement obligations of predecessor employers.[9] In addition, these cases gave successor employers easily adopted methods for structuring corporate transactions to avoid assuming *any* duty to recognize and bargain with the union that had represented a predecessor's employees. In short, this body of law has destabilized labor relations, deprived workers of hard-won representation rights, and erased the gains that workers had achieved in collective bargaining over many years. Moreover, the labor preemption doctrine, as the Supreme Court has developed it, has deprived local jurisdictions of the ability to provide a remedy.

Following some corporate transformation, a corporate entity may become a new employer for the employees of a former owner of a business. That transformation may occur, for example, through a merger or purchase of assets or after one company has taken over a service contract from another business entity, such as providing guard or janitorial services. When this occurs, important issues arise with respect to what is referred to as *successor liability*—the labor obligations owed by the corporate entity undergoing a change in corporate operations to the employees of the predecessor employer or to their union representative. These successor liability issues fall into four categories: (1) the duty to continue to recognize and bargain with the predecessor's union; (2) the duty to be bound by the terms of the predecessor's collective bargaining agreement; (3) the obligation to comply with the duty to arbitrate disputes contained in the predecessor's collective bargaining agreement; and (4) the duty to remedy the predecessor's unfair labor practices.

Debate over the optimal mix of successor liabilities centers on a desire not to "hamper capital mobility by discouraging takeovers and buyouts and by saddling purchasers with large costs." Yet national labor policy is (or should be) committed to minimizing the harm that workers and their union representatives suffer as a result of business transfers and acquisitions.[10] An appropriate way to understand and evaluate the Supreme Court's successorship cases is to evaluate how well the Court has accommodated these conflicting legitimate interests.

In 1964, the Supreme Court decided *John Wiley and Sons, Inc. v. Livingston*, the first case of what has become known as the successorship trilogy, the other two being *NLRB v. Burns International Security Services, Inc.* and *Howard Johnson Company v. Detroit Local Joint Executive Board*.[11] *Wiley* was decided in the last years of the Warren Court. It thus predated the onslaught of antiworker decisions in the 1970s, 1980s, and 1990s that emerged from the conservative majorities of the Berger and Rehnquist Courts. *Wiley* held promise that, by operation of law, a collective bargaining agreement would survive a corporate transformation. This worker-protective outcome turned out to be short-lived.

Wiley was a merger case. A smaller unionized publishing company (the predecessor employer) was purchased by and merged into Wiley, a nonunionized larger publishing company (the successor employer). The predecessor employer ceased to exist after the merger. The merger created the issue of the duty of Wiley, as successor employer, to honor the substantive provisions of the collective bargaining agreement that had been negotiated by the predecessor employer and the union representing its employees (the predecessor contract). The union that was a party to the predecessor contract brought a district court action against the successor employer to compel arbitration to resolve that issue. Wiley had hired all of the predecessor employer's unionized employees, and their job duties remained essentially unchanged. When the case reached the Supreme Court, the issue was whether the merger had voided the collective bargaining agreement and thus extinguished the duty to arbitrate.

Finding that there was a substantial continuity of the business operations, despite the change of ownership, the Court held that Wiley was required to recognize the predecessor union and arbitrate the issue of its duty to adhere to the provisions of the predecessor contract. The Court emphasized "the central role of arbitration in effectuating national labor policy" and concluded that this policy, which is designed to promote industrial peace, would be undermined if "a change in the corporate structure or ownership of a business enterprise had the automatic consequence of removing a duty to arbitrate previously established."[12] Justice John Harlan, writing for the majority, added:

> Negotiations [for a business transfer] will ordinarily not con-
> cern the wellbeing of the [predecessor's] employees [and while]
> national labor policy [needs to reflect] the rightful prerogative
> of owners independently to rearrange their businesses and even
> eliminate themselves as employers, [this must] be balanced by
> some protection to the employees from a sudden change in the
> employment relationship. The transition from one corporate
> organization to another will in most cases be eased and indus-
> trial strife avoided if employees' claims continue to be resolved
> by arbitration rather than by "the relative strength of the con-
> tending forces."[13]

Courts that have not tilted toward a pro-management viewpoint and are truly concerned with the interests of both employers and employees draft these kinds of decisions—and no informed person would challenge the fact that Justice Harlan was one of the Supreme Court's most respected conservative icons.[14] But that was in 1964. The Warren Court ended in 1969 and was succeeded by the conservative Burger Court (1969–86). By 1972, just eight years after the *Wiley* decision, much had changed, as evidenced by the Court's successorship decision in *NLRB v. Burns International Security Services, Inc.*

The *Burns* decision did not focus on things such as "concern [for] the well-being of the employees," "protect[ing] the employees from a sudden change in the employment relationship," or avoiding "industrial strife [by assuring that] employees' claims continue to be resolved by arbitration." Those values evaporated in *Burns* in favor of pro-business values that prioritize employers' freedom of contract and the importance of not hampering capital mobility by discouraging takeovers and buyouts or by saddling purchasers with large costs. Emphasis on these pro-business values underpins the *Burns* holding that successor employers are not required to honor the collective bargaining agreements negotiated by the predecessor employer. As the majority in *Burns* emphasized, "a potential employer may be willing to take over a moribund business only if he can make changes in corporate structure, composition of the labor force, work location, task assignment, and nature of supervision. [Accordingly,] saddling such an employer with the terms and conditions of employment contained in the old collective-bargaining contract may make these changes impossible and may discourage and inhibit the transfer of capital."[15] *Wiley* had said much the same but had added the need to balance these employer interests with those of the predecessor's unionized employees. The Court in *Burns* was presented with arguments regarding the need to address these countervailing employee interests. As the NLRB argued in *Burns* in support of its view that the successor must honor the predecessor's contract, "the stability of labor relations will be jeopardized and . . . employees will face uncertainty and a gap in the bargained-for terms and conditions of employment, as well as the possible loss of advantages gained by prior negotiations."[16] The *Burns* majority never responded to this claim but simply stated that *Wiley* was a section 301 action compelling arbitration while *Burns* was an unfair labor practice case where the NLRB was bound by section 8(d) of the Act not to impose a contract on an unwilling employer.[17]

Burns did hold that the successor has a duty to recognize the union that represented the predecessor's employees but only where (1) a majority of the employees hired into the workforce by the new employer are the union-represented employees of the predecessor and (2) the bargaining unit remains unchanged because there is a continuity of business operations before and after the corporate transaction. This might appear to represent a significant pro-worker aspect of the *Burns* holding. But the benefit to workers becomes far more fanciful once one understands that the successor employer is easily able to avoid a duty to recognize the predecessor union by the simple tactic of structuring the business transaction so that a majority of the employees hired by the successor are not the predecessor's employees. The trick is not to get caught making hiring decisions motivated by the goal of avoiding the duty to recognize the predecessor union by taking care that a majority of the workforce hired are not those who worked for the predecessor employer.[18] It hardly seems cynical to conclude that, "by not imposing a successorship obligation [that includes] at least [a duty] to recognize the union, if not to continue the terms of the collective agreement, the law encourages those corporate transformations undertaken in order to get rid of labor obligations."[19]

Two years after its decision in *Burns*, the Court formalized its retreat from *Wiley* in the asset sale case of *Howard Johnson Company v. Detroit Local Joint Executive Board.*[20] In *Howard Johnson*, following a unionized predecessor employer's sale of assets to another company, the predecessor union filed a judicial action to compel arbitration over the issue of the buyer's obligations under the collective bargaining agreement that the union had negotiated with the seller. The buyer hired only nine of the seller's fifty-three former employees. Distinguishing *Wiley* on two grounds, the Court refused to order arbitration. First, the buyer was not a "successor" because a majority of the employees hired into the new workforce by the buyer were not the union-represented employees of the seller; therefore, there was no substantial continuity of the workforce. Second, the Court pointed out that *Wiley* was a merger case. The predecessor employer ceased to exist after the merger; therefore, there was no entity in *Wiley* other than the successor against whom the union could assert its contract claims. By contrast, in *Howard Johnson*, a sale of assets case, the predecessor survived the transaction as a corporate entity and could be sued by the union for breach of contract.

Howard Johnson is unsatisfying to most who study the decision. On the one hand, its result can be explained by the fact that, unlike the surviving employer in *Wiley*, the buyer in *Howard Johnson* was not a successor, leaving unanswered the issue of whether the buyer in *Howard Johnson* would have had a duty to arbitrate had it been a successor. On the other hand, the Court in *Howard Johnson* distinguished *Wiley* on the second ground that, unlike *Howard Johnson*, *it* was a merger case leaving no surviving entity for the union to sue, suggesting that in merger cases where the surviving company *is* a successor, the duty to arbitrate survives. Really? What happened to the *Burns* view that national labor policy precludes imposing contract obligations on nonconsenting parties?

By 1987, the leadership torch had passed from the Burger Court to the arguably even more conservative Rehnquist Court (1986–2005). *Fall River Dyeing and Finishing Corporation v. NLRB* was the Rehnquist Court's contribution to successorship law.[21] *Fall River* added or confirmed three important aspects of the successorship doctrine, some beneficial to workers and some quite harmful. First, the Court confirmed that the appropriate yardstick for determining the presence of a continuity of the workforce was an evaluation of whether a majority of the new employer's workforce had worked for the predecessor. This test benefited workers because it resulted in more new employers being treated at law as "successors," compared to the alternative yardstick of whether the new employer had hired a majority of the predecessor's employees.[22]

Second, the Court in *Fall River* needed to clarify when the successor's obligation to bargain arose. Often there is startup period in successorship cases while the new employer gradually builds its operations and hires employees. In the mid-1970s, the Board was looking at the date when the predecessor union had made a demand to bargain, but some courts of appeal insisted that the composition of the successor's workforce should be measured when a "full complement" of employees had been hired.[23] In *Fall River*, the Board, with the approval of the courts of appeals, adopted a compromise, the "substantial and representative complement" rule, as the appropriate time for determining if a majority of the new workforce contained the predecessor's unionized employees. The Supreme Court agreed. While determining the duty to bargain by examining the composition of the new workforce once the new employer has hired a "substantial and representative complement" was not as beneficial to workers as determining the duty to bargain as of the date that a demand for bargaining was made, it was more beneficial for workers than waiting until a "full complement" of employees had been hired.

Third, the Court in *Fall River* clarified why the timing of when the duty to bargain commences is a critical factor in successorship cases. Until a duty to bargain arises, the new employer normally may set initial terms and conditions of employment free of any duty to first consult with the union.[24] But once a duty to bargain arises, except for changes already made, a successor may not set employment conditions that differ from those contained in the predecessor's collective bargaining agreement without first bargaining to impasse with the union.[25]

By agreeing that the duty to bargain commences as of the date that a "substantial and representative compliment" has been hired rather than waiting until a "full complement" of employees has been hired, the Court in *Fall River* shortened the time period during which a successor may unilaterally change working conditions from those that the workers enjoyed under the predecessor's collective bargaining agreement. One commentator has observed that, in this respect, "one detects [in *Fall River*] a modest resurgence of such policy considerations as continuity of representation and deterrence of industrial strife[,] . . . policies [that] had propelled the Court in *Wiley* . . . but in *Burns* and *Howard Johnson* they were subordinated to the efficient movement of capital and other competing interests."[26] While that is a valid observation, Justice Douglas notably described as "nonsense" the Court's successor cases that permit the new employer to avoid *any* bargaining obligation by deploying the simple device of hiring few, if any, of the predecessor's employees into its new workforce.[27] And even when the new employer is a successor who must recognize the predecessor union, these successorship cases destabilize labor relations by permitting the new employer to unilaterally make wholesale changes in conditions of employment, changes that erase many, perhaps most, of the gains that workers' had achieved in collective bargaining over many years. Moreover, it is unlawful for workers to strike to compel application of the predecessor contract to the new employer because such an application of the old contract by the new employer is not a mandatory subject of bargaining.[28] All of this in the name of protecting capital mobility.

A different type of successor liability—the duty to remedy the predecessor's unfair labor practices—was at issue in the fifth successorship case decided by the Supreme Court, *Golden State Bottling Company, Inc. v. NLRB.*[29] In *Golden State*, an employer who was subject to an NLRB reinstatement and backpay order to remedy an unfair labor practice sold its business. The NLRB ordered the purchasing company to reinstate the employee and ordered both firms to jointly or severally pay him a specified sum as backpay. The court of appeals enforced the order, and the Supreme Court unanimously upheld the Board order.[30] The key finding by the NLRB was that the successor had purchased the business with knowledge of the unfair labor practice litigation. The Court held that where a successor acquires a business with knowledge that the wrong remains unremedied, the Board properly exercised its discretion in issuing the order against the successor. Such derivative liability critically depends on whether a new employer has taken over the predecessor's operations with actual or constructive notice of unfair labor practice proceedings or an NLRB order involving the predecessor, something that often can be difficult to show.

Because the Supreme Court's successorship cases often have such a detrimental impact on unionized workers employed by the predecessor company, some states have attempted to provide a remedy. Three types of remedial state legislation operate differently and have different legal consequences. As the Supreme Court in *Wiley* noted, it is common for states to codify the general rule that, following a merger, the survivor business entity assumes the predecessors' contracts. This obligation may entail assuming the obligation of a predecessor's collective bargaining agreement. Such legislation is not problematic from a labor preemption perspective because this historic practice is labor neutral—it applies to all of the predecessor's contracts.[31]

Some states have enacted statutes that require the acquiring company to honor its predecessor's collective bargaining agreement. The obligation attaches in a variety of different types of corporate transactions, not just corporate merger transactions, such as consolidation, sale of assets, or other business combinations. For example, section 706, title 19, of the Delaware Code provides: "Notwithstanding [a] merger, consolidation, sale of assets or business combination, [a] labor contract [covering Delaware citizens] shall continue in effect until its termination date or until otherwise agreed by the parties to such contract or their legal successors.[32] A district court, however, has held that a similar Minnesota statute was unconstitutional, preempted by the NLRA to the extent that it applies to employers covered by the NLRA.[33]

A third type of state statute is referred to as a retention statute. These statutes typically require an employer to retain the former staff of a predecessor employer for a period of time, ordinarily ninety days, after a change in ownership. After the expiration of the retention period, the new owner has no obligation to retain any of the predecessor employer's employees. These statutes apply whether or not the predecessor employees were unionized. A growing number of jurisdictions have enacted these worker retention statutes, and they uniformly have been upheld against employer claims that they are preempted by the NLRA as interfering with federal successor rules.[34] As the district court reasoned in *Rhode Island Hospitality Association v. City of Providence*, the Supreme Court's successorship doctrine holds that the successor employer will be obligated to bargain with [a union] only if the successor employer retains its predecessor's employees beyond the [retention statute's] mandatory employment period or if it extends an offer for permanent employment prior to expiration of the mandatory retention period."[35] Until that point, the predecessor's employees are essentially probationary, and the new owner is free to decide whether its permanent workforce will contain a majority of the predecessor's employees.

Investment, Relocation, and Production Decisions: Narrowing the Duty to Bargain

James Brudney argues convincingly that, beginning in the 1970s, the Supreme Court's approach to workplace relations became less sympathetic toward group action.[36] Prior to that decade, the Court seemed to celebrate the ongoing vitality of worker collective action. For example, during the single decade of the 1960s, the Court reinforced the NLRA value of concerted activity by affirming nonunion employees' right to walk off the job to protest cold working conditions.[37] It also "conferred broad protection against sophisticated employer efforts to chill group action" through threats, through promised benefits, by granting super seniority to striker replacements, and by shutting down part of a business if a purpose was to discourage unionism.[38] Moreover, in the 1960s, "the Court also repeatedly recognized the importance of the collective bargaining process" by banning employer unilateral alteration of working conditions without bargaining, authorizing a Board-enforced bargaining order to remedy serious employer misconduct, and seeming to require bargaining over most entrepreneurial decisions.[39]

But beginning in the 1970s, as control shifted to the conservative Burger, Rehnquist, and Roberts Courts, the Supreme Court has shown a far less sympathetic attitude toward employee group action, choosing instead to endorse pro-business values. As I have discussed, the Court prioritized employer property rights in *Lechmere, Inc. v. NLRB*.[40] It also expressed distrust of the adversarial and political aspects of group action under the NLRA as evidenced by cases such as *NLRB v. Yeshiva University*, *NLRB v. Health Care and Retirement Corporation of America*, and *NLRB v. Kentucky River Community Care, Inc.*[41] This same pro-business, anti-group action mindset explains why today unions are unable, in most cases, to insist on collective bargaining over a company decision to relocate capital or other capital investment decisions, notwithstanding that these decisions often have a highly detrimental impact on workers' job security. This erosion of bargaining rights took hold in the Court's 1981 decision in *First National Maintenance Corporation v. NLRB*, which modified pre-1970s precedent that was highly favorable to workers' ability to demand bargaining over a wide-variety of a contemplated entrepreneurial decisions.[42]

Congress added section 8(d) to the NLRA in 1947, limiting the duty to bargain to "the mutual obligation of the employer and the representative of the employees to . . . confer in good faith with respect to wages, hours, and other terms and conditions of employment." Interpreting the scope of subjects contemplated by section 8(d), the Court in *NLRB v. Wooster Division of Borg-Warner Corporation* divided bargaining demands into "mandatory" and "nonmandatory" subjects of bargaining.[43] It held that insisting to impasse about adding a nonmandatory provision to a collective bargaining contract constitutes, "in substance, [an unlawful] refusal to bargain about the subjects that are within the scope of mandatory bargaining."[44]

Dividing subjects of bargaining into a mandatory-nonmandatory dichotomy has two significant implications. Employee-concerted activity in support of nonmandatory bargaining subjects is unprotected. Employers may respond with the self-help remedy of discipline. But "perhaps the greatest potential mischief arising from [the Borg-Warner dichotomy] is that it allows courts to remove basic employee concerns from required collective bargaining."[45] *Fibreboard Paper Products Corporation v. NLRB*, a case that the union "won," became the unwitting genesis for limiting the duty to bargain in the context of employers' investment and production decisions.[46]

Fibreboard involved an employer's decision to subcontract work without first bargaining with the union that represented its workers who had been doing the work. The Court held that the subcontracting decision was a mandatory subject of bargaining, that the employer had violated the NLRA duty to bargain by failing to bargain before subcontracting the work, and that the remedy was to return the subcontracted work to the bargaining unit to be performed by the bargaining unit employees. Perhaps more important than *Fibreboard*'s holding was its reasoning. Subcontracting was a mandatory subject of bargaining, the majority reasoned, because subcontracting was of "vital concern" to the workers affected. Subjecting the subcontracting decision to the bargaining process would advance the NLRA's policy of promoting industrial peace.

The *Fibreboard* majority opinion contained dicta that entrepreneurial decisions requiring major capital investment or a change in the company's "basic operation" might require a different outcome.[47] In his now-famous concurring opinion in *Fibreboard*, Justice Stewart argued that the duty to bargain should not attach to decisions that go to the "core of entrepreneurial control."[48] These caveats notwithstanding, the *Fibreboard* majority opinion adopted a sweeping vision of the duty to bargain that was consistent with the view of many scholars from the end of World War II until 1980, who "spoke of an expanding realm of collective bargaining that would eventually bring all matters of importance to labor into the arena of joint decision making, so that ultimately the duty to bargain would embrace most corporate decisions."[49]

In its post-*Fibreboard* decisions, the NLRB understood *Fibreboard* as having staked out an expansive realm for bargaining. The Board required bargaining over decisions regarding job categories, automation of the production process, relocation of work, sale of the business, and partial cessation of plant operations.[50] Robert Rabin sums up these developments by concluding that "the NLRB has required bargaining in connection with virtually every kind of decision that impairs employment security," with some pushback from the courts when decisions involve fundamental management rights.[51]

Revealing a stunning reversal of attitude and preferred values, the Burger Court's 1981 *First National Maintenance Corporation* decision adopted Justice Stewart's cramped vision of the duty to bargain, one that "radically altered the calculus that appeared to have been established in [*Fibreboard*]."[52] In *First National Maintenance*, a business provided housekeeping services for commercial customers on a cost plus fee basis. A dispute arose with a nursing home customer over the size of the management fee. Without first bargaining with the union, the company terminated its contract with the nursing home, resulting in the elimination of all bargaining unit jobs. The NLRB ordered bargaining over the decision to terminate the contract with the nursing home, and the court of appeals enforced the Board's order, holding that section 8(d) creates a presumption in favor of mandatory bargaining over an employer's decision to close part of its business. The presumption can be rebutted if the employer carries the burden to show that the purposes of the NLRA would not be furthered by imposing a duty to bargain.

The Supreme Court reversed. In holding that the employer had no duty to bargain over the decision to terminate the contract, the Court stated that it was adopting a balancing test—bargaining ordered only if "the benefit, for labor-management relations and the collective-bargaining process, outweighs the burden placed on the conduct of the business."[53] On its face, this balancing test takes into account only the interests of management; it fails to consider the legitimate employment interests of the workers and their union.[54] Indeed, in its discussion in *First National Maintenance* finding no duty to bargain, the Court focused almost exclusively on the interests of management, emphasizing (1) categories of decisions that need to remain exclusively management's prerogative ("retained freedom to manage its affairs unrelated to employment"); (2) convenience (need to be "free from the constraints of the bargaining process to the extent essential for the running of a profitable business"); and (3) efficiency (stressing the need for "speed, flexibility, . . . secrecy, [and] confidentiality"). It was pure speculation that bargaining would have provided minimal benefits to both the employer and the employees. As the Court acknowledged, the union might have been able to offer concessions, information, and alternatives that could have obviated or forestalled the canceling of the contract. In short,

First National Maintenance creates a calculus that is heavily biased in favor of finding no duty to bargain.

In the years since *First National Maintenance*, in cases that entail capital investment and production decisions, the NLRB has ordered bargaining only when the decision turns primarily on a desire to avoid contractual labor costs.[55] A savvy employer or its sophisticated labor counsel can almost always cast an entrepreneurial decision as turning on more than just contractual labor costs to include, for example, concerns regarding overall profitability. Accordingly, the post–*First National Maintenance* approach to determining the duty to bargain "insulates most employer decisions involving capital investment or corporate transformation. . . . The realm of mandatory bargaining has gotten very small and no longer encompasses most of the [investment, relocation, and production decisions] that unions need to influence."[56] "In most cases involving a plant closing, relocation, major subcontract, or sale of the business, the union and workers are, from a practical standpoint, helpless."[57] By assuring management the prerogative to control the introduction of new technology and redeployment of capital to new facilities or geographic locations, the Court endorsed a bargaining system that was inherently biased against unions, placed the impulse to choose unionization into an unworkable legal structure, and offered companies "new weapons to contain union power[, all of this] undercut[ting] the potency and appeal of American trade unionism."[58] It is difficult to disagree with James Brudney, who has argued that *First National Maintenance* is another example of the Court's choice to "emphasize the risks and costs of the collective bargaining process rather than its possibilities and benefits."[59] And some might agree with James Atleson, who views *First National Maintenance* as having converted the ideal of shared decision making between labor and management into a cynical myth.[60]

Bankruptcy

In congressional testimony, William B. Gould IV, a former NLRB chair and a law school professor, highlighted four judicial developments that he believed most "tilted the balance of power against labor." Among them was the Burger Court's 1984 decision in *NLRB v. Bildisco and Bildisco*, which Gould described as "another example of the pro-employer and antiunion approach to job security."[61]

In the 1970s, employers increasingly used the bankruptcy system to shed their wage-and-benefit obligations under collective bargaining agreements. This emerging trend undermined unions and the collective bargaining process. In *Bildisco*, yet another five-to-four decision, the Supreme Court affirmed that the bankruptcy code permits a debtor in possession to repudiate its existing collective bargaining agreements, thereby allowing employers to renege on obligations such as contractually negotiated wage increases and health and welfare contributions. News reports released when the *Bildisco* decision was pending stated that twenty-two corporations, including major ones, "had attempted to avoid their collective bargaining agreements through bankruptcy, and 19 had succeeded." In the early 2000s, bankruptcy cases flourished, enabling companies to shed labor costs and pension and retiree health costs.[62] After *Bildisco*, bankruptcy became "'a deliberate strategy used to broadly target costs associated with collective bargaining agreements and collectively-bargained pension and retiree health obligations.'"[63]

Bildisco prompted a public outcry, and Congress subsequently enacted legislation modifying it, now requiring bargaining over certain contract changes. But the bankruptcy code still contains provisions allowing employers to file an application seeking rejection of the collective bargaining agreement, and the agreement will be voided where "a balance of the equities" favors rejection.[64]

PART II

Diluting Statutory Protection of Employee Group Action and Enhancing Employers' Ability to Resist It

THE CASES

CHAPTER 4

Narrowing the Scope
of Protected Concerted Activities

Some years ago, Katherine Stone described a concept she called "the power broker effect of the labor laws."[17] By prescribing the actions that labor and management may each take during industrial disputes to further their individual interests, the NLRA actually is distributing relative power between management and labor. The Act "define[s] which . . . tactics are lawful and set[s] the ground rules for their exercise. Such rules cannot be avoided, and yet the content of each rule selected affects the power of each side relative to the other. [In this sense, the NLRA's rules] broker, or allocate, the relative power of management and labor."[18] The corollary to this observation is that those who interpret the NLRA are themselves powerbrokers. Judicial determinations shaping the scope of the Act's protections and prohibitions demonstrate this point.

By far, the most potent collective protection that the NLRA provides to workers is the section 7 right to engage in collective activities such as strikes and other forms of economic pressure to obtain favorable terms and conditions of employment. This right "form[s] the core of workers' ability to consolidate countervailing power against employers."[19] To fall within the protection of section 7, an activity must meet a three-part test: it must be (1) "concerted," (2) "protected," and (3) undertaken for employees' "mutual aid and protection"— that is, must be related to improving conditions of employment for specific workers or for workers as a class.[20] The Supreme Court has decided many cases involving the scope of the NLRA concept of protected concerted activities for mutual aid and protection. Evaluating these decisions through the lens of Court-as-powerbroker—as an entity that is allocating the relative power of management and labor—uncovers many of its latent value preferences.

Defining *Concerted*

Two post-1965 Supreme Court decisions demarcate the boundaries of the term *concerted* in section 7: *NLRB v. J. Weingarten, Inc.* and *NLRB v. City Disposal Systems, Inc.*[21] In each case, the Court stressed that the NLRA was designed to enhance workers' leverage vis-à-vis their employers in order to overcome the disparity in workers' bargaining power compared to their employers'.[22] By giving *concerted* a generous, expansive interpretation, each decision fortified labor law's ability to enhance workers' relative bargaining power.

In the 1975 *Weingarten* case, an employee asked for the presence of her union representative during an investigatory interview in which she was being interrogated by a management representative about reported thefts at the employer's store. The request was denied. The NLRB ruled that such a request for union representation is protected concerted activity and that disciplining an employee for refusal to participate in the investigatory interview without union representation violated the NLRA. The court of appeals refused to enforce the Board's order.

In a six-to-three opinion written by Justice Brennan, the Court upheld the NLRB's view that the NLRA's protection of concerted employee activities includes the right of an employee to refuse, without union representation, to submit to an interview that she reasonably fears may result in her discipline. The majority opinion reasoned that, though acting alone and having an immediate stake in the outcome, she was seeking her union's "aid or protection" against a perceived threat to her employment security. More fundamentally:

> The union representative whose participation she seeks is safeguarding not only her interest, but also the interests of the entire bargaining unit by exercising vigilance to make certain that the employer does not initiate or continue a practice of imposing punishment unjustly. The representative's presence is an assurance to other employees in the bargaining unit that they, too, can obtain [the union's] aid and protection if called upon to attend a like interview.[23]

In reaching these conclusions, Justice Brennan focused on the NLRA policy of enhancing workers' bargaining power relative to their employer's, concluding that the Act "is designed to eliminate the inequality of bargaining power between employees [and] employers [and that] requiring a lone employee to attend an investigatory interview which he reasonably believes may result in the imposition of discipline perpetuates the inequality the Act was designed to eliminate, and bars recourse to the safeguards the Act provided to redress the perceived imbalance of economic power between labor and management."[24] In this respect, the majority decision in *Weingarten* reminds us that, although the 1947 Taft-Hartly amendments strengthened management's hand in opposing unionization, it did not jettison the goal of national labor policy to "redress the perceived imbalance of economic power between labor and management."

Three of the Court's conservative justices—Powell, Stewart, and Burger—dissented in *Weingarten*. Justice Powell's dissenting opinion is instructive for both what it emphasizes and what it ignores. He stated he would provide a worker the right to union representation at a disciplinary interview only if the union were able to secure such a right for the worker as a concession in collective bargaining: "The power to discipline or discharge employees has been recognized uniformly as one of the elemental prerogatives of management. Absent specific limitations imposed by statute or through the process of collective bargaining, management remains free to discharge employees at will."[25] One might conclude from this dissenting opinion that Congress enacted the NLRA to preserve prerogatives of management. The viewpoint of the dissent is that, other than by requiring the employer to listen to a union's requests advanced in collective bargaining sessions, Congress, when designing the NLRA, never intended to lift workers' leverage vis-à-vis their employers in order to overcome the disparity in workers' bargaining power compared to their employers'. It is a startling and crabbed view of NLRA rights to limit the scope of section 7's protections simply to matters, as Justice Powell argued, that can be found in the "specific limitations imposed by statute." If section 7 protects only employee actions that already fall within the NLRA's "specific limitations," then section 7 is surplusage: there would no need for it in the Act. The political impulses that explain such a diminished view of section 7 rights become clearer, however, if we focus on NLRA judicial decisions as those of powerbrokers who are allocating power between workers and their employers and see the dissent in *Weingarten* as a transparent effort to shift power to employers.

NLRB v. City Disposal Systems, Inc. was a 1984 Burger Court case, and again Justice Brennan authored an opinion in a six-to-three decision. In *City Disposal*, the collective bargaining agreement between the employer and the union representing its garbage truck drivers stated that the employer would not require employees to operate any vehicle that was not in safe operating condition and that "it shall not be a violation of the Agreement where employees refuse to operate such equipment unless such refusal is unjustified." Nevertheless, one union employee, James Brown, was discharged when he refused to drive a truck that he honestly and reasonably believed to be unsafe because of faulty brakes. The question to be decided was whether Brown's honest and reasonable assertion of his right to be free of the obligation to drive an unsafe truck constituted "concerted activity" within the meaning of section 7 of the NLRA.

Weingarten and *City Disposal* shared the fact that in each case the employee was disciplined for acting alone in circumstances in which only he or she had an immediate stake in the outcome. The previous decision in *Weingarten* notwithstanding, the court of appeals in *City Disposal* emphasized that Brown's refusal to drive the truck was an action taken solely on his own behalf and thus did not involve concerted activity.[26] Again, as it had in *Weingarten*, the Supreme Court in *City Disposal* found that an act by an individual can constitute concerted activity for mutual aid and protection.

City Disposal was arguably a stronger case for finding concerted activity than was true in *Weingarten* because Brown's refusal stemmed from a right explicitly rooted in a collective bargaining agreement provision that management may not require employees to drive vehicles in an unsafe operating condition. Justice Brennan's opinion emphasized that fact. Congress added section 7's "concerted activities" language to the NLRA, he explained, in an effort to promote equal bargaining power between labor and management by "significantly enhancing workers' ability to assert countervailing power against employers." Brown's invocation of a right rooted in a collective bargaining agreement is an integral aspect of his and his co-workers' previous assertion of such countervailing power against their employer:

> Obviously, an employee could not invoke a right grounded in a collective-bargaining agreement were it not for the prior negotiating activities of his fellow employees. . . . Moreover, when an employee invokes a right grounded in the collective-bargaining

agreement, he does not stand alone. Instead, he brings to bear on his employer the power and resolve of all his fellow employees. [Invoking the collective bargaining contact right] was just as though James Brown was [physically] reassembling his fellow union members to reenact their decision not to drive unsafe trucks. A lone employee's invocation of a right grounded in his collective-bargaining agreement is, therefore, a concerted activity in a very real sense.[27]

Justice Brennan's opinions in *Weingarten* and in *City Disposal* contain the most elegant and powerful expressions of the NLRA's collectivist foundations found anywhere in the Supreme Court's cases, a recounting of Congress's recognition of a class struggle into which the U.S. government intervened by providing statutory protections designed to redress an imbalance of economic power between labor and management: *Weingarten* by upholding the right of an employee to refuse, without union representation, to submit to an interview that she reasonably feared might result in her discipline; *City Disposal* by finding concerted activity in Brown's solitary act of invoking the protections of the collective agreement. Each of these significant decisions enhanced workers' ability to assert collective countervailing power against employers, and each validated that an animating value in our national labor policy is to promote equal bargaining power between labor and management.

Defining *Protected* and *Unprotected*

The decision in *NLRB v. Jones and Laughlin Steel Corporation*, the Court's first case addressing the NLRA, made it plain that Congress did not intend to constrain an employer's prerogative to manage its business except to the extent that any exercise of management prerogative might interfere, restrain, or coerce employees in the exercise of their rights as protected by the NLRA.[28] In other words, the employer's "property right [including its derivative managerial prerogatives and entrepreneurial rights] stands in opposition to the employees' protected [NLRA] rights"[29] In the Supreme Court cases evaluating whether employee actions are "protected," employer property rights have unfailingly prevailed. The vast majority of them predate 1965, which is the start date of the cases examined in this study. Accordingly, they are discussed here in summary fashion. However, the Court has also decided a small number of post-1965 protected-unprotected cases, which receive a more comprehensive examination below.

In 1949, the Court explained in *United Auto Workers, Local 232, v. Wisconsin Employment Relations Board (Briggs-Stratton)* that, from its earliest NLRA decisions, it had followed the NLRB's lead (in *Harnischfeger Corporation*) regarding the appropriate measure for determining whether employee collective activity is protected or not.[30] That test is whether a particular activity "was so indefensible, under the circumstances," as to justify an employer's decision to discipline an employee for engaging in it.[31] Plainly, a "so indefensible" test is porous and thus an invitation for the Court to apply its own pro-business policy preferences, which it has done. The Court's decisions that hold employee conduct to be unprotected allocate power between workers and employers by uniformly prioritizing employer property interests.

For example, there is nothing in the language or legislative history of the NLRA suggesting that the duration, frequency, or intermittence of a strike determines whether it is protected. Accordingly, employees sometimes conduct "intermittent strikes"—a series of short, peaceful, unannounced strikes. Yet in *United Auto Workers, Local 232*, the Court stated in dicta what has become bedrock NLRA law: that the intermittent strike is "so indefensible" as to justify an employer's decision to discipline an employee for engaging in one. In the Court's words, it must be deemed "indefensible" because otherwise "management . . . would be disabled from any kind of self-help to cope [effectively] with these coercive tactics of the union."[32] Failing to cite any supporting evidence, the Court's conclusion that the employer was helpless in the face of an intermittent strike was *ipse dixit*. In any event, it is curious that the effectiveness of the union's peaceful and otherwise lawful collective strategy is what renders the intermittent strike unprotected concerted activity.[33] In prioritizing an employer's perceived need for effective options to resist a lawful union bargaining strategy, the majority left unacknowledged, and disregarded, Congress's intent in the NLRA to significantly enhance workers' ability to assert countervailing power against employers.[34]

One category of employee concerted activity that has been viewed as unprotected from the earliest days of the NLRA is activity that is illegal under state or federal law. This unprotected conduct includes mass picketing that blocks ingress and egress and disregard for state trespass laws when, for example, workers engage in so-called sitdown strikes in which strikers take possession of an employer's property and refuse to remove themselves during a strike.[35] From a political perspective, these outcomes were inevitable. As Ahmed White has observed, "were workers able to make unfettered use of sit-down strikes, mass picketing, and general strikes and sympathy walkouts, they could have very much challenged the sovereignty of capitalists in and about the workplace, and with this the bedrock institutions and norms of liberal society."[36] White concludes by arguing that the Supreme Court was never prepared to "endorse the . . . view that property rights might be sufficiently subordinate to labor rights [so] as to justify the[se] kinds of tactics. . . . [T]here is no reason to believe that any of this has changed or is poised to change today [given that our] culture and political system [are] more immersed than ever in the veneration of order and control [and] by the celebration of property rights."[37]

This veneration of property rights was on display in the Roberts Court's first protected-unprotected case, the 2023 decision in *Glacier Northwest, Inc. v. International Brotherhood of Teamsters*.[38] In *Glacier*, a union called a work stoppage against a ready-mix concrete company at a time when it knew the company was in the midst of mixing substantial amounts of concrete and delivering it to customers. The union directed drivers to ignore Glacier's instructions to finish the deliveries in progress. To delay the concrete's hardening process, drivers who had already set out for deliveries returned with fully loaded trucks and left the drums of their trucks rotating. By offloading the concrete before it hardened, the company prevented damage to its trucks. But as a perishable product, concrete that had been mixed that day became useless. The company sued the union for damages in state court, alleging various torts, including common-law conversion and trespass to chattels.

If the drivers' collective act of returning to the plant without delivering the concrete and then protecting it against hardening by keeping the drums rotating constituted protected concerted activity under the NLRA, or even "arguably protected" conduct, the state tort action would have been preempted. And, in fact, the state supreme court held unanimously that the tort action was preempted, thus leaving the NLRB to determine whether employees had taken reasonable precautions to protect Glacier Northwest's property from foreseeable, imminent harm.

The Roberts Court majority held that the work stoppage was neither protected nor even arguably protected and therefore the state tort action was not preempted. In the Court's view, by having the workers report to work and wait to strike until the concrete, or some of it, had been loaded into the trucks, the union "prompted the creation of the perishable product" and then ceased work when the concrete was in a vulnerable state. This constituted the unprotected act of "intentionally destroy[ing] the company's property during a labor dispute."[39]

A strong case can be made that the Court majority misapplied NLRB precedent, which had limited the principle regarding the duty to take reasonable precautions "to situations involving a danger of 'aggravated' injury to persons or premises," not a risk to property, as was the situation in *Glacier*.[40] The chilling effect of the *Glacier* decision on the right to strike has been inevitable, particularly in the food service industry, but also in other contexts when the employer's product is a perishable commodity.

Writing in dissent, Justice Ketanji Brown Jackson pointed out something that the majority opinion had chosen to ignore, except for a passing reference in a footnote. After the state court had found that the tort action was preempted by the NLRA but before the Supreme Court decided the case, the NLRB general counsel had issued a complaint against Glacier Northwest alleging that the NLRA protects the strike conduct that was at the center of the company's tort suit in state court. In addition, an NLRB administrative law judge had concluded that this complaint by the Board's general counsel "now independently establishes that the truck drivers' conduct was at least arguably protected under *Garmon*."[41] Moreover, the parties in the NLRB litigation had completed a post-hearing briefing to the NLRB administrative law judge the week prior to the Supreme Court's issuance of its *Glacier* decision.[42] In Justice Jackson's view, "the filing of the General Counsel's administrative complaint necessarily suffices to establish that the Union's strike conduct is 'arguably protected' within the meaning of *Garmon*[, and] because the General Counsel has now filed a complaint with the [NLRB] concerning the labor dispute at issue in this case, all courts—including this one—should stand down" and initiate a "*Garmon* pause" by remanding the case to the lower courts to decide the significance of the pending NLRB proceedings.[43]

In rejecting the dissent's make-sense suggestion for remanding the case to the lower courts to permit them to determine the legal significance of the

NLRB general counsel's conclusion that the drivers' strike had been protected concerted activity, the eight-to-one *Glacier* majority revealed a growing hostility to the NLRB's authority to determine even what strike activity was "arguably protected" by the NLRA. Without the benefit of the NLRB's or a court of appeal's consideration of the matter, the Court went out of its way to insert itself into the merits of the protected-unprotected issue.

Two realities may explain why part of the Court's liberal wing was willing to join such procedural irregularity in order to dispose of the case and support an outcome that creates a chilling effect on the right to strike. First, as I have discussed in chapter 2, they were influenced by *Cedar Point Nursery v. Hassid*, a 2021 case in which the Court struck down a forty-year-old California administrative regulation giving union organizers the right to meet with agricultural workers at their worksite on private property, calling that regulation an unconstitutional "taking."[44] *Glacier* was decided two years later. In this case, the employer advanced a "takings" theory, arguing that "construing the NLRA . . . to authorize unions to destroy employer property with no just compensation would put the law on a collision course with the Takings Clause."[45] The Court in *Glacier* was able to sidestep this challenge by concluding, contrary to the view of the NLRB general counsel and NLRB precedent, that the NLRA had not authorized the union's actions.

Second, the finding in the *Glacier* decision that the union's conduct was unprotected also avoided confronting "the elephant in the room—what to do with the [NLRB general counsel's] subsequent complaint, nine-day hearing, and hundreds of pages in post-hearing briefs. [These were matters that] engulfed oral argument."[46] Finding that the union's conduct in *Glacier* was unprotected deflected efforts by two members of the Court, Justices Thomas and Gorsuch, who urged in a concurring opinion that the Court reexamine NLRB preemption as an invasion of the state courts' prerogative to decide for themselves which actions in labor matters violate a state's tort laws.[47] The Court in *Glacier* left the doctrine of labor preemption undisturbed and deferred any reconsideration of the labor policy that tasks the NLRB with the primary jurisdiction to adjudicate the scope of the NLRA's legal protections.

But "the [*Glacier*] decision is a harbinger of more uncertain times ahead."[48] In this regard, the litigation in the case has been understood as an important addition to the Roberts Court's larger attack on the administrative state. In the post-Covid world of increased workplace activism, workers and their representatives, particularly in the service sector, endeavor to expand the administrative state's capacity to deliver social welfare goods, enforce workers' rights, and generally "play a larger role in shaping economic and social welfare policy. [But i]n so doing, labor's vision sharply conflicts with the . . . jurisprudence emerging from the conservative Supreme Court, which would eviscerate the administrative state, increase the power of the judiciary, and limit the government's capacity to regulate in the public interest."[49] Courtlyn Roser-Jones captures the significance of the *Glacier* decision when she explains why, in deciding to hear the case, the Roberts Court exposed its "crusade against the regulatory state" and its "proactive desire to . . . [appoint] itself—instead of Congress or the expert regulatory agency—as the decision-maker on labor policy."[50]

Another category of the Court's protected-unprotected cases (all except for one decided before 1965) entails employee conduct that is both legal and lawful but is deemed unprotected because it constitutes an alleged breach of a collective bargaining agreement's no-strike clause. The 1939 decision in *NLRB v. Sands Manufacturing Company* was decided the same day as *Fansteel* and just two years after the Court determined that the NLRA was constitutional.[51] The *Sands* decision moved the line of unprotected concerted activity beyond conduct that is illegal or tortious and into the more fluid category of conduct that contravenes public policy. In *Sands*, the collective bargaining agreement did not contain a no-strike clause, but the Court upheld the discharge of employees who had struck during the term of a contract to advance their goal of pressuring their employer to negotiate a replacement contract. The Court held that repudiating the provisions of a contract by striking is unprotected concerted activity. The majority drew a moral equivalency between such a strike and a tort: "The Act does not prohibit an effective discharge for repudiation by the employee of his agreement, any more than it prohibits such discharge for a tort committed against the employer."[52]

In *NLRB v. Rockaway News Supply Company*, decided more than a decade later, the Court addressed the question of an employer's right to limit by contractual waiver in a no-strike clause the otherwise protected concerted activity of refusing to cross a picket line maintained by another union against another employer.[53] The proviso to section 8(b)(4) of the Act declares that nothing in the NLRA prohibits a person's refusal to enter the premises of any employer (other than that person's own) that is engaged in a labor dispute approved by the union representing the employees of that employer. Accordingly, an employee of a secondary employer is engaged in protected activity when respecting a picket line established by employees of a primary employer.[54] The issue in *Rockaway News* was whether a no-strike clause in a collective bargaining agreement could waive this statutorily protected right of workers. The Court's answer was yes: it is lawful for a collective bargaining agreement's no-strike clause to ban employees' lawful act of refusing to cross picket lines at the premises of other employers. Breach of that ban constitutes a breach of the contract's no-strike clause and therefore is not conduct protected by section 7.[55]

Rockaway News substantially expands the *Sands* principle by endorsing the right of a union and an employer to agree to waive the statutory rights of employees. *NLRB v. Magnavox Company of Tennessee* holds, however, that the *Rockaway News* waiver principle is the exception.[56] The general rule is to proscribe contractual waivers of employees' protected statutory rights. In *Magnavox*, the Court refused to enforce a contractual limitation on employees' distribution of literature at the employees' workplace. Although *Rockaway News* upheld a waiver of the right to strike, it was "only in the area of the right to strike [that] the Court consistently [both] permitted—and, in fact, encouraged—contractual waivers."[57] Paul Barron has offered the explanation that the literature distribution that the employees desired in *Magnavox* had taken place on the employees' own time (breaks and their lunch period) but in *Rockaway News* the refusal to cross the picket line was on work time:

> [Under a contractual theory of labor relations,] the employer arguably purchases the employees' working time for a mutually agreeable price, and this consideration entitles the employer to require that employees follow his instructions during that time. Failure to comply with these instructions opens the employee to disciplinary action for breach of contract. . . . In other words, . . . activity that is protected when undertaken during an employee's own time loses its protection when it occurs during the employer's time [because there] seems a clear recognition that working time belongs to the employer.[58]

Barron's synthesis has a logical ring, but the Court's 1953 decision in *NLRB v. Local 1229, International Brotherhood of Electrical Workers (Jefferson Standard Broadcasting)* cannot be explained by claiming that employee conduct was illegal or tortious, nor that employees had breached a collective bargaining agreement, nor that the workers were violating the norm that working time belongs to the employer.[59] In *Jefferson Standard*, the Court upheld an employer's discharge of employees who distributed leaflets during their lunchbreak. The employees distributed the leaflets in an effort to obtain a favorable outcome with respect to an unresolved labor dispute with their employer following termination of their existing contract. The leaflets criticized the employer's television programming. Specifically, the criticism was that Jefferson Standard Broadcasting Company had failed to purchase the needed equipment to broadcast local programming such as local sporting events. Such local programming included "the same type of programs enjoyed by other leading American cities." The leaflets asked if the company considered Charlotte, North Carolina, a "second-class city."[60]

While truthful, the leaflets, which were signed "MBT Technicians," failed to disclose that the employees were then involved in a current labor dispute, something they easily could have remedied simply by adding the name of their union or the standard "Unfair to Labor" line to the leaflets. Discussions in the academic literature seldom mention that, in the weeks prior to the leaflet distribution, "the union [had begun] daily peaceful picketing of the company's station. Placards and handbills on the picket line charged the company with unfairness to its technicians and emphasized the company's refusal to renew the provision for arbitration of discharges. The placards and handbills [during the period of this initial picketing] named the union as the representative of the WBT technicians."[61] So when the "disloyal" leaflets criticizing Jefferson Standard's programming were later distributed, the ongoing labor dispute with Jefferson Standard Broadcasting was already public knowledge.

In a split decision, which rejected a contrary finding by the NLRB administrative law judge (then known as the trial examiner), the Board found the leaflet distribution that had precipitated the discharge to be "indefensible" unprotected activity, likening it to "acts of physical sabotage." The Board did not take into consideration the fact that the activity had been neither illegal nor tortious and that it had constituted concerted activity that was intended to secure a favorable outcome in ongoing collective bargaining negotiations. Yet while the employees' labor contract had expired and their leaflet distribution had been confined to their off-duty hours on their own time, they were not on strike but continued to draw full pay for the services they rendered during working time. Given these facts, the court of appeals remanded the case back to the NLRB "for a finding as to the 'unlawfulness' of the conduct of the employees which had led to their discharge."

The Supreme Court majority in *Jefferson Standard* rejected the court of appeals remand order and concluded that the employees' conduct, though lawful, was unprotected. The employees owed their employer a duty of loyalty that they had breached by publicly communicating honest criticism of the employer's product without disclosing that the criticism was in the context of a labor dispute. The Court described the leaflet's criticism as "a sharp, public, disparaging attack upon the quality of the company's product and its business policies, in a manner reasonably calculated to harm the company's reputation and reduce its income."[62] Apparently essential to the Court's decision was the fact that the leaflets had never disclosed a labor relations nexus to the employees' criticisms: "The employees purported to speak as experts, in the interest of consumers and the public at large. They did not indicate that they sought to secure any benefit for themselves, as employees, by casting discredit upon their employer."[63]

The reasoning in *Jefferson Standard* is a moving target: it is difficult to be certain just what would have been necessary for the employees' conduct to be judged as protected. Would adding "Unfair to Labor" to the top of the leaflet have led to a different outcome? Maybe. But the Court seemed more concerned with the disloyalty manifested by the content of the criticism:

> There is no more elemental cause for discharge of an employee than disloyalty to his employer. It is equally elemental that the Taft-Hartley Act seeks to strengthen, rather than to weaken, that cooperation, continuity of service and cordial contractual relation between employer and employee that is born of loyalty to their common enterprise. . . . Many cases reaching their final disposition in the Courts of Appeals furnish examples emphasizing the importance of enforcing industrial plant discipline and of maintaining loyalty as well as the rights of concerted activities."[64]

This statement reflects a vision of the NLRA that protects employee collective activity only to the extent that it promotes "cordial contractual relation[s] between employer and employee that is born of loyalty to their common enterprise." But then later in its decision, the Court emphasizes that "the attack . . .

was a continuing attack, initiated while off duty, upon the very interests which the attackers were being paid to conserve and develop. Nothing could be further from the purpose of the Act than to require an employer to finance such activities. Nothing would contribute less to the Act's declared purpose of promoting industrial peace and stability."[65] So if the employees had been on strike, would the Court have decided the case differently because the employees would have then been receiving no pay and the employer thus would not have been financing the leaflet distribution? The decision appears to be a case of a conclusion seeking a justification.

Far better than the majority opinion, the three-justice dissent in *Jefferson Standard* demonstrated an appreciation for core values embedded in our national labor policies:

> To suggest that all actions which in the absence of a labor controversy . . . should be unprotected, even when such actions were undertaken as "concerted activities for the purpose of collective bargaining," is to misconstrue legislation designed to put labor on a fair footing with management. Furthermore, it would disregard the rough and tumble of strikes, in the course of which loose and even reckless language is properly discounted. . . . More than that, to float such imprecise notions as "discipline" and "loyalty" in the context of labor controversies, as the basis of the right to discharge, is to open the door wide to individual judgment by Board members and judges. One may anticipate that the Court's opinion will needlessly stimulate litigation.[66]

The dissent was prescient in predicting that the decision would create confusion and much fodder for future litigation. Even now, seventy years after the decision in *Jefferson Standard*, it is difficult for those of us who teach labor law to give students clear guidance regarding the boundaries of unprotected employee conduct due to "disloyalty." And the Board and the courts have yet to corral the concept into a workable and predictable standard that the parties can use to guide clients.[67]

But the decision in *Jefferson Standard* is also troubling for a less pragmatic but arguably more important reason. The majority seemed to adopt, for workers, a Marquess of Queensberry Rules vision of labor relations in which the union is required to exhibit sportsmanship and an eagerness for fair play while the employer retains the right to aggressively harm employees economically by locking them out, permanently replacing economic strikers, unilaterally imposing contract terms following an impasse in bargaining, rewarding with priority in job retention those who quit the strike and cross picket lines, and structuring various strategies that permit withdrawal of union recognition.[68] Justice Felix Frankfurter, who was no stranger to the rough and tumble of labor relations, stated in dissent in *Jefferson Standard*:

> [The 1947 Taft-Hartley amendments do not] speak of discharge "for disloyalty." If Congress had so written that section [in the amendments], it would have overturned much of the law that had been developed by the Board and the courts in the twelve years preceding the Taft-Hartley Act. [Under the majority's approach of using disloyalty to find conduct unprotected,] many of the legally recognized tactics and weapons of labor would readily be condemned for [encompassing the] "disloyalty" [that might be] employed between man and man in friendly personal relations.[69]

Jefferson Standard should be exhibit 1 for the proposition that the Supreme Court has sometimes lost its way in its NLRA labor cases. It has periodically forgotten, as Justice Frankfurter explained, that our national labor policy is "designed to put labor on a fair footing with management [in the] rough and tumble of strikes."[70]

The Mandatory-Nonmandatory Subjects of Bargaining Distinction and Unprotected Means

Supreme Court cases that limit the scope of mandatory subjects of bargaining also shrink section 7's protection for employees to engage in concerted activities. During the pre–Taft-Hartley era, the Wagner Act did not create an explicit dichotomy between mandatory and nonmandatory subjects of bargaining. Accordingly, the NLRB assumed the role of deciding the scope of the duty to bargain and defined that duty so broadly that, in 1964, Justice Stewart was able to reflect, "There was a time when one might have taken the view that the [NLRA] gave the Board and the courts no power to determine the subject about which the parties must bargain."[71] That was never literally true, but under the NLRB's pre-1947 precedent, a union could demand bargaining over any topic deemed to be an "integral part of the employment relationship"—not much of a restriction.[72] This meant that employees could lawfully strike to demand bargaining over virtually any topic that affected their work lives, a right that gave them substantial potential influence over workplace decisions and thereby advanced the NLRA's goal of industrial democracy: empowering workers by altering the top-down, management-dominated structure of U.S. industry through some democratic restructuring of the organization of work.[73]

The 1947 Taft-Hartley amendments added section 8(d) to the Act, which the Court in *NLRB v. Wooster Division of Borg-Warner Corporation* found had created a dichotomy between mandatory and nonmandatory (permissive) subjects of bargaining.[74] In *Borg-Warner*, the Court held that an insistence on inclusion of a nonmandatory (permissive) subject of bargaining in a collective bargaining agreement is, in effect, a refusal to bargain in good faith, which, of course, is an unfair labor practice. In *Borg-Warner*, it was the employer who had insisted on a nonmandatory bargaining subject, but unions, which have a parallel duty to bargain in good faith, similarly violate their duty by insisting on bargaining over a nonmandatory subject of bargaining. Moreover, employees who engage in concerted activities to force bargaining over nonmandatory bargaining subjects forfeit their own section 7 protection because engaging in concerted activity to secure an employe's acquiescence to a demand for inclusion in a contract of a nonmandatory subject of bargaining is unprotected activity.[75]

There is a certain irony here. The *Borg-Warner* case, which determined that an employer engaged in bad faith bargaining by insisting on bargaining over a nonmandatory subject, has had one of its greatest impacts by adding yet another limitation on employees' section 7 right to strike. The Court's 1971 decision in *Allied Chemical and Alkali Workers, Local 1, v. Pittsburgh Plate Glass Company* expands this ban on striking.[76] In this case, during the term of a collective bargaining agreement an employer unilaterally modified a health and insurance plan for retired employees. If benefits for retired employees were a mandatory subject of bargaining, the unilateral change would have constituted an employer refusal-to-bargain unfair labor practice, and a protest strike over this unfair labor practice would not have breached a no-strike clause, rendering the strike unprotected.[77] But the Court held that the subject of benefits for already-retired employees was not a mandatory subject of bargaining. It ruled that matters involving individuals outside the bargaining unit can qualify as mandatory bargaining subjects but only if those matters "vitally affect" the terms and conditions of bargaining unit employees. The health benefits of already-retired employees, the Court held, have an insubstantial and speculative impact on active workers, so they do not "vitally affect" the conditions of employment of active workers. If the workers were to strike to protest the employer's unilateral modification of retired employees' health and insurance plan benefits, the strike would violate the no-strike clause if it occurred during the term of the contract and, in any event, would be unprotected because it concerned matters that are not a mandatory subject of bargaining. This "vitally affects" test is calculated to chill employees' exercise of section 7 rights and invites judges to apply their individual policy predilections. For who can predict with any degree of certainty the boundaries of a "vitally affects" limitation on workers' right to demand bargaining?

First National Maintenance Corporation v. NLRB was analyzed in chapter 3.[78] The Court's decision held that the employer had no duty to bargain over the decision to terminate a contract with a customer that resulted in the loss of all bargaining unit jobs. The Court stated that it was adopting a balancing test—bargaining ordered only if "the benefit, for labor-management relations and the collective-bargaining process, outweighs the burden placed on the conduct of the business."[79] As I explained, the *First National Maintenance* approach to determining the duty to bargain now "insulates most employer decisions involving capital investment or corporate transformation. . . . The realm of mandatory bargaining has gotten very small and no longer encompasses most of the [investment, relocation, and production decisions] that unions need to influence."[80] Moreover, workers can be fired for striking to protest these managerial decisions that are not mandatory subjects of bargaining.

THE CASES

The Right to Hire Striker Replacements
    NLRB v. Mackay Radio and Telegraph Company[1]
    Radio Officers' Union v. NLRB[2]
    NLRB v. International Van Lines[3]
    Mastro Plastics Corporation v. NLRB (again)[4]
    NLRB v. Erie Resistor Corporation[5]
    NLRB v. Great Dane Trailers, Inc.[6]
    NLRB v. Fleetwood Trailer Company[7]
    TWA, Inc. v Flight Attendants[8]
The Right to Conduct a "Defensive" Lockout
    NLRB v. Truck Drivers, Local 449 (Buffalo Linen)[9]
    NLRB v. Brown[10]

CHAPTER 5

Creating Reactive Economic Pressure

As I have discussed, outcomes in labor law litigation allocate power between workers and employers. Chapter 4 demonstrated how the Supreme Court's judge-made rules in its section 7 protected-unprotected cases bolstered employers' ability to resist employees' efforts to better their conditions of employment. Section 7 creates a zero-sum game. The employer retains all of its common law property rights to control the workplace, including the power to discipline, except to the extent that the NLRA limits that autonomy. Thus, whenever the Court holds that a category of employee conduct is unprotected by section 7 of the Act, it is creating employer rights: the right to discipline without NLRA restraint.

The Court has created additional employer rights through another body of judge-made rules that narrow the effectiveness of section 7's protection. Through these cases, the Court has enabled employers to impede employees from effectively engaging in section 7 activities by upholding the lawfulness of certain retaliatory actions that employers direct at employees who engage in *protected* concerted activities. In other words, without the need to find that employee activity is unprotected, the Court has developed judge-made doctrine that "allow[s it] . . . to shape employment relationships under the NLRA in ways substantially different from that which would have been possible if employers could respond [adversely] only to unprotected activities."[11] This chapter examines the Court's cases that create employer rights to deploy *reactive* economic pressure to resist protected employee group action. Then chapter 6 will explore the Court's cases that endorse employer use of *preemptive* retaliatory economic pressure.

The Right to Hire Striker Replacements

The decision in *NLRB v. Mackay Radio and Telegraph Company* is a paradigmatic example of a judge-made rule that permits an employer to undermine the efficacy of protected section 7 rights through reactive economic pressure.[12] The Court decided *Mackay Radio* in 1938, just one year after the constitutionality of the NLRA was established. In this case, an employer reinstated most strikers following a failed strike effort but refused to reinstate four who were union officers and activists. The NLRB concluded that the company's refusal to reinstate these four because of their union activities violated the NLRA. The remedy was to reinstate the four strikers to their jobs. The NLRB specifically declined to address the question of whether the Act grants employers the right not to reinstate strikers at all when they have been replaced during the strike, for that was not an issue in the case. The court of appeals refused to enforce the Board's order, reasoning that, by striking, workers had voluntarily severed their contractual relationship with the employer. The NLRB's reinstatement order compelled the employer to enter into new contracts of employment and thus was an unconstitutional invasion of the employer's liberty interest in freedom of contract.

At the Supreme Court, the NLRB attempted to limit the question to discrimination: whether the NLRA authorizes the NLRB to order reinstatement of economic strikers whom the employer refused to reinstate because they were strike leaders. The company insisted on framing the question as to whether the NLRB retained the general power to order the reinstatement of economic strikers under any circumstances. To be certain that the Supreme Court understood that the NLRB in *Mackay Radio* was only litigating the right to order reinstatement of economic strikers who were the victims of discrimination in reinstatement, the Board's general counsel, Charles Fahy, wrote a reply brief that conceded that an employer could replace economic strikers with permanent replacements—replacements whom the employer was privileged to retain following the termination of the strike. In short, the Board conceded an issue not before the Court, stating that the employer had no general duty to reinstate economic strikers who had been permanently replaced.[13] In the course of upholding the NLRB's right to order reinstatement as a remedy for discrimination in choosing which striking employees to reinstate, the Court in *Mackay Radio* declared in dicta that the NLRA grants employers the right to permanently replace strikers in the absence of antiunion discrimination.

Ahmed White has written that the *Mackay Radio* rule "came out of the blue. It was set forth in a case which required no such question to be resolved, in a manner that drew no support from the text of the Wagner Act, and on the basis of legislative history that was ambiguous at best. Worse, . . . the rule is in direct conflict with the . . . statutory principle of barring discrimination on the basis of a worker's assertion of the basic labor rights laid out in § 7."[14]

As the following list demonstrates, the *Mackay Radio* rule has many deficiencies.[15]

- In the NLRA, Congress protected the right to strike to enhance employee bargaining power, but since *Mackay Radio* workers' right to strike has served as a source of *employer* bargaining power. First, during organizing, employers routinely remind workers that employers have no duty to agree to any bargaining demand, unions often must strike to achieve bargaining goals, and in the face of a strike the employer reserves the right to permanently replace the strikers. Moreover, *Mackay Radio* creates an incentive for employers to engage in hard bargaining in order to precipitate a strike, for then the employer can substitute its unionized workforce with permanent replacements.[16]

- *Mackay Radio* has "rendered the strike useless and virtually suicidal for many employees."[17] Unions and worker groups, largely led by organizations of low-wage service workers, many of them women and people of color, have recently been engaging in more work stoppages and protests.[18] But as employers increasingly rely on permanent replacements, the frequency of major work stoppages has diminished. The 2023 United Auto Workers strike against the big-three auto companies is the exception.[19]

- *Mackay Radio* negates the NLRA's ban on employer "discrimination" based on union activity as well as the prohibition on "coerc[ing]" employees in the exercise of their section 7 rights. When an employer rewards those who cross picket lines by offering them permanent jobs while punishing workers with job loss when they exercise their section 7 right to strike, the employer coerces workers: that is, forces them to choose between exercising their statutory rights and losing their jobs to permanent replacements. "Whether the loss of a job

comes as a result of a discharge (concededly illegal) or of 'permanent replacement,' it certainly constitutes a powerful disincentive
to engage in protected activity."

- Employers are able to operate during strikes without the need to hire
  permanent replacements. The Court in *Mackay Radio* never argued
  to the contrary. In any event, those who have examined the question
  have concluded that employers do not need to make such offers.[20]
- *Mackay Radio* is inconsistent with current NLRA section 8(a)(3) doctrine. Since at least 1954, with the Court's decision in *Radio Officers'
  Union v. NLRB*, it has been clear that the NLRB may find that an
  employer has engaged in proscribed section 8(a)(3) "discrimination"
  without acting with the specific intent of discouraging union membership or activity.[21] The Court's decision in *NLRB v. Erie Resister
  Corporation* reiterated that point.[22] In *Erie Resister*, the employer
  granted striker replacements superseniority, ostensibly on the basis
  of business necessity, not antiunion animus. The Court upheld the
  NLRB's finding of an 8(a)(3) violation notwithstanding the absence
  of proof of antiunion motive. The Court held that the NLRA bans
  employer reactive economic pressure that is "inherently destructive"
  of section 7 rights. Granting superseniority to striker replacement
  qualifies because it causes a permanent cleavage among bargaining
  unit employees that compromises their ability to work together for
  "mutual aid and protection." This shift away from a motive-centric
  analysis of section 8(a)(3) in favor of an impact emphasis was reiterated in two post-1965 cases: *NLRB v. Great Dane Trailers, Inc.* and
  NLRB v. Fleetwood Trailer Company.[23] In short, the current approach
  to section 8(a)(3) renders the outcome in *Mackay Radio* indefensible
  today. In *Erie*, the Court stated: "Superseniority by its very terms
  operates to discriminate between strikers and non-strikers, both
  during and after the strike, and its destructive impact upon the
  striker and union activity cannot be doubted."[24] How is permanent
  replacement any different?

Mackay Radio has been understood as a defense of property rights. Ahmed
White argues that, had the case come out differently and had instead barred
employers from replacing economic strikers, strikes most likely would have

proliferated as workers would have fully understood that they had a right to be restored to their jobs, no matter the outcome. White believes that, in such a case, Congress would have concluded that workers now possessed excessive power and would have intervened with its own rule. "Ultimately, it is difficult to imagine a much more liberal alternative to the *Mackay Radio* rule."[25] However, a more liberal alternative to *Mackay Radio* has actually been advanced, one that is politically plausible: permit an employer to use permanent replacements after a strike has continued for six months, if the employer is able to demonstrate business necessity.[26]

In *Mastro Plastics Corporation v. NLRB* and *NLRB v. International Van Lines*, the Court refined the application of the *Mackay Radio* rule and ameliorated some of its harshness.[27] In *Mastro Plastics*, it added a major limitation on the employer's right to hire permanent replacements. The Court held that employees who, at least in part, protest an employer's unfair labor practice rather than strike to advance economic demands are entitled to reinstatement upon an unconditional offer to return, even if replacements for them have been hired. In other words, the employer may hire replacements, but only temporary ones, when employees are engaged in an unfair labor practice strike.

NLRB v. International Van Lines provides an expansion of the *Mastro* rule. In this case, employees were engaged in a lawful economic strike by refusing to cross a picket line formed in connection with a union's organizational campaign. The employer advised them that because of their failure to report for work, they were being permanently replaced. In fact, however, the employer had not then hired permanent replacements. The Court concluded that this misrepresentation was a discharge of the strikers that constituted an unfair labor practice directed at them, entitling the strikers to reinstatement and back pay. The strike continued, in part as a protest of the employer's unfair labor practice, and thus was converted into an unfair labor practice strike. The strikers made an unconditional offer to return that the employer refused. For this additional reason, the strikers were entitled to reinstatement with back pay. They had become unfair labor practice strikers, and the employer's refusal to reinstate them upon their unconditional offer to return violated the *Mastro* rule.

Prior to about 1980, employers seldom chose to operate with permanent replacements. The norm was not to use this tactic as an economic weapon. Then, by the mid-1970s, "the labor movement found itself . . . locked in bitter conflicts [with employers] increasingly over . . . fundamental issues, including the movement's very right to exist in a meaningful way."[28] This emerging no-holds-barred assault on unions, combined with the Reagan administration's willingness in 1981 to fire more than 10,000 striking air traffic controllers, made resistance to unions more fashionable and the permanent replacement of strikers less stigmatizing.[29] There is no question that, beginning in the 1980s, the permanent replacement of strikers occurred in proportionately more strikes than it previously had.[30]

In *TWA, Inc. v. Flight Attendants*, the Court decided a case that has created strong incentives for strikers to break ranks during a strike and return to work.[31] *TWA* held that strikers who made an unconditional offer to return to work at the end of a strike not only may not displace permanent replacements but also may not insist on exercising their seniority to displace less-senior strikers who crossed the picket line to return to work during the strike. Strikebreaking after the *TWA* decision provided a way for less-senior workers to retain their jobs after the termination of the strike by surmounting the seniority rights of more senior workers who did not choose to become crossovers. Employers benefit from the incentives that the *TWA* holding creates. Strikers are encouraged to quit the strike and become strikebreakers because doing so becomes an effective way to protect their own jobs once the strike ends.

The majority in *TWA* distinguished *Erie Resistor*. Granting crossovers reinstatement priority over noncrossovers, in the view of the majority, would not be "inherently destructive" of section 7 rights because, unlike the cleavage in the bargaining unit that the grant of superseniority in *Erie Resister* created, no cleavage would be created here. The *TWA* majority reasoned that full-term strikers at TWA, once reinstated, would lose no seniority either in absolute or relative terms and would be able to displace junior flight attendants—whether new hires, crossovers, or full-term strikers—with regard to future reductions in force, vacancies in desirable assignments or domiciles, or periodic bids on job scheduling. That was true, but only once full-term strikers were reinstated. The delay prior to such reinstatement may entail years of unemployment in the industry. For a considerable period of time following the termination of the TWA strike, flight attendants were widely aware of which junior flight attendants had quit the strike, crossed the picket line, and used strikebreaking to retain their jobs while more senior flight attendants who maintained solidarity lost their jobs.[32]

The Right to Conduct a "Defensive" Lockout

Two cases, *NLRB v. Truck Drivers, Local 449 (Buffalo Linen)* and *NLRB v. Brown*, litigated the question of an employer's right to assert reactive economic pressure against employees who had engaged in protected concerted activities by initiating a "defensive" lockout of its employees.[33] In *Buffalo Linen*, an association of eight employers in the linen supply business and the union representing their truck drivers had for many years negotiated successive multiemployer collective bargaining agreements. In one of those negotiations, after six weeks of unproductive bargaining, the union put into effect a whipsaw plan. Whipsawing is the process of striking one at a time, or in small groups, against the employer members of a multiemployer association. Whipsawing is a lawful way to increase bargaining leverage on an employer whose workers are striking while its competitors' are not. The strike against the one employer necessarily carries with it an implicit threat of future strike action against other members of the association, with the calculated purpose of causing successive individual employer capitulations. In this case, on the day after the union began the whipsaw strike against one member of the association, the other seven members laid off their truck drivers after notifying the union that the layoff action had been taken because of the strike against one association member. The union was advised that the laid-off drivers—the locked-out drivers—would be recalled if the union withdrew its picket line and ended the strike. A week later, agreement on a new contract was reached, the union ended the strike, the locked-out drivers were recalled, and normal operations were resumed.

The union filed a claim of unfair labor practices against the non-struck employers, alleging that locking out their drivers was unlawful. The NLRB general counsel agreed and issued a complaint; the NLRB trial examiner also agreed and recommended that the Board find a violation. The NLRB dismissed the complaint, reasoning that a strike by employees against one employer-member of a multiemployer bargaining unit constitutes a threat of strike action against the other employers. Thus, the threat constitutes the type of economic action that justifies their resort to a temporary lockout of employees.

The Court of Appeals for the Second Circuit reversed the NLRB order that had dismissed the complaint. The appeals court held that the lockout constituted an unlawful interference with the statutory rights of nonstriking employees to choose whether or not to engage in concerted activity and also constituted discrimination that could be justified only if there were an unusual economic hardship. On these facts, there was no economic justification for the lockout.

The Supreme Court unanimously agreed with the NLRB that the non-struck members of a multiemployer bargaining association did not commit an unfair labor practice by locking out their employees. The temporary lockout during contract negotiation was justified, the Court reasoned, "as a defense to a union strike tactic which threatens the destruction of the employers' interest in bargaining on a group basis."[34] The premise of the Court's reasoning was that the preservation of bargaining on a group basis trumps the union's right to call a strike without the employees of the non-struck employers suffering the risk of retaliation resulting from the non-struck employers' lockout. The *Buffalo Linen* decision allocates power to employers in the name of promoting the advantages that they—especially small employers—gain from group bargaining. The decision is a paean to the small American entrepreneur whose bargaining position the Court chose to prioritize over the interests of workers who temporarily lose their jobs and income stream when locked out. As the Court said, "conflict may arise between the right to strike and the interest of small employers in preserving multi-employer bargaining as a means of bargaining on an equal basis with a large union and avoiding the competitive disadvantages resulting from nonuniform contractual terms. The ultimate problem is the balancing of the conflicting legitimate interests."[35] Then the Court fell back on the old chestnut that Congress had committed primarily to the NLRB the function of striking the balance to effectuate national labor policy and the Court needed to defer to the Board.

The next stage in the defensive lockout saga was predictable. In *NLRB v. Brown*, the union initiated a whipsaw strike against one member of a multi-employer bargaining unit.[36] The non-struck employers exercised their *Buffalo Linen* right to lockout. But then all members of the employer group continued operations with temporary replacement employees. The issue litigated in *Brown* was the lawfulness of combining a *Buffalo Linen* lockout with the hiring of temporary replacements. Irrespective of motive, under the rationale of *Erie Resistor*, if the impact of this combination was "inherently destructive" of employees' section 7 rights, then the combination of locking out followed by hiring replacements violated the NLRA.

This time, NLRB found that the employer had violated the NLRA by locking out their regular employees and then using temporary replacements to carry on business. The NLRB distinguished *Buffalo Linen* where all members of the employer group shut down operations. In *Brown*, all of the employers continued operations with temporary replacements and it was reasonable to infer that the employers did so *not* to protect the multiemployer group from disintegration, but rather acted "for the purpose of inhibiting a lawful strike."

The court of appeals disagreed and refused to enforce the Board's order. The Supreme Court affirmed the court of appeals:

> The Board's decision does not rest upon independent evidence that the [employers] acted either out of hostility toward the [union] or in reprisal for the whipsaw strike. [The Board's decision] rests upon the Board's appraisal that the [employers'] conduct carried its own indicia of unlawful intent, thereby establishing, without more, that the conduct constituted an unfair labor practice. It was disagreement with this appraisal, which we share, that led the Court of Appeals to refuse to enforce the Board's order.[37]

The Court concluded that the non-struck employers had the right to lock out and replace employees to protect the multiemployer bargaining unit from destruction. The Court reasoned as follows: (1) *Buffalo Linen* gave the non-struck employers in a multiemployer unit a right to lock out whenever a member of the unit is struck so that a parity of economic advantage or disadvantage between the struck and non-struck employers can be maintained. (2) In order to maintain that parity where the struck employer hires replacements, the non-struck employers must also be free to hire replacements, lest the right to lock out to protect the multiemployer bargaining unit be illusory.(3) The non-struck employers need not offer these jobs to the locked-out employees desiring to work, lest the parity between the struck and non-struck employers be lost and the right to lock out be meaningless.[38]

This reasoning in *Brown* is flawed because its premise is unsound. *Buffalo Linen* did not give employers the unqualified right to lock out. Rather, it held, notwithstanding the lockout's severe adverse effects on employee protected rights, that the non-struck employers in that case could cease operations by means of a lockout after the union had successfully shut down the operations of one of the employers. This right to lockout was needed to avoid the destructive effects on multiemployer bargaining resulting when one employer is unable to operate due to being struck while the others maintain full operations. In short, *Buffalo Linen*'s rationale is that the NLRA does not require the non-struck employers to contribute to this pressure by being forced to maintain full operations.

But when the struck employer itself resumes operations with replacements, the threat to the integrity of the multiemployer unit, the decisive consideration in *Buffalo Linen*, is dramatically different. Indeed, in the *Brown* case, the NLRB found that there was "no economic necessity . . . for the other members shutting down."[39] The majority opinion in *Brown* is built on the faulty premise that *Buffalo Linen* established the non-struck members' unencumbered right to lock out, absent any motivation linked to antiunion animus. The self-evident way to protect the integrity of the multiemployer bargaining unit when the struck employer continues operations by hiring replacements is for the other employers also to continue operations by not locking out. It was reasonable, therefore, for the NLRB to conclude that when the non-struck employers do choose to lock out and then replace, they are motivated by factors other than preserving the integrity of the multiemployer association. As Justice White argued in his dissent in *Brown*, any "disparity between the struck employer who resumes operations and the non-struck employers who choose to lock out to maintain a united front is caused by the unilateral action[s] of [those] employer members of the [multiemployer bargaining unit who chose to lockout] and not by the union's whipsawing tactic."[40]

It certainly was not unreasonable, arbitrary, or capricious for the NLRB to have adopted the "assessment" in *Brown* that dismissing non-striking union members who desired to work and hiring temporary replacements simply because other union members working for a different employer have struck is "inherently destructive" of protected employee rights. *Buffalo Linen* and *Brown* demonstrate again, as has been true in many other cases discussed throughout this book, that the Court's reliance on the duty to defer to the NLRB is a toggle switch: only when the value preferences underpinning a Board decision seem compatible with the Court's preferences does the Court conclude that it must defer to the Board because Congress committed primarily to the NLRB the function of striking the balance to effectuate national labor policy. Otherwise, the Court finds reasons not to defer.

THE CASES

The Right to Threaten Plant Closing or Relocation
  Textile Workers v. Darlington Manufacturing Company[1]
  NLRB v. Gissel Packing Company[2]
The Right to Conduct an "Offensive" Lockout
  American Ship Building Company v. NLRB[3]
The Right to Make Unilateral Changes in Conditions of Employment
  NLRB v. Katz[4]
The Right to Litigate a Retaliatory Lawsuit against a Union
  Bill Johnson's Restaurants, Inc. v. NLRB[5]
  BE & K Construction Company v. NLRB[6]
The Right to Withdraw Recognition
  Charles D. Bonanno Linen Service, Inc. v. NLRB[7]
  NLRB v. Curtin Matheson Scientific, Inc.[8]
  Auciello Iron Works v. NLRB[9]
  Allentown Mack Sales and Service, Inc. v. NLRB[10]

CHAPTER 6

Employer Preemptive Economic Pressure

Chapter 5 analyzed Supreme Court decisions that shaped rules permitting employers to deploy retaliatory economic pressure in response to employees' engagement in protected group action. This chapter examines a number of related Court decisions, with the difference that, in these cases, the economic pressure that employers asserted cannot be explained by a need to defend themselves from employees' collective efforts. Rather, employers deployed averse actions preemptively to impede employees from being able to engage effectively in protected section 7 activities.[11]

The Right to Threaten Plant Closing or Relocation

Those familiar with the Court's labor law cases might find it unusual to link *Textile Workers v. Darlington Manufacturing Company* and *NLRB v. Gissel Packing Company* as examples of cases in which the Supreme Court created rules empowering employers to act preemptively to deter employees from engaging in protected section 7 rights.[12] That's because each case contains a holding that seemingly supports employee rights. *Gissel* provided broad protection against sophisticated employer efforts to chill group action through threats, and *Darlington* banned shutting down part of a business if a purpose of that closure is to discourage unionization. But each case also gave employers rights that can be used to coerce employees.

Darlington is an excellent example of the Court's choice to prioritize managerial prerogative and employer property rights over the rights of workers and the collective bargaining process. In this case, the Court upheld an employer's right to permanently close its plant in response to its employees' decision to choose union representation. Such an antiunion-motivated shutdown clearly interfered with the employees' right to self-organization: they lost their jobs. The issue in *Darlington* was not whether the plant would be reopened (the NLRB did not order that) but whether the Deering Milliken Corporation "had the right to close to punish the employees and be *free* of any [backpay] obligation for the affected employees."[13] The Court found no NLRA violation because "[the] proposition that a single businessman cannot choose to go out of business if he wants to would represent such a startling innovation that it should not be entertained without the clearest manifestation of legislative intent."[14] Moreover, the Court reasoned, a complete liquidation is lawful regardless of motivation because it yields no future benefit for the employer.[15] In contrast, "a partial closing is an unfair labor practice under [section] 8(a)(3) if motivated by a purpose to chill unionism in any of the remaining plants of the single employer and if the employer may reasonably have foreseen that such closing would likely have that effect."[16] So, in the Court's view, a partial closing is a protected employer right, even if it is a response to employees' protected concerted activity, so long as it cannot be proved that the employer used the closing to chill unionism among other employees. Missing here is the slightest concern for the employees who lost their jobs as a result of the plant closure. Paul Barron writes:

> Unquestionably, the plant closing discourages [these] employees from future membership in a union and [thereby prospectively] interferes with, restrains, and coerces them in the exercise of their section 7 rights. More importantly, when coupled with the employer's right to announce prior to an election its decision to close [as the Court in *Darlington* held was lawful], this right to close may have a chilling effect on the election itself.[17]

In short, *Darlington* hollowed out employees' ability to protect their jobs when an employer liquidates a business to escape the economic consequences of a union. An antiunion plant closing is lawful unless there is proof that the employer "occup[ies] a relationship to [some] other business which makes it realistically foreseeable that its employees will fear that such business will also be closed down if they persist in organizational activities"—in other words, proof that the employer has discharged some in order to intimidate others.[18]

Gissel is derivatively complicit with *Darlington* in chilling employees' section 7 activity because it reiterates the point made in *Darlington* that the NLRA permits an employer to announce in advance of a union election a decision already reached by the board of directors to close the plant, should the employees choose to unionize. In *Gissel*, the Court explained this right as follows: "[The employer] may even make a prediction as to the precise effects he believes unionization will have on his company. In such a case, however, the prediction must be carefully phrased on the basis of objective fact to convey an employer's belief as to demonstrably probable consequences beyond his control or to convey a management decision already arrived at to close the plant in case of unionization."[19] If the union wins the election and the company does not retaliate by closing the business, who is going to complain? *Darlington* and *Gissel* have enabled the company to launch with impunity a preemptive false threat to close the business, should employees unionize.

The Right to Conduct an "Offensive" Lockout and the Right to Make Unilateral Changes in Conditions of Employment

The Court completed its lockout trilogy in its decision in *American Ship Building Company v. NLRB*.[20] *Buffalo Linen* and *NLRB v. Brown* were discussed in chapter 5. Both concerned defensive lockouts initiated in response to a union's whipsaw strike. In *American Ship Building*, there was no pretense that the employer needed the lockout as self-defense. Rather, the employer initiated the lockout as a preemptive bargaining tactic, an economic weapon to coerce employees into acceding to the employer's bargaining demands. The offensive lockout in *American Ship Building* occurred following an impasse in bargaining, but it is easy to recognize the intimidation that can take place throughout the bargaining process, inherent in employees' knowledge that their employer is permitted to control whether or not they would lose their income as a result of their decision to engage in collective bargaining. Julius Getman captures the reality when he observes: "It requires a narrow focus to ignore the pressure on employees and the fear that might follow the employer's message that[, due to the labor dispute, employees were to be laid off until further notice]. The message to employees undoubtedly conveyed—as it [would normally be] intended to—[wa]s that insisting on their collective bargaining positions was a dangerous business whether or not they struck."[21] The simple truth is that employees suffer retaliation as a result of the offensive lockout because they choose to protect their interests through the "practice and procedure of collective bargaining," which is the core activity that our national labor policy encourages. Because of its inherently destructive impact on protected section 7 activity, the NLRB held that the offensive lockout violated the NLRA. In *American Ship Building*, however, the Supreme Court disagreed, characterizing the offensive lockout as simply one of the economic weapons available to employers in the give-and-take of collective bargaining.

The coercive impact of the *American Ship Building* decision is best appreciated in the context of another 1960s Supreme Court decision, *NLRB v. Katz*.[22] The decision in *Katz* provides that an employer may lawfully make unilateral changes with respect to mandatory subjects of bargaining not contained in an existing collective bargaining contract once impasse in bargaining occurs. Ellen Dannin has convincingly argued that the *Katz* unilateral implementation rule, combined with the offensive lockout and the employer's right to permanently replace strikers, "gives employers the power to destroy collective bargaining."[23]

These judge-made rules operate in tandem to harm employees. Because section 8(d) provides that the duty to bargain does not entail any duty to agree, an employer can engage in "hard bargaining" until an impasse in bargaining is reached and then advance a final offer to the union that provides little of value for the employees. The union, of course, can accept those terms but does so at great risk; for by doing so, it demonstrates its impotence and becomes a ripe candidate for a successful decertification challenge.

If the union chooses to do nothing in the face of an employer's post-impasse final offer, the employer can lawfully exercise its post-impasse right under *American Ship Building* and lock out the employees as an offensive weapon to pressure the union to accept its offer. A bargaining impasse might not be needed for the offensive lockout to be lawful, but that currently is an unsettled issue.[24] Following a lawful offensive lockout, the employer may hire temporary replacements and continue operations.[25] The employer may add conditions to the locked-out employees' right to return to work by clearly communicating that it will refuse to offer reinstatement until a new agreement is reached.[26]

If a union receives what it considers to be an inadequate final offer from the employer and chooses to resist by striking for a better contract, the strikers risk losing their jobs to permanent replacements under the *Mackay Radio* rule.[27] And if impasse in bargaining has been reached, the employer can rely on the *Katz* implementation-upon-impasse rule to unilaterally set conditions of employment. The employers' trifecta of economic weapons—the implementation-upon-impasse rule of *Katz*, the offensive lockout of *American Ship Building*, and the right to permanently replace of *Mackay Radio*—places them in a commanding position during bargaining and can be an effective way for an employer to rid itself of the union entirely.

The Right to Litigate a Retaliatory Lawsuit against a Union

Beginning in the late 1970s and early 1980s, unions broadened their organizing strategies and methods of asserting economic pressure on employers. Unions continued to rely on picketing and striking but increasingly designed "comprehensive campaigns" to develop leverage. These innovative campaigns relied on the creative use of a wider range of techniques, such as forging ties with community organizations and environmental groups, legislative lobbying and lawsuits, shareholder actions, creative media work, and "urging regulatory agencies to target employers for health and safety and environmental violations, and oppose building and zoning permits."[28] Employers retaliated to the labor movement's broadened array of campaign tactics by taking unions, their officials, and individual workers to court. "This litigation relied on . . . state tort claims [such as defamation] . . . and the development of new federal antitrust and RICO claims."[29] Even when unsuccessful—and this litigation habitually lacked merit—such suits can kill the momentum of a union's campaign and inflict substantial costs on the defendants.[30] Many unions filed unfair labor practice charges against employers who brought this litigation, alleging that the employers had filed baseless suits motivated by retaliatory animus in response to employees having exercised protected section 7 rights. Out of this conflict arose two important Supreme Court cases: *Bill Johnson's Restaurants, Inc. v. NLRB* and *BE & K Construction Company v. NLRB*.[31] Employers prevailed in each case at the Supreme Court. Both cases, but especially *BE & K Construction*, have given employers great freedom to retaliate preemptively against unions and workers by bringing nonmeritorious litigation.

For more than forty years, the NLRB treated retaliatory employer suits as a threat to workers' rights. In *Bill Johnson's Restaurants*, the Supreme Court agreed with the NLRB that an employer's lawsuit could be a powerful tool of coercion. In that case, the Court held that the NLRB may find the prosecution of an *ongoing lawsuit* unlawful if the suit lacks a reasonable basis in fact or law and was brought with a retaliatory motive.[32] The Court also considered the circumstances under which the Board might find a *concluded suit* to be an unfair labor practice. It explained that if the concluded proceedings resulted in a judgment adverse to the plaintiff or if the suit had been withdrawn or otherwise shown to be without merit, then the Board could proceed to find a violation if the suit had been filed with a retaliatory intent. In determining whether the suit had been filed in retaliation for the exercise of employees' section 7 rights, the Board could take into account that the suit lacked merit.[33] After *Bill Johnson's*, the Board's policy with respect to ongoing suits was to await the outcome of the litigation. The NLRB's view was that to do otherwise would deprive the plaintiff of its First Amendment right to have legal questions decided by the state or federal judicial system. [34]

BE & K Construction involved a completed lawsuit. The union's conduct at issue included lobbying for the adoption and enforcement of environmental standards, picketing and striking, suits under health and safety codes, and grievances against a joint venture partner of the plaintiffs. Applying the "concluded suit" standard of *Bill Johnson's*, the Board found that the suit was "unmeritorious" because all of the petitioner's claims had been rejected by the district court on the merits or had been voluntarily withdrawn with prejudice. The Board then concluded that retaliatory intent could be inferred from three factors: (1) the petitioner's federal suit was directed at the conduct that the Board had found was protected under section 7, and the litigation tended to discourage similar protected activity; (2) the lawsuit's attempt to have the district court impose liability on unions that had not engaged in the conduct at issue in the litigation showed an intent to "[harass] the Unions, not to [obtain] justice"; and (3) certain of the petitioner's claims were completely baseless.[35]

In *BE & K Construction*, the Supreme Court unanimously rejected the NLRB's standard for finding retaliatory motive in nonmeritorious cases. Expanding opportunities for employers to bring retaliatory lawsuits against unions and workers with impunity, the Court adopted the view that a non-meritorious lawsuit may enjoy First Amendment protection if the plaintiff reasonably believes the conduct is unprotected and illegal.[36] Even when moti-vated by animus, the Court concluded, a plaintiff's "purpose [may be] to stop conduct he reasonably believes is illegal."[37] Accordingly, the Court adopted a two-part test for completed suits challenged as retaliatory under the NLRA. The NLRB cannot impose NLRA unfair labor practice liability based on an employer's reasonably based but unsuccessful lawsuit against a union, even when the employer had a retaliatory purpose in filing the lawsuit. Rather, the NLRB must find that a plaintiff both brought an "objectively baseless" lawsuit and had a subjectively retaliatory motivation for bringing it. Justice O'Connor, writing for the Court, left open the possibility that the NLRB "may declare unlawful any unsuccessful but reasonably based suits that would not have been filed but for a motive to impose the costs of the litigation process, regardless of the outcome, when brought in retaliation for NLRA protected activity."[38] One wonders what proof would be required and could be developed to prove such a motive.[39]

The Right to Withdraw Recognition

Another way that employers initiate a preemptive attacks on protected employee rights is to imperil the stability of an established bargaining relationships by withdrawing recognition from the union. In four cases, the Court confronted this tactic and generally limited this employer option. The four cases were *Charles D. Bonanno Linen Service, Inc. v. NLRB*; *NLRB v. Curtin Matheson Scientific, Inc.*; *Auciello Iron Works v. NLRB*; and *Allentown Mack Sales and Service, Inc. v. NLRB*.[40]

It is common in certain industries for employers to form associations and for the association and a union representing its members' employees to mutually consent to negotiate on a multiemployer basis. These negotiations are intended to produce a single contract that binds all of the association's employer members and their unionized employees. The NLRB will not order such multiemployer bargaining; all parties must consent to its commencement. Legal issues arise, typically, when one of the employers desires to withdraw from bargaining on a multiemployer basis. Such a withdrawal can be destabilizing, especially when one of the largest employers in the group concludes that it can negotiate a more favorable contract on its own and thus wishes to withdraw from group bargaining. Whether such a withdrawal is permitted depends in significant measure on whether or not withdrawal is sought after the union and the employers have commenced multiemployer bargaining.

In its landmark 1958 *Retail Associates* decision, the NLRB ruled that either the union or an employer may withdraw from group bargaining but only under certain circumstances and only by following certain procedures.[41] Prior to the contractually established date for modification of the collective agreement or prior to the agreed-upon date for commencement of multiemployer negotiations, either party may withdraw after giving adequate, unequivocal written notice. Thereafter, either party may withdraw only by mutual consent or under "unusual circumstances." Two circumstances are widely viewed as "unusual": (1) dire economic circumstances that bring the economic viability of the employer as a business into doubt and (2) fragmentation, in which the integrity of the association has been dissipated by a series of consensual withdrawals and negotiation of separate agreements.[42] The circuits were split over whether the development of an impasse in bargaining constituted an "unusual circumstance." The Supreme Court resolved that circuit split in *Charles D. Bonanno Linen Service, Inc. v. NLRB* by agreeing with the Board that impasse does not constitute an unusual circumstance. As the Court explained, an "impasse is only a temporary deadlock or hiatus in negotiations, which in almost all cases is eventually broken, through either a change of mind or the application of economic force."

Prior to the Court's decision in *Bonanno Linen*, some courts of appeals had concluded that impasse constitutes an unusual circumstance. They were concerned that, post-impasse, the union would initiate a whipsaw strike against one employer or a small group of employers and subsequently negotiate separate agreements with the members of the association who were struck. The specter of the remaining members being forced to watch their withdrawing competitors resume business while they were still in the throes of an economic strike was destabilizing. In *Bonanno Linen*, the Supreme Court approved the NLRB's solution. The Board distinguished between, on the one hand, temporary interim agreements between the union and individual members of the multiemployer group and, on the other hand, permanent individual agreements. An interim agreement is not destabilizing: to qualify as a lawful interim agreement, it must terminate at the conclusion of group bargaining when a multiemployer contract is negotiated. All members of the association are then bound to the final multiemployer contract. In contrast, without circumstances permitting lawful withdrawal from group bargaining, permanent individual agreements are unlawful. They "effectively [fragment] and [destroy] the integrity of the bargaining unit," and this fragmentation, not an impasse, can be an unusual circumstance justifying withdrawal from the other association members.[43]

The Court's 1990 decision in *NLRB v. Curtin Matheson Scientific, Inc.* its 1996 decision in *Auciello Iron Works v. NLRB*, and its 1998 decision in *Allentown Mack Sales and Service, Inc. v. NLRB* also contributed to maintaining the stability of bargaining units because they all limited an employer's right to withdraw recognition. For many years, the rule had been that there are certain times when an employer may not lawfully withdraw recognition from the union because, as a matter of law, the union enjoys a *conclusive presumption* of majority support. When that is not the case, the union enjoys a *rebuttable presumption* of majority support. To rebut the presumption and lawfully withdraw recognition, the employer must demonstrate that either (1) the union has clearly lost majority support or (2) the employer has a good faith doubt reasonably grounded on objective evidence that the union has lost majority support. In its *Allentown Mack Sales* decision, the Court affirmed these rules and thereby contributed to the stability of bargaining relationships.[44] Three year earlier, in *Auciello Iron Works*, it had affirmed another rule that provides stability in bargaining relationships, the contract bar rule, which provides that even a good faith doubt regarding a union's majority status is inadequate to support withdrawal of recognition because a conclusive presumption of majority status arises at the moment a collective bargaining contract offer had been accepted, as was the case in *Auciello Iron Works*.

As useful and important as *Allentown Mack Sales* and *Auciello Iron Works* are to promoting stability in bargaining relationships, they pale in comparison to the Court's decision in *NLRB v. Curtin Matheson Scientific, Inc.* Here, the employer sought review of an NLRB decision finding that the company had committed unfair labor practices by withdrawing its recognition of the union. The company objected to the NLRB's refusal to apply a presumption that striker replacements opposed the union for the purpose of determining whether the employer had good faith doubts about the union's continuing majority status, which would allow it to lawfully withdraw its union recognition after hiring those permanent replacements. The court of appeals denied enforcement, and

NLRB appealed. Writing for the Supreme Court's majority, Justice Marshall reasoned that the NLRB's refusal to adopt a presumption that striker replacements opposed the union was rational and consistent with the NLRA. The majority opinion added a rare pragmatic observation reflecting labor relations reality: the NLRB's refusal to assume that workers hired to replace striking employees would be against union representation eliminates any incentive for an employer to delay good faith bargaining, precipitate an impasse in bargaining, and then hire striker replacements in an effort to undermine union strength and ultimately withdraw recognition from the union.

PART III

Impeding Workers' Ability to Counter
Employer Opposition to Group Action

CHAPTER 7

Banning Secondary Strikes and Picketing

Legal Framework and Recurring Issues

Since 1965, the Supreme Court has decided eleven cases involving the ban on secondary boycotts and hot cargo agreements. Many arose out of labor disputes in the construction industry, and all involved peaceful protest, mostly picketing. These cases have rebounded on workers in three important ways. First, they affect solidarity among workers as a class and thus ultimately societal views regarding the NLRA's commitment to worker collective action. Second, they affect the lawfulness of efforts to deploy work preservation provisions in collective bargaining agreements as workers struggle to preserve or recapture some of the thousands of jobs threatened by technological change. Finally, they raise the specter of a constitutional double standard: that twenty-first-century free-speech doctrine protects peaceful secondary boycotts in many contexts (civil rights protests, for example) but fails to protect the same conduct during labor disputes.

Section 8(b)(4)(B) of the Act was added as section 8(b)(4)(A) in 1947 and amended and renumbered in 1959. Section 8(b)(4)(B) makes it an unfair labor practice for a union (1) to strike, induce, or encourage any individual employed by any person to engage in a work stoppage; (2) to engage in other conduct that threatens, coerces, or restrains; and (3) to engage in such conduct when the object is to force or require one person to cease doing business with another person.[13] The section 8(b)(4)(B) ban is referred to as a ban on secondary boycotts.

Early on, the Court made it clear that "whatever may have been said in Congress preceding the passage of the Taft-Hartley Act concerning the evil of all forms of secondary boycotts, . . . , it is clear that no such sweeping prohibition was in fact enacted . . . . [S]ection 8(b)(4)(B) does not speak generally of secondary boycotts. It describes and condemns specific union conduct directed to specific objectives."[14] The "specific objective" that is principally banned is exerting economic pressure against a secondary employer (one who is unconcerned with the underlying labor dispute) to bring economic pressure on the primary employer (one who has the power to resolve the underlying dispute). But section 8(b)(4)(B) permits economic action directed at a primary employer, even when that economic pressure has secondary effects, even predictable ones. For example, it is clear that employees engaged in a labor dispute with an employer may seek to induce any person approaching the employer's facility to not enter and thereby to cease doing business with the employer. The inducement is literally to ask a person employed by a secondary employer to "cease doing business" with the primary employer. But such an inducement does not fall within section 8(b)(4)(B)'s ban because the employer who controls the premises where the job action is taking place is the one with whom the workers have a primary dispute.[15]

The Court's post-1965 section 8(b)(4)(B) cases have mostly wrestled with clarifying this primary-secondary distinction in a variety of contexts: that is, they address the question of which union actions have or do not have the proscribed secondary (cease doing business) object. The Court has stated that the task is to draw "lines that are more nice than obvious," a difficult endeavor that also requires "preserving the right of labor organizations to bring pressure to bear on offending employers in primary labor disputes and shielding unoffending employers . . . from pressures in controversies not their own."[16] For example, in *NLRB v. Local 825, International Union of Operating Engineers (Burns and Roe, Inc.)*, the Court considered the scope of the term *cease doing business*.[17] It clarified that a cease-doing-business objective is proven if the goal of a union's actions is any significant secondary disruption of a business relationship between a neutral and a primary. A complete cessation of a neutral's business with a primary is not required.[18]

Notably, the ban on secondary pressure has had an adverse effect on worker solidarity. As I've shown in previous chapters, one theme of these post-1965 labor cases has been the Court's recurring disillusionment with the collectivist underpinnings of the NLRA in favor of prioritizing pro-business values such as property rights and the need for greater management control of the workplace. This bias is apparent, for example, in the Court's union-access-to-employer-property cases as well as in its decisions that exclude from the duty to bargain a broad swath of subjects that the Court deems to fall within the "core of entrepreneurial control." In addition, the Court's "allied-with-management" cases have excluded thousands of workers from NLRA coverage by shifting them across the class line from worker to manager. This class-shifting process has so reduced those who are now covered by the NLRA that unions gradually have been placed in a "legal straightjacket," with union organizing largely "consigned to a roughly static geographic and demographic terrain, an archipelago [of] one blue-collar community to another in the Northeast, the Midwest, and on the Pacific Coast."[19]

The Taft-Hartley Act's secondary boycott provisions have contributed to the redefinition of the sociological boundaries of worker solidarity. Prior to Taft-Hartley, stronger unions assisted weaker unions: the stronger could boycott the products produced by workers who were striking or attempting to organize but who were in a relatively weak position. This stronger-assisting-the-weaker reality was deployed, for example, by the transport and longshore unions in an effort "to extend unionism into retail trade, food processing, and warehouse work[, thereby] provid[ing] fertile terrain for the growth of cross-class, cross-union social movements."[20] As Christopher Tomlins has explained:

> [The Act's provisions] formed a major barrier to the extension of American unionism beyond the "social and regional terrain that it had won in the previous decade." [T]he legislation . . . widened drastically the . . . limitations hindering the institution of collective bargaining from penetrating and collectivizing facets of the employment relationship other than wages, hours, and benefits. [In service of expanding the corporate political economy], the [Taft-Hartley secondary boycott] innovations imposed explicit limits on the sphere of labor-management relationships to be governed by collective bargaining.[21]

A striking example of how class solidarity has fared poorly in the Supreme Court's secondary boycott cases is the Court's decision in *International Longshoremen's Association v. Allied International, Inc.*[22] In this case, unionized workers refused to load and unload ships engaged in trade with Soviet Union. In a majority opinion written by Justice Powell, the Court held that, although the refusal to handle was intended to protest the Soviet Union's invasion of Afghanistan, it violated the secondary boycott provisions of the Act. In reaching this conclusion, the Court applied the secondary boycott ban broadly to include political boycotts that have no nexus to any labor dispute, reasoning that it is "more rather than less objectionable" for a union to pursue nontraditional objectives rather than the traditional demands for better wages and conditions of employment for its own members.[23]

The protection of employers' legitimate interests does not require weakening workers' class solidarity through an expansive interpretation of the Act's secondary boycott bans, as was exhibited in *International Longshoremen's Association v. Allied International, Inc.* Many nineteenth- century and early-twentieth-century common law courts deemed secondary boycotts unlawful, an expression of both their zealous quest to promote market efficiency and their "devotion to competition and freedom of contract."[24] But these common law courts did not uniformly condemn secondary boycotts.[25] Exceptions varied widely, and "the decisions were in hopeless conflict."[26] Even today, unions regulated by the Railway Labor Act—those representing employees of railroads and airlines—are free to advance lawful union objectives by means of secondary boycotts.[27] "In practice, the Railway Labor Act, enacted in 1926, has worked well without the need for a secondary boycott ban. . . . The real oddity in federal labor law . . . is not the lawful status of secondary boycotts in the airline and railroad industries, but the illegality of secondary boycotts in nearly all other industries."[28]

Work Preservation Doctrine

Many of the Court's post-1965 cases addressing issues of unions' alleged use of unlawful secondary pressure arose from union efforts to adapt to job loss resulting from technological change. One strategy has been for unions to negotiate provisions in collective bargaining agreements that preserve work for bargaining unit employees. An important question has been whether these agreements constitute proscribed so-called "hot cargo agreements."

Prior to 1959, collective bargaining agreements sometimes had provisions that gave bargaining unit employees the right not to handle certain goods—often, but not necessarily, goods produced by nonunion workers. In *Carpenters, Local 1976, v. NLRB (Sand Door Plywood Company)*, the Supreme Court ruled that nothing in the Act prohibits an employer from voluntarily consenting to such a hot cargo agreement, but compliance must remain voluntary.[29] Accordingly, a union violates the ban on secondary boycotts by striking to enforce a hot cargo agreement.

In 1959, Congress added two provisions to the NLRA in an effort to thwart negotiation and enforcement of hot cargo agreements. The new section 8(e) declared that such agreements are unlawful and thus unenforceable, defining them as any agreement whereby one employer agrees to refrain from dealing in any of the products of any other employer.[30] In addition, a newly enacted section 8(b)(4)(A) prohibited union efforts to obtain or enforce a proscribed section 8(e) agreement. Section 8(e) does not in terms distinguish between primary and secondary objects, but, as I will discuss, the Court has held that, as with section 8(b)(4)(B), Congress intended in section 8(e) to reach only hot cargo agreements that have secondary objectives.

Automation and other workplace technological innovations have the effect of replacing human labor, thereby forcing workers to confront unemployment, downward reclassification, and psychological dislocation.[31] Union efforts to deploy the collective bargaining process to preserve work threatened by technology has inevitably resulted in a literal cease-doing-business impact on secondary employers. For example, when a collective bargaining agreement in the construction industry grants unionized carpenters the right not to work on prefabricated doors that have been precut and prefitted at a factory prior to shipment to a job site for installation, compliance requires that the signatory employer-contractor purchase only blank doors and not do business with door manufacturers that precut and prefit doors offsite.[32] Or a collective bargaining agreement between an employer association and a union may reserve as onsite work the cutting of stainless steel bands used to fasten asbestos material around pipes to be insulated. Compliance requires that employer-contractors not do business with companies that sell precut steel bands.[33] Or a union contract may provide that pipe threading and cutting for the internal piping in climate control units is to be performed on the jobsite by bargaining unit employees, requiring the employer-contractor not to do business with manufacturers whose products contain pipe that is cut, threaded, and installed in a factory.[34] The NLRB and the courts have decided several cases that adjudicate if these work preservation agreements are prohibited by section 8(e). They have a secondary effect but do they have a secondary object?

The lead case was the Warren Court's decision in *National Woodwork Manufacturers Association v. NLRB*.[35] In that case, a carpenters' union had negotiated an agreement providing that bargaining unit employees working on construction projects would not be required to work on prefitted doors. Reversing the NLRB, the court of appeals concluded that, due to the cease-

doing-business effect on companies that produce prefitted doors, this agreement violated section 8(e). The Supreme Court reversed, reasoning that the
object of the agreement was primary, not secondary, because the goal was to
preserve work that was fairly claimable by the unionized workers who had
customarily performed the work. The Court explained: "The touchstone is
whether the agreement or its maintenances is addressed to the labor relations
of the contracting employer vis-à-vis [its] own employees."[36]

It is all too easy to forget how precarious workers' rights are in the hands of
a politically conservative leaning Supreme Court. Notably, *National Woodwork*
was a five-to-four decision. A vigorous dissent written by Justice Stewart insisted
that, irrespective of the object, section 8(e) is to be read literally to ban all
agreements, including work preservation agreements, that have a cease-doing-
business/will-not-handle effect.[37] This approach disregards the 1947 legislative
history showing that Congress intended only to ban secondary objects. Yet
a single changed vote would have dramatically altered the course of 8(e) law.

The precariousness of workers' rights came into bold relief within ten years
of the *National Woodwork* decision when the Burger Court, in 1977, decided
NLRB v. Enterprise Association, Pipefitters, Local 638.[38] In this case, conservative
forces on the Court hollowed out most of the gains made in *National Woodwork*
by adopting the right-to-control doctrine. *Pipefitters, Local 638* was, in many
ways, a typical work preservation dispute. Relying on a work preservation
agreement between the union and a plumbing and pipefitting subcontractor,
the union induced the subcontractor's unionized employees to refuse to handle
climate control equipment whose internal piping had been cut, threaded, and
installed in a factory. It was undisputed that cutting, threading, and installing
this piping on the jobsite was traditional bargaining unit work performed by
pipefitters and that the work preservation provision of the parties' collective
bargaining agreement prohibited the plumbing subcontractor from contracting to install climate control equipment whose internal piping had been cut,
threaded, and installed in a factory.

Nevertheless, the NLRB, composed of a Nixon-appointed majority, held
that the union had engaged in unlawful secondary activity. The court of
appeals, sitting *en banc*, disagreed. The Supreme Court, in a six-to-three decision written by Justice White, agreed with the NLRB, holding that the work
preservation agreement was not an adequate defense to the secondary boycott
charge because the general contractor's job specifications provided for the use
and installation by the plumbing subcontractor of the climate control equipment

that contained the factory-installed piping. According to the NLRB and the Court, because the general contractor possessed the "right to control" which products were to be installed, that contractor was the primary employer and the employer-subcontractor was the secondary one—a neutral. Accordingly, the union's attempt to enforce an otherwise valid work preservation agreement against the subcontractor that was signatory to the work preservation agreement constituted unlawful secondary activity. The majority reasoned that the union's object must have been to influence the general contractor—who had the right of control—by exerting pressure on the subcontractor, an employer who had no power to award the work to the union.

But the villain here was the subcontractor. In violation of an otherwise lawful work preservation clause in its collective bargaining agreement with the union, the subcontractor bid on a contract that it knew would require it to violate the collective bargaining agreement's work preservation provision and subsequently contracted with a third party to install prefabricated products. Thus, the contract-breaching subcontractor was the primary employer with whom the union had a dispute. That employer could have resolved the dispute by not taking on work requiring a violation of the collective bargaining agreement. But when the contract-breaching subcontractor undertook to install those prefabricated products using its unionized workforce, its employees suffered the very loss of work that the work preservation agreement had been designed to avoid.

The majority in *Pipefitters, Local 638* rejected the defense that the contract-breaching subcontractor was not a neutral. But Justice Brennan, dissenting, focused on the essential inquiry required by *National Woodwork*: whether the union's object was to benefit its own bargaining unit members or whether "in fact the activity [was] directed against [the immediate employer [but] was carried on for its effect elsewhere."[39] Unquestionably, the union's sole concern was protecting its members against loss of traditional work. Indeed, as in *National Woodwork*, the NLRB in *Pipefitters, Local 638* had made a finding that the union's actions were taken "for the purpose of preserving work [that its members] had traditionally performed."[40] Following is the principle adopted by the Court in *National Woodwork* but later abandoned by the majority in *Pipefitters, Local 638*:

> If the purpose of a contract provision, or of economic pressure
> on an employer, is to secure benefits for that employer's own

employees, it is primary; if the object is to affect the policies of some other employer toward his employees, the contract or its enforcement is secondary. . . . Pressure undertaken in order to preserve work traditionally performed by unit members aims at benefits for those members, and centers on a conflict between the employees and their employer, which, although it has secondary effects on other employers, as does the use of almost any economic weapon in a labor dispute, can only be regarded as primary.[41]

Justice Stewart joined most of Justice Brennan's dissent in *Pipefitters, Local 638* but wrote a separate and unique one-paragraph dissent—one of the more interesting dissents to be found in the Court's post-1965 labor cases. He reminded readers that "I disagreed with the Court in *National Woodwork* [but] until that decision is overruled . . . it stands as an authoritative construction of section 8(b)(4)(B). . . . I agree that the Court's decision today is 'patently precluded' by the *National Woodwork* case."[42] Within the constraints of collegiality norms at the Supreme Court, the Stewart dissent comes perilously close to accusing the majority in *Pipefitters, Local 638* of *sub silentio* reversing *National Woodwork* and amending the NLRA, which in effect is what occurred. As Justice Stewart's dissent makes clear, the majority in *Pipefitters, Local 638* adopted exactly the literal reading of section 8(e) that Justice Stewart had unsuccessfully advocated in his *National Woodwork* dissent but then abandoned in *Pipefitters, Local 638* in order to respect the principle of *stare decisis*.

It is worth emphasizing that the decision in *Pipefitters, Local 638* created a loophole that consumes most of the benefit that *National Woodwork* provided workers who were attempting to redress through the collective bargaining process the risk of job loss from technological change. Since *Pipefitters, Local 638*, all that is needed to defeat the protections of a work preservation agreement is for the architect or the general contractor of a building project to draft construction specifications that require prefabricated products. Once that is done, the subcontractor employer can violate the lawful work preservation agreement by bidding on the installation of prefabricated items with complete confidence that any responsive job action by the union will be found to be unlawful. True, a subcontractor employer may lose its neutral "unoffending employer" status if it affirmatively initiates the restrictions on work that result in its loss of the "right to control."[43] But as with other areas of labor relations law examined in this book, there is a disconnect between what the law proscribes and the conduct that a law-violating employer realistically can fear being caught doing.

What are the distinguishing differences between work preservation and work acquisition? On the one hand, it is clear that the work preservation doctrine provides generally that efforts to preserve work for employees displaced by technological innovation are not unlawful secondary activities and that collective bargaining contracts with the same purpose are not proscribed hot cargo agreements. By contrast, activities and agreements that seek not to preserve the traditional work of displaced workers but to acquire work of other employees are unlawful under section 8(e). Containerization, a technological change in the longshore industry, generated complex issues with respect to whether certain rules on containers agreed to by shipping companies and the International Longshoremen's Association (ILA) were an effort by the ILA to acquire work or merely an attempt to preserve its members' traditional responsibilities in the era of containerized shipping.

At issue in *NLRB v. International Longshoremen's Association (Dolphin's Forwarding) (ILA I)*[44] and *NLRB v. International Longshoremen's Association (New York Shipping Association) (ILA II)*[45] were collectively bargained rules that reserved to longshoremen the loading and unloading of certain containers performed within a fifty-mile radius of the port. The rules are complex, but gaining a general familiarity with them is essential to understanding the holdings in these two ILA cases.

The new technology involved specially designed ships that transport containers—large, reusable metal receptacles that can be lifted on and off a vessel unopened; each container can also be attached to a truck chassis and transported intact to and from the pier. Containerization lowers costs considerably and also reduces the time spent loading and unloading ships and warehousing cargo. However, it drastically cuts the amount of traditional ILA on-pier work, which in the past has largely involved handling loose cargo on conventional ships. The amount of work available for longshoremen has been further reduced by the shipping companies' practice of making their containers available for loading (stuffing) and unloading (stripping) away from the pier by shippers and freight consolidators who combine the goods of various shippers into a single shipment.

The rules on containers negotiated by the ILA and certain employer associations permitted the great majority of containers to pass over the piers intact, reserving to the ILA the right to stuff and strip at the pier only those containers that would otherwise be stuffed or stripped locally (within a fifty-mile radius of the port) by anyone except employees of the beneficial owner of the cargo. The shipping company was liable for specified liquidated damages for any container handled in violation of the rules.

The NLRB held that, by enforcing the rules on containers, the ILA had engaged in a secondary boycott because it was attempting to secure work not traditionally performed by the ILA. The Board defined the work as loading and unloading containers rather than the unloading and loading of goods transported by ship. Stuffing and stripping containers was work traditionally done off-pier either by the shippers themselves or by consolidation companies, not work that the ILA had traditionally performed on-pier. Thus, the NLRB held that the rules on containers were an illegal effort by the ILA to acquire work, not to preserve traditional work.

In *ILA I*, the Supreme Court disagreed. The focus, the Court concluded, should not be on the actual tasks that the union claims for bargaining unit members but on the "work patterns that the parties are seeking to preserve" and how, under the changed circumstances of technological developments, the agreement seeks to retain those patterns. The Board erred in focusing on the work done by consolidators when its focus should have been the scope of the work traditionally performed by ILA members to onload and offload ships and whether the object of the rules on containers was no more than preserving that traditional bargaining unit work. The Court stated that the Board's reasoning was seriously defective because the very reason for negotiation of the rules on containers was that the ILA had never performed this particular work away from the pier. Agreeing with the court of appeals, the Court concluded that, under the Board's analysis, the "work preservation doctrine is sapped of all life."[46] The Court remanded the case to the NLRB to reevaluate the rules on containers in light of the guidance provided by the Court in *ILA I*.

On remand, the Board found that much of the work covered by the rules on containers was functionally related to traditional ILA work.[47] But the Board also ruled that other claimed work (referred to as shortstopping and warehousing) was both traditionally performed by the longshoremen at the pier and historically duplicated by truckers and warehousers. With the advent of containerization, this duplicated work "no longer existed as a step in the cargo handling process."[48] Thus, claiming this eliminated work through the rules on containers constituted an unlawful work acquisition objective.

In *ILA II* the Supreme Court again rebuffed the NLRB, holding that it was wrong to conclude that eliminated work can never be the lawful object of a work preservation agreement. Critically, the object of the rules on containers was preservation of traditional longshore work, and the employer possessed the power to assign that work. The Court held that it is lawful for a union to recapture or reclaim traditional work, for "when the objective of an agreement and its enforcement is so clearly one of work preservation, the lawfulness of the agreement under [the Act's secondary boycott and hot cargo provisions] is secure absent some other evidence of secondary purpose."[49] This follows irrespective of adverse effects on persons beyond the ILA bargaining unit.

Provisions Specific to the Construction Industry

Section 8(e) contains a proviso that exempts certain agreements between a union and an employer in the construction industry concerning the contracting or subcontracting of work to be performed at a construction jobsite. In *Woelke and Romero Framing, Inc. v. NLRB,* a construction industry employer and the union reached an impasse during bargaining negotiations over the union's demand for a clause that would prohibit Woelke from subcontracting work at any construction jobsite "except to a person, firm or corporation, party to an appropriate, current labor agreement with the appropriate Union, or subordinate body signatory to this Agreement."[50] Following picketing at its construction sites in support of the union's demand for the subcontracting clause, Woelke filed unfair labor practice charges with the NLRB, asserting that subcontracting clauses are sheltered by section 8(e)'s construction industry proviso only if they are limited in application to particular jobsites at which both union and nonunion workers are simultaneously employed. The NLRB held that subcontracting clauses are lawful whenever they are sought or negotiated in the context of collective bargaining relationships, even when not limited in application to particular jobsites at which both union and nonunion workers are employed. The court of appeals agreed. The Supreme Court upheld the NLRB's view, reasoning that the plain language and the legislative history of section 8(e) and the construction industry proviso clearly indicates that it shelters union signatory subcontracting clauses that are sought or negotiated in the context of a collective bargaining relationship. The protection provided by the construction industry proviso to section 8(e) is not limited to jobsites where union workers are forced to work alongside nonunion workers. The

Court acknowledged that broad subcontracting clauses such as those at issue in *Woelke* create top-down pressure for unionization by requiring subcontractors, in order to obtain work, to force their employees to become union members. But by adding the construction industry proviso, Congress had decided to accept whatever top-down pressure for unionization that might occur.

Section 8(f) of the NLRA is another provision that is specific to the construction industry. Like any other employer, an employer in the construction industry is free to refuse to bargain with a labor organization that does not represent a majority of its employees, and it normally is unlawful for the employer to extend recognition to a minority union—one that does not represent a majority of the employer's employees. But unlike most other employers, a construction industry employer may, by operation of section 8(f), sign a contract with a union whose majority status has not been established, without risking liability for interfering with the organizational rights of employees by recognizing a minority union. In short, section 8(f) permits unions and employers in the construction industry to enter into what are referred to as pre-hire agreements.

In *NLRB v. Local Union No. 103, International Association of Bridge, Structural, and Ornamental Iron Workers (Higdon Construction Company)*, a construction industry employer entered into a lawful section 8(f) pre-hire agreement with the union but thereafter undertook construction projects with nonunion labor.[51] The union picketed those projects with signs stating that the employer was violating the pre-hire agreement with the union. At no time did the union represent a majority of the employees at the jobsites. Nor had the union petitioned for a representation election. The construction employer filed a charge with the NLRB alleging that the union had engaged in unlawful recognition picketing in order to force the employer to bargain with a union when it was not currently the majority representative of the employees. The NLRB found the picketing unlawful, but the court of appeals denied enforcement, holding that the valid section 8(f) pre-hire contract had created the union's right to enforce the contract by picketing.

The Supreme Court, in an opinion written by Justice White, upheld the NLRB in a six-to-three decision. The majority reasoned that (1) the general prevailing statutory policy is that a union should not be recognized to act as the employees' collective bargaining agent unless it represents a majority of employees and (2) the NLRB reasonably concluded that the picketing to enforce a pre-hire agreement was the legal equivalent of unlawful picketing to require recognition of the union as exclusive bargaining agent, when in fact a majority of the employees had never indicated a desire to be represented by the union. The *Higdon* case holds, in sum, that a union that is party to a pre-hire agreement is not excused from the obligation to achieve majority support before it can use economic pressure to require the employer to bargain with the union.

Dissenting, Justice Stewart argued that the majority opinion in effect dismisses section 8(f) agreements as nullities: "The Board in this case concedes that the employer could lawfully have voluntarily chosen to adhere to the [pre-hire] agreement even though the union had not attained majority status. Thus even if [the employer] was under no legal duty to abide by the terms of the pre-hire agreement, that fact does not establish that [the employer] was immune from economic pressure aimed at encouraging it to do so."[52] The picketing was peaceful primary economic pressure in pursuit of a lawful objective. Even when undertaken by a minority union, such economic pressure is not forbidden by the NLRA unless it falls within an express statutory prohibition, and the picketing here was not barred by any NLRA language.[53] Not only does the majority in *Higdon* add a limitation to unions' peaceful economic activity that is found nowhere in the Labor Management Relations Act, but it does so in a context that invites employers to abandon contractual commitments without any adverse consequences.

Secondary Pressure and the First Amendment
PICKETING THE PRODUCT

In the landmark *NLRB v. Fruit and Vegetable Packers and Warehousemen, Local 760 (Tree Fruits)* case, the Supreme Court confronted a robust First Amendment free speech challenge to the regulation of union picketing.[54] The Court avoided the constitutional claims in *Tree Fruits* through strained reasoning that has been characterized as a "virtuoso performance in judicial policymaking."[55] The *Tree Fruits* majority held that the NLRA's secondary boycott provisions do not proscribe all peaceful consumer picketing at secondary sites. Some limited struck product picketing is permitted.

The *Tree Fruits* case arose out of a strike that occurred in Washington State following an impasse during collective bargaining negotiations involving a multiemployer bargaining association (Tree Fruits), representing fresh fruit packing and warehousing firms, and Fruit and Vegetable Packers and

Warehousemen, Local 760. To assert economic pressure on Tree Fruits and its employer members, Local 760 initiated a consumer boycott of Washington State apples that included picketing and hand billing the entrances of forty-six Safeway stores in Seattle, all of which were then selling apples obtained from Tree Fruits members. The picketers were given written instructions: (1) they were to picket only customer entrances, not any entrance set aside for the use of store employees and delivery persons; (2) they were not to make any statement to the effect that the stores were unfair or on strike, and they were instructed not to request that customers refuse to patronize the stores but only to ask shoppers not to buy Washington State apples; and (3) they were not to interfere with the work of any employees in the store or truck drivers making any pickups or deliveries and were to tell all such drivers that the pickets did not intend to interfere with pickups or deliveries.

The NLRB concluded that the union's picketing constituted an unlawful secondary boycott because it had the illegal object of coercing Safeway into ceasing to sell Tree Fruits products. In addition to citing certain Taft-Hartley Act legislative history, the NLRB relied heavily on the language of the second proviso to NLRA section 8(b)(4)(ii)(B), which permits a union to engage in some secondary consumer actions but only "publicity, other than picketing." In the view of the Board, it was clear that Congress had decided to ban all consumer picketing in front of a secondary establishment.

While acknowledging that the language of the second proviso to section 8(b)(4)(ii)(B) and the Taft-Hartley Act's legislative history lend some support to the NLRB's NLRA statutory interpretation, the court of appeals nevertheless refused to enforce the order. The court reasoned that, while the NLRB could reasonably conclude that the section 8(b)(4)(ii)(B) language, "threaten, coerce, or restrain any person," is broad enough to ban all peaceful consumer picketing at the premises of a neutral employer when conducted for a cease-doing-business object, the Board's literal interpretation of statutory language posed serious constitutional questions that could have been avoided if a reasonable alternative reading of the NLRA had been available. The court of appeals then interpreted subsection ii of section 8(b)(4) as barring only peaceful consumer picketing that was shown to have actually had a coercive effect upon the neutral employer. The case was remanded to the Board to make that determination.

In a seven-to-two decision drafted by Justice Brennan, the Court agreed with neither the NLRB nor the court of appeals.[56] When enacting subsection ii of section 8(b)(4)(B), the majority explained, Congress had expressed great concern that banning all peaceful picketing at a secondary site would violate the free speech guarantees in the Constitution. The Court concluded that the secondary boycott legislative history failed to "reflect with the requisite clarity a congressional plan to proscribe all peaceful consumer picketing at secondary sites." On the contrary, that legislative history is awash with evidence that the "evil" addressed by the secondary boycott ban was limited to the use of consumer picketing at secondary sites, having the object "to persuade the customers of the secondary employer to cease trading with [the picketed neutral] in order to force him to cease dealing with, or to put pressure upon, the primary employer."[57] Acknowledging that the legislative history is somewhat opaque, the Court concluded that Congress did not intend that the NLRA should ban consumer picketing that was focused only on requesting persons not to purchase products of the primary employer. In such limited consumer picketing, "the union's appeal to the public is confined to its dispute with the primary employer, since the public is not asked to withhold its patronage from the secondary employer, but only to boycott the primary employer's goods."[58]

Nor, according to the majority in *Tree Fruits*, does the second proviso to NLRA section 8(b)(4)(ii)(B), which permits some secondary consumer actions by a union but only "publicity, other than picketing," require a contrary result. That proviso, also reflecting free speech concerns, permits some peaceful communication directed to consumers that is intended "to shut off all trade with the secondary employer unless he aids the union in its dispute with the primary employer" but only by means of "publicity, other than picketing." That "is poles apart from . . . picketing which only persuades his customers not to buy the struck product."[59]

Justice Black wrote an important concurring opinion.[60] It concluded that subsection ii of section 8(b)(4)(B) bans all consumer picketing but, in so doing, violates the free speech provisions of the Constitution. When picketing does not threaten public order and when its object seeks neither an unlawful nor a criminal object, it becomes clear that the picketing is being banned due to the viewpoint expressed—specifically, the union's viewpoint regarding a labor dispute as shown through its picketing. "The result is an abridgment of the freedom of these picketers to tell a part of the public their side of a labor controversy, a subject the free discussion of which is protected by the First Amendment."[61] To Justice Black, the principle was clear: "The object of the picketing was to ask Safeway customers to do something which the section itself recognizes as perfectly lawful . . . while others are left free to picket for other reasons[.] [T]hose who wish to picket to inform Safeway customers of their labor dispute with the primary employer, are barred from picketing—solely on the ground of the [content of the] lawful information they want to impart to the customers."[62] Implicit in Justice Black's reasoning is that the Constitution would protect persons who wanted, for example, to picket the Safeway stores and urge customers to purchase Washington State apples as a means of aiding Tree Fruits in its labor dispute with Local 760. The union suffers legal liability, but only due to the contrary viewpoint it chooses to express.

Within fifteen years of its *Tree Fruits* decision, the Burger Court began a process of undercutting the free speech protections that the case had provided to unions. In *NLRB v. Retail Store Employees Union, Local 1001 (Safeco Title Insurance Company)*, the Court held that a union may not engage in consumer picketing if the sales of the neutral employer being picketed are largely sales of the struck product.[63] Safeco Title Insurance Company did business with several title companies that were deriving more than 90 percent of their gross incomes from the sale of Safeco insurance policies. When contract negotiations between Safeco and Local 1001, the bargaining representative for certain Safeco employees, reached an impasse, the employees went on strike. Local 1001 picketed each of the title companies, urging customers to support the strike by canceling their Safeco policies. Safeco and one of the title companies filed charges with the NLRB, alleging that the union's picketing constituted an unlawful secondary boycott. The NLRB found that the union's product picketing violated section 8(b)(4)(ii)(B) of the NLRA. The court of appeals refused to enforce the Board's order, finding that the picketing constituted lawful product picketing within the protection confirmed in *Tree Fruits*.

In a six-to-three decision (a plurality and two concurring opinions), the Court, in an opinion written by Justice Powell, held that, although the picketing constituted product picketing, it violated the ban on secondary activity because the picketed secondary title insurance companies derived so much of their gross income from the sale of Safeco's policies. The Court reasoned that successful secondary product picketing would force the neutral title companies to choose between surviving and severing their ties with Safeco. Accordingly, distinguishing *Tree Fruits*, the Court concluded that, because the picketing threatened neutral parties (the title companies) with ruin or substantial loss, it predictably encouraged those parties to boycott the primary employer, Safeco, altogether. In addition, Justice Powell, joined by Chief Justice Burger and Justices Stewart and Rehnquist, concluded that, as applied to picketing that predictably encourages consumers to boycott a secondary business, section 8(b) (4)(ii)(B) imposes no unconstitutional restrictions upon speech protected by the First Amendment. Two additional justices, in concurring opinions, also found no First Amendment violation.[64]

Justice Brennan, dissenting, protested the vagueness of the majority's "ruin or substantial loss" test for distinguishing lawful from unlawful product picketing, leaving it to unions to guess when picketing is lawful or not. More fundamentally, he explained how the majority in *Safeco* had altered the analytical underpinnings of *Tree Fruits*. Under *Tree Fruits*, the test for determining the legality of product picketing turned on an evaluation of whether the pickets urged only a boycott of the primary employer's product or a boycott of all products carried by the neutral. *Tree Fruits* reasoning did not entail an examination of the extent of economic harm to a neutral as a result of the picketing. Now, after *Safeco*, the legality or illegality of product picketing varies depending on the composition of the secondary's business. "*Tree Fruits* expressly rejected the notion that the coerciveness of picketing should depend upon the extent of loss suffered by the secondary firm through diminished purchases of the primary product."[65]

In 1984, Lee Modjeska wrote a thorough, carefully reasoned evaluation of *Tree Fruits*.[66] In that article, following an extensive review of Taft-Hartley Act's legislative history, he concluded that the "literal construction of the statutory language [and the legislative history] propelled the *Tree Fruits* Court toward the inevitable conclusion that section 8(b)(4)(ii) proscribed consumer picketing at neutral premises irrespective of actual impact, and without distinction between limited struck product and general neutral picketing. Equally clear, however, was the Court's disinclination, for constitutional and policy reasons, to reach such a result."[67]

The constitutional challenge to an across-the-Board ban on all consumer picketing is indeed formidable. Two lines of constitutional attack, grounded in well-established precedent in place at the time that the Court decided *Tree Fruits*, provide a compelling argument that a total ban on product picketing would be unconstitutional. First, the breakthrough case of *Thornhill v. Alabama* acknowledged that picketing entails a form of speech. *Thornhill* held that a state's blanket ban of all peaceful picketing is unconstitutional.[68] As is widely understood, the Court subsequently undercut its *Thornhill* decision by holding that states are constitutionally free "to enjoin peaceful picketing aimed at preventing effectuation of [some valid] policy."[69] Subsequently, the Court held that the federal government has the same immunity from constitutional challenge when banning picketing as a means to advance some valid federal policy.[70]

Judge David Bazelon's decision for the D.C. Circuit in the *Tree Fruits* case contains the most cogent argument to date of why, notwithstanding the above-cited post-*Thornhill* cases, it would be unconstitutional for Congress to ban all consumer product picketing.[71] The key is the difference between consumer picketing and labor picketing and why that renders the post-*Thornhill* cases' retreat from *Thornhill*'s free speech–based protective view of labor picketing as inapposite to consumer picketing.[72] The Supreme Court has discounted the First Amendment protection afforded to labor picketing when it is viewed as "signal picketing": more than just speech, "the very presence of a picket line may induce action of one kind or another, quite irrespective of the nature of the ideas which are being disseminated. [It is] those aspects of picketing [that] make it the subject of restrictive regulation."[73] Judge Bazelon, in his D.C. Circuit Court decision in *Tree Fruits*, argued that discounting the free speech protection accorded to labor picketing makes sense because "[union-ized] employees are subject to group discipline based on common interests and loyalties, habit, fear of social ostracism, or the application of severe economic sanctions. [For these reasons, labor] picketing is more than 'pure' speech."[74] Picketing addressed solely to the public, on the other hand, lacks such signal effects. With consumer product picketing, "each prospective patron could read the Union's signs and literature and determine, in the light of his own interests and convictions, what course he would follow. . . . Thus it may well be that [consumer product picketing] is closer to the core notion of consti-tutionally protected free speech than the picketing the Supreme Court has held may be banned."[75]

Justice Black's concurrence in *Tree Fruits* advances a powerful additional argument for why banning peaceful labor consumer picketing but not pro-hibiting other consumer picketing is unconstitutional: a total ban on all labor consumer picketing would constitute unconstitutional viewpoint discrimina-tion. As Mojeska has explained Justice Black's view:

> If picketing on local streets or adjacent to local business premises was the substantive evil warranting governmental regulation, why then a proscription aimed only at discussion of one side of a particular kind of labor dispute? If secondary consumer appeals were the substantive evil warranting governmental regulation,

why then the proviso's tolerance of publicity other than picketing
for the same object? If the consumer appeal object is otherwise
lawful, why then a proscription on picketing?[76]

It is hard to escape the conclusion, as Justice Black explained in his *Tree Fruits*
dissent, that a total ban on consumer picketing would be a proscription on
"picketing, otherwise lawful, [that] is banned only when the picketers express
particular views."[77]

HANDBILLING

Eight years after its decision in *Safeco*, the Court unanimously held, in *Edward J.
DeBartolo Corporation v. Florida Gulf Coast Building and Construction Trades
Council*, that it is lawful for unions to peacefully distribute handbills outside
a shopping mall, urging the public not to patronize the mall's stores until the
mall's owner agrees to use only contractors who pay fair wages.[78] The Court
decided that the NLRA did not proscribe such peaceful handbilling and thus
avoided "deciding whether a congressional prohibition of handbilling on the
facts of [DeBartolo] would violate the First Amendment."[79] Soon thereafter,
in two related but different contexts, the lower courts began the process of
eroding the victory that unions had achieved in *DeBartolo* by finding that (1)
handbilling at the site of a secondary employer to communicate the existence
of a labor dispute to secondary workers necessarily constituted an unlawful act
of "inducing" those workers to quit and 2) peaceful picketing of a secondary
employer, whether directed at communicating a viewpoint to the public or
to workers, necessarily constituted "coercion" in violation of subsection ii of
section 8(b)(4).

 DeBartolo did not address whether section 8(b)(4) could prohibit handbilling and other nonpicketing publicity that had the effect of causing secondary
employees to refrain from working. That issue was addressed in 1999 by a
split three-judge panel of the D.C. Circuit Court of Appeals in *Warshawsky
and Company v. NLRB*.[80] In *Warshawsky*, a union had a labor dispute with
a nonunion employer at a construction site. The union distributed handbills
to all who approached the site, explaining that the nonunion employer was
paying substandard wages but also stating: "We are appealing only to the
general public. We are not seeking any person to cease work or stop making
deliveries." Some employees of secondary employers at the site nevertheless

responded by not performing work. The NLRB held that union handbilling was lawful because the union did not intend the handbills to induce persons to cease work.

The D.C. Circuit denied enforcement of the Board's decision. The court concluded that when a union communicates a labor dispute to the employees of secondary employers, even by means of distributing handbills, that communication will be found to have the proscribed unlawful intent to induce or encourage secondary employees to cease doing work, at least when such cessation of work in fact occurs. Dissenting in *Warshawsky*, Judge Patricia Wald understood the majority rational as concluding that "the First Amendment is not implicated at all when a union communicates solely with neutral employees [and that] the majority jump[ed] from the Supreme Court's holding that the prohibition under section 8(b)(4) of the inducement or encouragement of a secondary work stoppage does not constitute an unconstitutional abridgment of free speech to its conclusion that any kind of union speech directed to neutral employees carries no First Amendment protection."[81]

It may be that the two judges comprising the *Warshawsky* majority were later victimized by the reality that "any principle once announced may in time gain a momentum not warranted by the exigencies of its creation," as Justice Douglas once observed.[82] Yet as Judge Wald's dissent in *Warshawsky* presciently predicted, the majority opinion in *Warshawsky* was written in such broad terms that the opinion has been interpreted subsequently to ban any communication concerning a labor dispute that takes place at a construction site not open to the general public, even when neutral employees do not respond by ceasing work. The *Warshawsky* principle, as it has developed among conservative decisionmakers is that, de facto, such communication constitutes an unlawful inducement or encouragement for employees to engage in a work stoppage, notwithstanding any disclaimers to the contrary contained in the handbill and notwithstanding an absence of work stoppage by any secondary employees.[83] The D.C. Circuit's view that unions have no First Amendment freedom to communicate the existence of a labor dispute to secondary employees is "especially important because the D.C. Circuit is the only federal appellate court to which all decisions of the NLRB can be appealed, and thus the only such court to which any and all parties "aggrieved" by a Board decision can turn.[84]

Regarding the notion that peaceful picketing of a secondary employer necessarily constitutes "coercion" in violation of subsection ii of section 8(b)(4), scholars have advanced sound, even compelling, arguments demonstrating that if binding precedent in nonlabor cases were evenly applied, labor picketing would qualify for greater protection than is currently provided. Yet these arguments have "gain[ed] little traction before the federal courts, particularly the current Supreme Court."[85] The standard explanation for why "the Supreme Court has granted less First Amendment protection to labor picketing than to virtually identical picketing by civil rights and other organizations" is that, when banning labor picketing, government proscribes "only that aspect of the union's efforts to communicate its views that calls for an automatic response to a signal, rather than a reasoned response to an idea."[86] As discussed, Judge Bazelon's decision for the D.C. Circuit in the *Tree Fruits* case explained that courts conclude that, in labor picketing, "[unionized] employees are subject to group discipline based on common interests and loyalties, habit, fear of social ostracism, or the application of severe economic sanctions. [These forces, more than the message, explain why] they may refuse to work or to make pickups and deliveries for a secondary employer."[87]

As I will detail more fully in chapter 9, in the past sixty years, the Court has dramatically modified the law of union discipline. Today, union members are free to disregard labor pickets through the simple act of resigning from the union. As the Court concluded in *NLRB v. Granite State Joint Board, Textile Workers Union, Local 1029*, "the union has no more control over the former member than it has over the man in the street."[88] Accordingly, Cynthia Estlund could not have been more clear, or more correct, when she concluded that the "union power to discipline" rationale for limiting First Amendment protection for union speech is now "illusory."[89] Yet courts continue to characterize union picketing as signal picketing to justify the viewpoint discrimination inherent in the rules that govern union picketing.

The staying power of the view that union communication to secondary employers is inherently an unlawful signal to cease work can be found in cases adjudicating unions' peaceful communication of a labor dispute at the location of a secondary employer by displaying symbols of protest (such as an inflatable rat). Courts have found this activity to be unlawful signal picketing irrespective of the symbol used to express protest, the viewpoint contained in the symbol, any disclaimers that the union has no intent to urge cessation of work, or the absence of any cessation of work by secondary employees. Outcomes vary, but many courts continue to conclude that displaying banners and symbols of protest at a location where secondary employees can view them constitutes unlawful picketing that signals a request that workers cease work.[90]

THE CASES

Inadequate Remedy

H. K. Porter Company v NLRB[1]
NLRB v. Food Store Employees Union, Local 347[2]
NLRB v. Transportation Management Corporation[3]
ABF Freight System, Inc. v. NLRB[4]
Starbucks Corporation v. McKinney, Regional Director of Region 15, NLRB[5]

Arbitration as the Preferred Remedy

Textile Workers Union v. Lincoln Mills[6]
Steelworkers Trilogy[7]
Cary v. Westinghouse[8]
Republic Steel Corporation v. Maddox[9]
NLRB v. C & C Plywood Corporation[10]
NLRB v. Acme Industrial Company[11]
NLRB v. Strong Roofing and Insulating Company[12]
Boys Market, Inc. v. Retail Clerks, Local 770[13]
Gateway Coal Company v. United Mine Workers[14]
Buffalo Forge Company v. Steelworkers[15]
Nolde Brothers v. Bakery and Confectionery Workers, Local 358[16]
Litton Financial Printing Division v. NLRB[17]
AT&T Mobility, LLC, v. Concepcion[18]
Epic Systems Corporation v. Lewis[19]
Lamps Plus, Inc. v. Varela[20]

Section 301 Preemption and the Erosion of Individual Employment Rights

Local 174, Teamsters, v. Lucas Flour Company[21]
Avco Corporation v. Aero Lodge No. 735[22]
Allis-Chalmers Corporation v. Lueck, 89[23]
Caterpillar, Inc. v. Williams[24]
International Brotherhood of Electrical Workers v. Hechler[25]
Lingle v. Norge Division of Magic Chef[26]
Steelworkers v. Rawson[27]
Livadas v. Bradshaw[28]

CHAPTER 8

Thwarting the Effective Enforcement of Statutory Rights

Inadequate Remedy

The four Supreme Court cases decided since 1965 that address the NLRB's remedial authority have two things in common.[29] First, they highlight Congress's decision that it is the NLRB's responsibility to exercise wide discretion in "tak[ing] such affirmative [remedial] action . . . as will effectuate the policies' of the Act."[30] Second, these cases also show that, at points that are crucial to workers, the Court has undermined the effectiveness of the NLRA by denying worker-friendly remedies proposed by the NLRB, remedies calculated to help secure the Act's commitment to encouraging the "practice and procedure of collective bargaining."

The 1970 decision in *H. K. Porter Company v. NLRB* is a good example. This was a clear case of an employer's refusal to bargain in good faith. The NLRB, the court of appeals, and the Supreme Court all agreed that the employer's refusal to agree to a checkoff provision in the collective bargaining agreement was motivated by a desire to avoid reaching *any* agreement with the union.[31] The NLRB remedied this egregious unfair labor practice by ordering the employer to bargain in good faith going forward and to grant the union a contract clause providing for the checkoff of union dues. The court of appeals enforced the NLRB's remedial order, observing that the employer was trying to destroy the union. As one commentator has observed, the NLRB's order "might [have] promote[d] a measure of institutional security for the union and the growth of the collective bargaining process."[32] In short, it was the only efficacious remedy available to achieve the purposes of the Act.

The Supreme Court granted *certiorari* and then reversed, holding that the NLRB is "without power to compel a company or a union to agree to an substantive contractual provision of a collective bargaining agreement."[33] The

Court relied on legislative history and Supreme Court precedent supporting the conclusion that the NLRA is grounded in a commitment to the freedom of contract and that, when enacting the NLRA, Congress rejected a system of government that would determine workers' conditions of employment. Accordingly, the NLRB may not, for example, compel concessions or otherwise attempt to settle terms of collective bargaining agreements. But all of this legislative history and Court precedent was addressing how the NLRB could determine *if* a bad faith bargaining violation had occurred; it was not considering the scope of the Board's remedial authority to cure violations based on the complete absence of an employer's subjective willingness to engage in good faith bargaining. The Court's majority in *H. K. Porter* agreed that the NLRA's language addresses the principle of freedom of contract only in the context of determining whether bad faith bargaining has occurred. Nevertheless, the Court concluded explicitly that the freedom of contract principle is an overarching tenet of NLRA policy. This commitment precludes the NLRB from ordering even a recalcitrant employer to grant the union any contract clause, such as providing for the checkoff of union dues.

Dissenting, Justice Douglas focused on the NLRA's language, specifically the broad remedial authority granted to the NLRB "to take such affirmative action . . . as will effectuate the policies of the Act." Nothing in the language of the NLRA limits the Board's "affirmative action," as the majority concluded in *H. K. Porter*. Moreover, the remedy the NLRB chose was reasonable, given that the employer's bargaining strategy was clearly and solely aimed at avoiding any agreement.

Glaringly absent from the majority opinion in *H. K. Porter* is any meaningful consideration of the need to accommodate the NLRA's freedom of contract principle with the Act's policy to encourage the practice and procedure of collective bargaining. The Court recognized that the case had lingered before the NLRB and the courts for more than eight years, due to a delay that "appears to have occurred chiefly because of the skill of the company's negotiators in taking advantage of every opportunity for delay in the [NLRA]."[34] With the NLRB armed only with the remedial authority to order the employer, who was trying to destroy the union, to cease and desist from future bad faith bargaining, why would anyone conclude that good faith bargaining would now take place? Concurring in *H. K. Porter*, Justice Harlan observed that the employer might be subjected to a bargaining order enforceable by a citation for contempt if bad faith bargaining were to continue.[35] True, but contempt litigation provides yet one more legal proceeding that will generate several additional years of delay, during which time the bargaining unit employees will have no collective bargaining agreement. Inevitably, the employees will likely become disillusioned and pessimistic, and soon the union's majority support will erode.

NLRB v. Food Store Employees Union, Local 347 was another Supreme Court decision that foiled an attempt to bolster the effectiveness of the remedies available to deter employer unfair labor practice conduct.[36] After finding that Heck's, Inc., had engaged in pervasive unfair labor practices, the NLRB issued a standard cease-and-desist order against the employer. The Board rejected the union's argument for additional remedies, including reimbursement of litigation expenses and excessive organizational costs incurred as a result of Heck's illegal conduct. The court of appeals enforced the NLRB's order but remanded the case to the Board for further consideration of additional remedies. The NLRB again refused to order reimbursement, reasoning that its orders must be remedial, not punitive, and that collateral losses are not considered in framing a reimbursement order.

The court of appeals enforced the NLRB's amended order but noted that, in *Tiidee Products, Inc.*, the Board had modified its policy on ordering reimbursement to a victim of an employer's unfair labor practices.[37] Accordingly, the court of appeals enlarged the NLRB's order by requiring Heck's to reimburse the union for any extraordinary organizational costs that the union had incurred because of Heck's policy of resisting organizational efforts, refusing to bargain, and refusing to pay the Board's and the union's costs and expenses connected with the litigation.

Notwithstanding that sections 10(e) and (f) of the NLRA authorize courts of appeals to "make and enter a decree . . . modifying and enforcing as so modified" an NLRB order, the Supreme Court held that the court of appeals had erroneously exercised its section 10(e) and (f), authority by enlarging the Heck's order without first affording the NLRB an opportunity to evaluate the case in light of the changed policy enunciated in *Tiidee* and to decide whether that policy should be applied retroactively. The Court's decision was unanimous.

In *Food Store Employees Union, Local 347*, the Court missed a rare opportunity to strengthen NLRA remedies. Had it enforced the order of the court of appeals, it could have set the standards for when, as a matter of law, an NLRB order may provide for extraordinary remedies. By not providing that guidance, the Court left development of the Board's authority to issue extraordinary remedies to the vagaries of subsequent NLRB panels and courts of appeals throughout the United States. As a result, the development of the extraordinary remedies doctrine since the decision has been disastrous. An order for an employer to pay litigation costs could have been available to remedy vexatious and wanton unfair labor practices designed to destroy a union. But since *Food Store Employees Union, Local 34*, that remedy has been limited to cases in which the employer's defense to the unfair labor practice is "frivolous"—that is, the employer advances a "transparently nonmeritorious defense."[38]

More significantly, however, in 2016, the D.C. Circuit decided *HTH Corporation v. NLRB*, holding that the NLRB lacks the legal authority to remedy unfair labor practices by ordering reimbursement of litigation expenses.[39] In *this case*, the NLRB determined that the employer had committed "severe and pervasive unfair labor practices" in its dealing with the union and, as a remedy, awarded litigation expenses to the Board's general counsel and the union. The D.C. Circuit agreed with the employer that the NLRB lacks the authority to order such reimbursement, noting that the Board is a "creature of statute, . . . has only those powers conferred upon it by Congress[, and that no provision of the NLRA] explicitly or implicitly [grants the NLRB the power to apply the bad-faith exception."[40] Subsequently, the circuit again held that the NLRB has no authority to require the reimbursement of litigation costs but upheld its award of negotiation expenses. The court of appeals explained that litigation expenses are punitive in nature and thus beyond the Board's remedial power. An award of bargaining expenses, it noted, is a primarily compensatory remedy, designed to restore "the economic status quo that would have obtained but for the Companies' wrongful acts" and thus falls within the Board's section 10(c) remedial authority.[41] All of this erosion of the NLRB's remedial authority would have been avoided had the Supreme Court upheld the court of appeals order in *Food Store Employees Union, Local 34*.

The Biden NLRB created more efficacious remedies. In *Thryv, Inc.*, the NLRB held that "in all cases in which [the Board's] standard remedy would include an order for make-whole relief, [the Board] shall expressly order that the respondent compensate affected employees for all direct or foreseeable pecuniary harms suffered as a result of the respondent's unfair labor practice." On review, the court of appeals described this expanded make-whole remedy as "draconian [and] a novel, consequential-damages-like labor law remedy" but never ruled on whether the remedy was lawful because the court found that the employer had not committed any unfair labor practices.[42] The Supreme

Court's 2024 decision in *Securities and Exchange Commission v. Jarkesy* might thwart efforts to expand make-whole remedies.[43] In *Jarkesy*, the Court held that a defendant is entitled to a trial by jury if civil penalties are imposed, raising the question of whether the NLRB's expanded make-whole remedy is unconstitutional because it is an administratively imposed "civil penalty." In the summer of 2024, this constitutional argument was advanced by Space Exploration Technologies Corporation (SpaceX) in a complaint filed in the Southern District of Texas.[44]

Two additional post-1965 Supreme Court cases litigated remedies: *NLRB v. Transportation Management Corporation* and *ABF Freight System, Inc. v. NLRB*.[45] *Transportation Management* created a loophole for employers who discriminate against workers for engaging in rights protected by NLRA section 7. The case held that even with proof that an adverse action was motivated by an employer's antiunion animus, the NLRB is permitted to withhold a remedy if the employer can carry the burden of proving, as an affirmative defense, that the adverse action would have been taken even if the employee had not been involved in protected activities. Nothing in the NLRA provides such an affirmative defense for an employer when antiunion animus is a substantial motivating factor in the adverse action. But the Court approved the NLRB's decision to create this defense for an employer.

ABF Freight System presented an issue that is unlikely to recur: the question of the NLRB's authority to grant reinstatement to an employee who was discharged for protected activities but then engaged in the misconduct of falsely testifying during an NLRB proceeding. The Board held that the false testifying did not preclude granting the remedy of reinstatement with back pay, and the Supreme Court upheld the NLRB's choice to decline adopting a rigid rule denying reinstatement and back pay in these circumstances. *ABF Freight System* is significant not for the impact it will have in day-to-day labor relations but as evidence of the Court's inclination to defer to the NLRB with respect to crafting remedies for violations of the NLRA.

The most recent Supreme Court decision addressing NLRA remedies is the Court's 2024 decision in *Starbucks Corporation v. McKinney, Regional Director of Region 15, NLRB*.[46] The Court in *Starbucks* weakened the ability of the NLRB to obtain preliminary injunctive relief pursuant to NLRA section 10(j). That section's precepts on preliminary relief are particularly important because, in *Starbucks*, the NLRB deployed the injunction to obtain temporary reinstatement of employees whom the Board's general counsel had concluded were discharged for protected union activities. Unlawful discharge of the union leadership can be a very effective way for an employer to crush an organizing effort. Likewise, ordering that these leaders be reinstated pending the NLRB's adjudication of the charge that they were unlawfully fired often has the effect of bolstering the organizing effort. In other words, the outcome of section 10(j) litigation can greatly influence the success or failure of workers' effort to obtain union representation.

Federal courts hearing NLRB requests for section 10(j) preliminary injunctive relief require the Board to show the likelihood of success on the merits: that is, the likelihood that Board will ultimately conclude that the general counsel's complaint alleging an unfair labor practice is meritorious. Acknowledging the Board's primary role in adjudicating labor disputes, most district courts prior to the *Starbucks* decision found that this likelihood-of-success factor had been satisfied so long as the Board presented "some evidence to support the unfair labor practice charge, together with an arguable legal theory."[47] However, the Court in *Starbucks* rejected this deferential approach to evaluating requests for a section 10(j) injunction. The *Starbucks* majority held that district courts must apply the same traditional equitable authority that is used in all requests for injunctive relief, which means that courts must wade into the merits of the underlying claims and use their unbounded judicial discretion to determine the likelihood of success. No deference to the informed judgment of the NLRB is needed or warranted, the Court concluded, thus ceding increased power to the lower federal courts to impose their own policy predilections in section 10(j) litigation. *Starbucks* represents a shift to judicial substitution of agency expertise, notwithstanding that the NLRA was enacted to limit the role of the judiciary, in part due to the backdrop of an "ignominious history of [judicial] abuse [in which] 'the federal courts generally were regarded as allies of management in its attempt to prevent the organization and strengthening of labor unions.'"[48] In short, *Starbucks* weakens the NLRB's ability to remedy, through section 10(j) litigation, employers' unfair labor practices that are designed to foil union organizing efforts while they are still in their embryonic stage. Time will reveal the impact as district courts take up the *Starbucks* Court's invitation to undertake an independent review of merits of a pending NLRB claim of antiunion discrimination and use their unfettered discretion to decide section 10(j) cases. One suspects that the NLRB will be hobbled, at least to a degree, in temporarily reinstating unlawfully discharged organizing leadership during an organizing drive before a vote on union representation.

Arbitration as the Preferred Remedy

Of the approximately one hundred significant labor and management relations decisions that the Supreme Court decided during the sixty years between 1965 and 2025, twelve address the role of arbitration as a means of resolving industrial disputes.[49] In addition, there are six pre-1965 cases that address the arbitral process, including three pivotal 1960 cases comprising what is known as the *Steelworkers Trilogy*.[50] Taken as a whole, these eighteen cases enshrine arbitration in our national labor policy as the preferred forum to resolving labor-management conflict. Establishing the primacy of labor arbitration offers benefits to workers but also exacts costs that are seldom discussed.

By the end of World War II, voluntary arbitration occupied a secure role in the collective bargaining process as a credible dispute-resolution mechanism. Ideologically, voluntary arbitration united collective bargaining with free enterprise and its commitment to the private ordering of wages and working conditions. Pragmatically, the World War II experience with labor arbitration had demonstrated its efficiency and wide acceptance. Arbitration of collective bargaining contract disputes not only developed as an alternative to industrial strife but was also viewed by many as a preferable alternative to the courts for resolving industrial disputes.[51]

In her monumental and still timely article "The Post-War Paradigm in American Labor Law," Katherine Stone explained how the 1947 enactment of the Taft-Hartley Act's section 301 created a crisis for advocates of labor arbitration.[52] These advocates feared that, by creating federal court jurisdiction to enforce collective bargaining agreements, section 301 would result in judicial displacement of voluntary, private arbitration, thereby positioning the federal government to set the terms and conditions of employment. "Hence, [advocates of arbitration] urged the courts not to use section 301 to preempt private arbitration or to expand government control of the workplace [but to] affirm the . . . vision of the democratic, self-determined workplace. The Supreme Court, over the next twenty-five years, did just that."[53]

By 1965, the Court had laid the foundation for "arbitration [to be] elevated to the center stage of national labor policy."[54] This initial transformation of arbitration's role was accomplished primarily in four cases that are among the most liberal, even visionary, of the Court's decisions and reflect the highpoint of its investment in industrial democracy—what Justice Douglas referred to as viewing "[a] collective bargaining agreement [as] an effort to erect a system of industrial self-government."[55] The traditional literature heaped praise on the elevation of labor arbitration as a bedrock of our national labor policy.[56] Yet, as I will show, even when the Court's liberals perceived themselves to be championing labor's cause, they did so in a way that contained seeds of future defeat.

Decided in 1957, *Textile Workers Union v. Lincoln Mills* not only upheld the constitutionality of section 301's grant of federal jurisdiction to enforce collective bargaining agreements but also held that section 301 mandated the federal courts to create a federal common law setting the substantive rules for the enforcement of collective bargaining agreements.[57] Then, in the pivotal 1960 *Steelworkers Trilogy*, the Court exercised its section 301 authority to create a common law of collective bargaining contract enforcement. First, it held that courts should enforce arbitration agreements without consideration of the merits of the underlying grievance.[58] Second, it held that national labor policy creates a presumption of arbitrability. Thus, in litigation over whether the parties had agreed to arbitrate a particular grievance, all "doubts should be resolved in favor of [the arbitrability of the dispute in question]."[59] Finally, and further truncating the role of the judiciary, it held that when the issue is whether the judiciary should enforce an arbitration award, the award should be enforced, even when arbitrators fail to clearly articulate their rationale, as long as the award can plausibly be viewed as "draw[ing] its essence from the collective bargaining agreement."[60] It is difficult to disagree with the conclusion that, by 1965, *Lincoln Mills* and the *Steelworkers Trilogy* had "elevated arbitration to a favored position by requiring courts to promote arbitration, without permitting them to scrutinize the outcomes of the disputes [and had] substitute[d] the arbitral forum for the judicial forum."[61]

In the journey to achieving arbitral supremacy—promoting arbitration in most cases as the sole forum for adjudicating collective bargaining disputes—the Court needed to confront the problem of an overlap of jurisdiction between the NLRB and arbitration. In *Carey v. Westinghouse Electric Corporation*, a dispute arose that could have been resolved as an NLRB representation dispute or in arbitration as a dispute over collective bargaining contract interpretation. The Court held that NLRB jurisdiction over the dispute should not preclude an arbitral remedy. Moreover, "if by the time the dispute reaches the Board, arbitration has already taken place, the Board [should show] deference to the arbitral award."[62] Over time, the NLRB developed a deferral-to-arbitration doctrine, concluding that in cases that could be resolved through arbitration, it would defer to arbitration by dismissing an unfair labor practice complaint and later defer to any arbitral decision if the hearing was "fair and regular."[63] In short, by the end of the 1960s, the Court had effectively elevated the arbitral forum over the courts and the NLRB as the preferred mechanism for resolving collective bargaining disputes.[64]

The guidance in *Carey v. Westinghouse*—that the NLRB has concurrent jurisdiction with private arbitration but should defer to an arbitral award— was an important development in the process of shaping the boundaries of the overlapping jurisdictions of the NLRB and arbitration and establishing arbitration as the primary forum for resolving industrial disputes. But much more was needed to clarify the accommodation of NLRB unfair labor practice jurisdiction with the role of labor arbitration. For example, does the NLRB have contract interpretation authority when it needs to interpret a labor contract in order to adjudicate an unfair labor practice? This question arose in *NLRB v C & C Plywood Corporation*.[65] In that case, the union had filed an unfair labor practice charge against an employer alleging that the employer's inauguration of a premium pay plan during the term of a collective agreement, without previously consulting the union, violated the duty to bargain. The employer claimed that the action had been authorized by the collective agreement. The disagreement over the correct interpretation of the labor agreement was the gravamen of the dispute. Interpreting the contract, the NLRB rejected the employer's contract claim. The court of appeals refused to enforce the Board's finding that the employer's unilateral change constituted bad faith bargaining, reasoning that the Board lacked jurisdiction to interpret a provision of a labor agreement that "arguably" allowed the employer to institute the premium pay plan. The Supreme Court reversed. While Congress determined that the NLRB should not have general jurisdiction over all alleged violations of collective bargaining agreements, the Board is charged with the duty to enforce the provisions of the NLRA, and the Board may interpret collective bargaining agreements "so far as [is] necessary to . . . to decide th[e] unfair labor practice case [before it]."[66]

There was no arbitration provision in the contract involved in the *C & C Plywood* litigation, raising the question of whether the NLRB possesses juris- diction to interpret a contract that has an arbitration provision. The Court resolved that question in two cases: *NLRB v. Acme Industrial Company* and

NLRB v. Strong Roofing and Insulating Company.[67] In each case, the parties' labor agreement contained a grievance-arbitration provision. The employer argued that, although interpreting the labor contract might be necessary for the NLRB to adjudicate an unfair labor practice, when the contract contains an arbitration provision, all interpretation issues must be resolved through arbitration. The Court rejected the employer's argument, reasoning that section 10(a) of the NLRA provides that "the Board is empowered . . . to prevent any person from engaging in any unfair labor practice. . . . This power shall not be affected by any other means of adjustment or prevention that has been or may be established by agreement, law, or otherwise."[68] Thus, the constricted role for courts in enforcing collective bargaining agreements, as described in the *Steelworkers Trilogy*, is inapplicable to the NLRB.

In its most recent decision in this series of cases, *Litton Financial Printing Division v. NLRB*, the dispute arose from an employer's refusal to arbitrate a grievance arising from an expired contract.[69] The underlying unfair labor practice dispute arose with respect to whether the parties intended the arbitration provision to survive the expiration of the contract. Although disagreeing with the NLRB's interpretation of the contract in that case, the Court again confirmed the Board's authority to interpret provisions of a collective bargaining agreement, notwithstanding that the contract contains an arbitration provision. Even with the Supreme Court's repeated holdings that the NLRB possesses the authority to interpret labor contracts that contain arbitration provisions, some judicial resistance continues. One leading treatise on labor and management relations law has stated that, even after *Litton*, the lower courts "are cautious to point out that arbitrators and courts, not the NLRB, are the primary interpreters of contracts."[70]

Assigning labor arbitration a central role in enforcing national labor policy has had consequences harmful to workers. One example is the implied no-strike clause. For a labor policy to successfully channel the resolution of disputes through the arbitral process, it is important to limit workers' ability to attempt to resolve disputes through strikes rather than arbitration. Accordingly, to substitute arbitration for striking, the Court has found ways to abrogate workers' right to strike. One way is to hold as a matter of law that even in the absence of a no-strike clause in a collective bargaining agreement, a strike over a dispute covered by a collective bargaining agreement's arbitration provision violates the labor agreement.[71] But finding that a contract, by implication, contains a no-strike obligation, required the Court to rewrite the parties' collective bargaining agreement. The Court's willingness to add an implied no-strike obligation to a collective bargaining agreement thus disregarded the commitment to private ordering that the Court has often referred to as a bedrock NLRA policy.

Furthermore, elevating arbitration as the preferred dispute resolution process has harmed workers because the Supreme Court has used this cornerstone position of labor arbitration to justify permitting federal courts to enjoin certain strikes. A policy to resolve industrial disputes through arbitration rather than through strikes requires not only that workers be placed under a no-strike obligation but also that there will be an effective way to enforce that no-strike obligation. Workers and their union representatives must be coerced, if necessary, to choose to resolve disputes by arbitrating rather than by attempting to obtain a favorable outcome via striking in breach of the contract's no-strike clause. The labor injunction is the enforcement mechanism that the Supreme Court chose in its post-1965 cases to prevent workers from engaging in strikes that breach a contract's no-strike clause.

But deploying the labor injunction for this purpose initially confronted a major hurdle: section 4 of the 1932 Norris-LaGuardia Act.[72] That act deprives the federal courts of jurisdiction to issue injunctions arising out of most labor disputes.[73] Initially, the Court had held that this bar precluded enjoining strikes in breach of a no-strike clause.[74] However, in *Boys Market, Inc. v. Retail Clerks, Local 770*, it found an efficient solution for overcoming the Norris-LaGuardia hurdle.[75] Overruling a case it had decided just eight years previously, the Court discovered an implied exception to the Act's ban on federal court labor injunctions.[76] This implication was grounded in the 1947 Taft-Hartley Act's preference for dispute resolution through arbitration—Congress's desire that labor disputes be resolved through voluntary arbitration. The *Boys Market* decision reasoned that, in 1947, Congress must have intended to amend the Norris-LaGuardia Act *sub silentio* to permit federal courts to enjoin breaches of a collective bargaining agreement's no-strike provisions. The reason is that, without the ability to secure such an injunction, an employer would be disinclined to agree to arbitration as a substitute for the strike, thus undermining Congress's preference to channel industrial disputes through arbitration.

The Court's 1976 decision in *Buffalo Forge Company v. Steelworkers* is grounded in this link between promoting the arbitral process as the preferred means to resolve industrial disputes and authorizing federal courts to enjoin breaches of no-strike clauses.[77] In *Buffalo Forge*, the Court held that the federal court lacked jurisdiction to enjoin a strike in breach of a no-strike obligation in a collective bargaining agreement. Here, the strike was not over a dispute covered by the arbitration clause contained in the striking union's collective bargaining agreement. Rather, it was a sympathy strike in support of another union that was striking over a dispute with its employer. Thus, denying the employer an injunction in *Buffalo Forge* did not create any disincentive for that employer to agree to arbitration in the future. In short, the *Boys Market*–discovered exception to Norris-LaGuardia did not apply because "the strike had neither the purpose [n]or effect of denying or evading an obligation to arbitrate."[78]

As it emerged from its World War II roots, labor arbitration under a collective bargaining agreement developed as a voluntary, bilateral process: unions and employers jointly agreed to arbitrate their disputes. But arbitration has assumed a more sinister face in the form of forced arbitration among nonunionized workers.[79] In this take-it-or-leave-it approach to the arbitration of workplace disputes, an increasing number of corporations are unilaterally requiring their nonunion workforce to sign employment contracts that waive the employees' rights under civil rights, minimum wage, and other protective laws. Instead, disputes must be resolved through arbitration. Employees lose access to the courts in a wide array of employment contexts, including disputes under laws prohibiting employment discrimination, protecting employees with disabilities, allowing workers to take maternity and medical leaves, and guaranteeing minimum wages and overtime. As of 2017, forced arbitration provisions had been added to more than half of private sector, nonunion employees' contracts.[80] It is estimated that, by 2025, more than 80 percent of private sector, nonunion workers will be blocked from court by forced arbitration provisions.[81] "Mandatory [forced] arbitration is more common in low-wage work and in industries with higher proportions of women and Black workers."[82]

These forced arbitration agreements typically contain two related provisions. First, they waive an employee's right to initiate or join litigation challenging an employer's unlawful conduct and instead limit relief to whatever redress may be available in arbitration. Second, they typically contain a class waiver provision that precludes groups of employees from joining similar claims in arbitration. In short, they bar group actions via either litigation or arbitration, thus eliminating "the most basic mechanism used by workers to hold employers accountable: the class-action lawsuit."[83]

Forced arbitration agreements with class-action waivers create an insurmountable obstacle for effecting systemic change at the workplace, particularly for nonunion employees. Two examples make the point. Misclassification of employees as independent contractors under the Fair Labor Standards Act (FLSA) is a widespread source of wage theft, as is failure to pay minimum wage or overtime pay.[84] The FLSA does not provide private litigants with the remedy of prospective injunctive relief, but groups of litigants can combine individual claims for monetary relief by bringing a collective action to redress past FLSA violations.[85] Forced arbitration agreements bar this option to secure systemic change at the workplace. Further, "because Title VII pattern-or-practice claims must be brought as group actions rather than as individual claims, arbitration agreements prevent employees from bringing [such] pattern-or-practice claims."[86]

In three landmark cases, the Supreme Court has encouraged this trend toward forced arbitration. The Roberts Court's 2011 decision in *AT&T Mobility, LLC, v. Concepcion* was decisive.[87] There, the Court upheld the enforceability of class waivers in arbitration agreements, notwithstanding that the waivers were unenforceable under state law. *Concepcion* gave employers incentives to add forced arbitration agreements with class waivers to employees' contracts as an efficient way to eliminate class-action litigation. In *Lamps Plus, Inc. v. Varela*, another five-to-four decision, the Roberts Court's conservative majority became even more zealous in its effort to preclude workers from working jointly to remedy an employer's denial of their legal rights.[88] In this case, the Court held that, even if a forced arbitration provision in an employment contract contains no class waiver provision or does not clearly waive collective action, employees may only arbitrate a dispute on an individual rather than a classwide basis: workers are assumed to have "consented" to individualized arbitration. The legal presumption is that a forced arbitration provision in an employment contract includes an implied class waiver, and courts "may not infer [an employer's] consent to participate in class arbitration absent an affirmative 'contractual basis for concluding that the [employer] agreed to do so.'"[89]

In *Epic Systems v. Lewis* the Court consolidated several cases.[90] In two of them, an employee's employment contract provided for individualized arbitration to resolve employment disputes between the parties. In each case, the employee brought a collective and class action in federal court against an employer, alleging that the employer had violated both the FLSA and state law. Invoking the employment contract's arbitration clause, the defendant employer in each case then filed a motion to dismiss and to compel individual arbitration. In one case, the federal district court denied the employer's motion; in the other, the district court granted it. In both cases, appeals were taken, and in each a U.S. court of appeals denied the employer's motion to dismiss and compel individual arbitration.

In a split five-to-four decision, the Roberts Court ruled in *Epic Systems* that the employer's motion to dismiss and to compel individual arbitration should have been granted because the Federal Arbitration Act (FAA) mandates that federal courts enforce arbitration agreements, even with respect to alleged violations of statutory rights arising under federal and state law. The FAA has a "saving clause" that removes a federal court's obligation to enforce an arbitration provision if an arbitration agreement violates some other federal law. The employees in *Epic Systems* argued that, by requiring individualized proceedings, the arbitration agreements barred employees from joining with others in collective and class actions and thereby violated the NLRA, specifically the right to engage in concerted activities for mutual aid and protection. The NLRB agreed with the employees' interpretation of the Act.[91] The majority in *Epic Systems* disagreed, holding that combining together in collective or class actions does not constitute concerted activity for mutual aid and protection. Rather, "the term 'other concerted activities' [in section 7] should, like the terms that precede it, serve to protect things employees 'just do' for themselves in the course of exercising their right to free association in the workplace, rather than 'the highly regulated, courtroom-bound activities of class and joint litigation.'"[92] Accordingly, an employer does not violate the NLRA by forcing employees to waive the right to act jointly to litigate workplace violations of protective labor legislation.

While forced arbitration is framed as a more efficient alternative to litigation, its opponents argue that the real purpose is to "suppress legal claims and avoid accountability [because arbitration clauses may] impose costly fees on workers, shorten periods for initiating a claim, limit workers' ability to collect evidence to prove their case, and prevent arbitrators from awarding the level of relief that would be available in court." [93] As Justice Brennan once explained, "arbitral factfinding is not generally equivalent to judicial factfinding. . . . [T]he record of the arbitration proceedings is not as complete; the usual rules of evidence do not apply; and rights and procedures common to civil trials, such as discovery, compulsory process, cross-examination, and testimony under oath, are often severely limited or unavailable."[94]

A factor that makes forced arbitration suspect is that most employees are likely to press a claim in arbitration only once in their work life, while employers may have a recurring future need to hire arbitrators. This difference creates at least the appearance that arbitrators have an incentive to find for employers in the hope of obtaining future business. The most careful study of forced arbitration to date concludes that, compared to judicial relief, mandatory arbitration is a less satisfactory option for vindicating workplace rights: employees bring fewer claims, win less often, and receive lower awards.[95]

In an amicus brief to the Second Circuit Court of Appeals, a dozen law professors argued that allowing the National Football League's arbitration system, with commissioner Roger Goodell serving as arbitrator, to determine the merits of racial discrimination and civil rights disputes arising within the league is "unconscionable" and an "egregious" violation of fundamental fairness." The brief compares this to "allowing a referee to officiate a professional football game where the referee owns one of the teams."[96]

Congress has begun to take notice. In 2021, it enacted the Ending Forced Arbitration of Sexual Assault and Sexual Harassment Act. The legislation makes pre-dispute arbitration agreements unenforceable "with respect to a case which is filed under Federal, Tribal, or State law and relates to [a] sexual assault dispute or [a] sexual harassment dispute." [97] The outcomes in early cases suggest that courts are taking a worker-friendly approach to the arbitration ban.[98] Broader statutory bans on the judicial enforcement of pre-dispute forced arbitration agreements have been introduced in Congress.[99]

Section 301 Preemption and the Erosion of Individual Employment Rights

Few workers, indeed few judges and law professors, are familiar with the intricacies of section 301 preemption doctrine, the poison pill of U.S. labor relations. Employers use this doctrine as an argument to discourage employees from choosing union representation. The argument works because even as federal, state, and local governments have vastly expanded individual employee rights, such as unemployment insurance, workplace safety regulations, anti-discrimination protection, and protection against unjust dismissal (to cite just a few examples), "the broad § 301 preemption doctrine has placed union workers at a disadvantage relative to nonunion workers, by denying the former the benefit of [statutory] employment rights."[100] This discrimination against unionized workers is the product of eight Supreme Court decisions, all but one decided since 1965.

In most cases, when a unionized worker sues to enforce an individual statutory employment right—for example, a state statutory ban on unjust dismissal—the section 301 preemption doctrine extinguishes (preempts) the worker's statutory right. As the Supreme Court has held, "when resolution of a state-law claim is substantially dependent upon analysis of the terms of an agreement made between the parties in a labor contract [almost always the case when a unionized employee sues to enforce a statutory employment right] that claim must either be treated as a § 301 claim [and litigated as a collective bargaining contract dispute] or dismissed as pre-empted by federal labor-contract law."[101] The rules resulting in this discrimination against unionized workers are complex but can be summarized as follows.

As I discussed briefly above, NLRA's section 301, on its face, does no more than provide federal courts with subject matter jurisdiction to enforce collective bargaining agreements. But early on, the Court held that section 301 also has a substantive component: it provides the rules of labor contract enforcement as determined by the federal courts.[102] Section 301's preemption doctrine developed from this humble beginning. The doctrine's foundation decision was *Local 174, Teamsters, v. Lucas Flour Company*, which gave section 301 a broad preemptive scope.[103] *Lucas Flour* held that state courts have concurrent jurisdiction with federal courts to adjudicate collective bargaining disputes. However, to promote uniformity, state courts adjudicating a dispute arising under a collective bargaining agreement must apply section 301's federal substantive rules, not state contract rules.

As the Court made clear soon thereafter in *Avco Corporation v. Aero Lodge No. 735*, in litigation to resolve disputes arising under collective bargaining agreements, section 301 preempts all substantive state law: there is no enforceable state law setting substantive rules of labor contact enforcement.[104] Any litigation adjudicating a dispute arising under a collective bargaining agreement, whether brought in a state or a federal court, notwithstanding how it is styled, is a section 301 action to be resolved applying federal substantive law.

Section 301's broad preemptive scope is well illustrated in the Court's far-reaching 1985 decision in *Allis-Chalmers Corporation v. Lueck*, initially brought as a state law *tort action*.[105] In that action, the employee alleged that his employer and an insurer that administered a nonoccupational disability insurance plan included in Lueck's collective bargaining agreement had violated the state tort of bad faith in handling an insurance claim. The lower state courts dismissed the action, but the state supreme court reversed, and the U.S. Supreme Court agreed to hear the case. The Court, in a decision by Justice Blackmun, held that adjudicating the state tort required proving bad faith by the employer. But because the employer's duty of good faith when processing insurance claims was "defined by the contractual obligation of good faith, any attempt to assess liability here inevitably would involve contract interpretation."[106] Accordingly, the tort action was section 301 preempted. The complaint should have been dismissed for failure to use contract grievance procedure or dismissed as preempted by section 301—that is, dismissed because section 301 displaces all state causes of action requiring for their adjudication interpretation of a collective bargaining agreement, even if the state law claim was pleaded as a tort.[107]

Caterpillar, Inc. v. Williams, decided two years after *Lueck*, addressed the issue of whether the contract interpretation issue that triggers section 301 preemption must arise solely from the plaintiff's claim or whether section 301 preemption can also arise because the employer raises a defense that requires an interpretation of a collective bargaining agreement.[108] In *Williams*, former employees brought a state court action against an employer for breach of individual employment contracts negotiated while they were managerial employees, thus prior to their having been assigned to unionized positions covered by a collective bargaining agreement. Their state court action required no interpretation of a collective bargaining agreement. The employer removed the case to federal court and moved to dismiss pursuant to section 301 preemption. The district court found section 301 preemption based on the employer's defense that, as a matter of federal substantive labor law, all individual contracts of employment were merged into and superseded by the collective bargaining agreement. Thus, the dispute could not be resolved without interpreting the superseding effect of that agreement. The court of appeals reversed. Agreeing with the court of appeals that there was no section 301 preemption, the Supreme Court majority reasoned:

> Section 301 governs claims "substantially dependent on analysis of a collective-bargaining agreement." [The state court complainant here] does not rely upon the collective agreement indirectly, nor does it address the relationship between the individual contracts and the collective agreement. "[I]t would be inconsistent with congressional intent under [§ 301] to pre-empt state rules that proscribe conduct, or establish rights and obligations, independent of a labor contract."[109]

Caterpillar seemed to have resolved that section 301 preemption arises when resolution of a state law claim is "substantially dependent on analysis of a collective-bargaining agreement" and not from employer defenses that alone introduced the need for contract interpretation.

Decided during the same term as *Caterpillar, International Brotherhood of Electrical Workers v. Hechler* reinforced the core holdings of both *Caterpillar* and *Lueck*.[110] A union member had brought a suit against her union in state court, alleging that the union had breached its duty to ascertain that she had essential training and experience before being assigned work at an electrical substation of a utility company that resulted in a workplace injury. The Supreme Court's Justice Blackmun held that the tort claim under state law was not sufficiently independent of the collective bargaining agreement to withstand the preemptive force of section 301 because any duty of care the union owed to the union member had arisen from the collective bargaining agreement. Accordingly, as *Lueck* had directed, the case was 301 preempted because its outcome was "substantially dependent on analysis of a collective-bargaining agreement."[111]

Section 301 preemption cases seemed to be coming to the Court every term or two during the late 1980s as the lower courts attempted to develop novel ways to use the preemption to extinguish individual employment rights for union-represented state court plaintiffs. *Lingle v. Norge Division of Magic Chef,* decided the year after the decision in *Hechler,* is a good example.[112] A unionized employee filed a state court action under a state law governing the tort of retaliatory discharge for filing a worker's compensation claim. None of the proof required to establish the elements of the tort required the state court to interpret any term of a collective bargaining agreement. A finding of no section 301 preemption would have appeared to be self-evident. Nevertheless, the lower courts did find 301 preemption. According to their reasoning, because the plaintiff's collective bargaining agreement's grievance-arbitration clause would have provided the plaintiff with the same relief as could be achieved through the state law tort action, the claim was section 301 preempted. The Supreme Court unanimously reversed, emphasizing that the availability of parallel relief through the contract's grievance-arbitration procedure does not determine 301 preemption. Rather, "as long as the state-law claim can be resolved without interpreting the collective-bargaining agreement itself, the claim is 'independent' of the agreement for § 301 pre-emption purposes."[113]

Livadas v. Bradshaw is an extreme example of how lower courts (here, a state official) have attempted to deploy 301 preemption to deny union-represented employees individual employment rights provided by state law.[114] California law requires employers to pay all wages due immediately upon an employee's discharge and imposes a penalty of three days' pay for failure to pay those wages promptly. The law places responsibility for enforcing these provisions on the state's commissioner of labor. Livadas's employer refused to pay her the wages owed upon her discharge, and she filed a penalty claim. The commissioner replied that the labor code barred him from enforcing Livadas's claim because her terms and conditions were governed by a collective bargaining agreement containing an arbitration clause. Livadas brought a section 1983 action against the state labor commissioner, alleging that denial of enforcement of the state labor code had deprived her of her rights under NLRA to bargain collectively. The commissioner argued that Livadas's claim was section 301 preempted because if the commissioner were to find a violation and impose a penalty requiring the employer to pay Livadas three days' worth of pay, the commissioner would need to consult the collective bargaining agreement to decide how much Livadas had been paid in order to compute the amount of money owed. Once again, the Supreme Court majority needed to explain that section 301 does not broadly preempt employee rights conferred by state law but preempts claims whose legal character depends on rights under the collective bargaining agreement. When liability is governed by independent state law and the meaning of contract terms is not in dispute, the bare fact that a collective bargaining agreement is consulted for damage computation is no reason to extinguish the state-law claim.

A 1990s-era survey of 301 preemption cases revealed "a very broad tendency for courts to preempt unionized workers' state law claims. Indeed, with very few exceptions, courts always preempt unionized workers' attempts to assert state law employment rights. The broad trend, as well as the narrow exceptions, are apparent."[115] More recent studies have concluded that "a section 301 preemption question arises each time a union worker brings a lawsuit alleging the violation of a state law employment right that arguably involves the [collective bargaining] agreement[. And] although the Supreme Court has addressed this issue [repeatedly] in its line of section 301 preemption cases, lower federal courts and state courts have failed to develop a uniform rule for the preemption of a union employee's state law claims [and continue to struggle]."[116]

THE CASES

The Union Security Cases
    The Pre-1965 Cases[1]
    Abood v. Detroit Board of Education[2]
    Ellis v. Brotherhood of Railway Clerks[3]
    Chicago Teachers Union v. Hudson[4]
    Communication Workers of America v. Beck[5]
    Lehnert v. Ferris Faculty Association[6]
    Air Line Pilots v. Miller[7]
    Knox v. Service Employees International Union, Local 1000[8]
    Harris v. Quinn[9]
    Friedrichs v. California Teachers Association[10]
    Janus v. American Federation of State, County, and Municipal Employees, Counsel 31[11]
The Union Fine Cases
    NLRB v. Allis-Chalmers Manufacturing Company[12]
    NLRB v. Industrial Union of Marine and Shipbuilding Workers of America, AFL-CIO, Local 22[13]
    Scofield v. NLRB[14]
    NLRB v. Granite State Joint Board, Textile Workers Union of America, Local 1029[15]
    NLRB v. Boeing Company[16]
    Booster Lodge No. 405, International Association of Machinists and Aerospace Workers, AFL-CIO v. NLRB[17]
    Pattern Makers League of North America v. NLRB[18]
    NLRB v. International Brotherhood of Electrical Workers, Local 340[19]

CHAPTER 9

The Union's Relationship
with Those It Represents

The Union Security Cases

Union members pay financial support to a union per their union's governing documents, which set forth the obligations of union membership. But unions and employers also enter into union security agreements that require all employees in union-represented bargaining units, as a condition of employment, to contribute to the cost of union representation. These agreements have spawned much litigation. Since 1965, the Supreme Court has decided ten union security cases, and that is in addition to four pre-1965 adjudications.

The Court's union security cases center on disagreement over the fairness of compelling financial support for a union from those in a bargaining unit who are not union members and object to providing that support. The tension arises from two competing cultural norms. On the one hand, unions represent all employees in a bargaining unit, they are obligated to represent all of those employees fairly, and all employees who benefit from union representation should pay their fair share of that representation. Otherwise, members become a free riders. On the other hand, basic to our legal culture is the value of not forcing persons into unwanted association and, relatedly, not requiring persons to finance views with which they disagree.

In public sector cases where state and local governments are the employers, this tension is resolved by applying constitutional free speech and free association principles. In contexts related to the Railway Labor Act (RLA), union security disputes also are resolved as constitutional problems, although employers are private entities. That was the Court's holding in *Railway Employees v. Hanson*.[20] In cases arising under the NLRA, *Communication Workers of America v. Beck* is the lead case.[21] It holds that union security disputes are not controlled by constitutional principles but are analyzed as duty-of-fair-representation disputes.[22] But in *Beck*, the Court held that precedents arising in RLA litigation are applicable to NLRA union security disputes.

Machinists v. Street, Railway Clerks v. Allen, and *NLRB v. General Motors Corporation* are the three most important pre-1965 Supreme Court union security cases, laying the foundation for most of what came later.[23] *General Motors* addressed the freedom of association/free rider tension for NLRA union security agreements by holding that, while the Act refers to permitting unions and employers to agree to require union membership as a condition of employment, the NLRA concept of membership is limited to requiring employees to pay their prorated share of the financial core of union membership—that is, periodic union dues and fees. Union security agreements may not require that a bargaining unit employee actually join the union and thereby be bound by its rules. The phrase that entered the labor relations lexicon in *General Motors* was "agency fee" payers. Employees can satisfy the requirements of a union security agreement by paying an agency fee but not otherwise owing any fealty to the union. But disagreement over which union expenses fall within the chargeable financial core and how to calculate those expenses has dominated the Court's union security cases for the past sixty years.

The other two pre-1965 cases, *Street* and *Allen*, were RLA cases. In each, nonmembers of the union who were subject to a union security agreement charged that the RLA was unconstitutional to the extent that it permitted unions to use union security–generated money collected from nonmembers to promote political candidates and ideologies that plaintiffs opposed. The Court avoided the constitutional questions in the cases by holding that the RLA does not permit a union, over the objections of nonmembers, to expend agency fees collected from them on political causes. In its 1988 decision in *Communication Workers v. Beck*, the Rehnquist Court explained that the Court's *Street* decision had concluded that the RLA authorization of union security agreements "'contemplated compulsory unionism to force employees to share the costs of negotiating and administering collective agreements, and the costs of the adjustment and settlement of disputes,' but that Congress did not intend 'to provide the unions with a means for forcing employees, over their objection, to support political causes which they oppose.'"[24]

It then became necessary for the Court to decide how dues objectors are to remedy a union's alleged use of their money for objectionable political purposes. In *Allen*, nonmembers who had refused to pay any agency fees obtained injunctive relief in state court against enforcement of the union security agreement. The Court found the injunction improper. The Court had held that "dissent is not to be presumed—it must affirmatively be made known to the union by the dissenting employee. . . . The union receiving money exacted from an employee under a union-shop agreement should not in fairness be subjected to sanctions in favor of an employee who makes no complaint of the use of his money for such activities."[25] In *Allen*, the plaintiffs had not made their objection known to the union prior to suing, but the Court held that the complaint filed in the lawsuit provided the union notice. However, the injunction was improper because dissenting employees are not entitled to an injunction relieving them of all obligation to pay the money due under the union security agreement. Objectors remain obliged, as a condition of continued employment, to make the payments to their respective unions called for by the agreement. Their grievance stems from the spending of their funds for purposes not authorized by the Act in the face of their objection, not from the enforcement of the union shop agreement by the mere collection of funds. The Court remanded the case for determination of which expenditures were properly characterized as political and the percentage of total union expenditures that they constituted.

Street and *Allen* provided little guidance with respect to which union expenditures are political and which are chargeable to objectors because they are germane to the union's representational function. That question lingered for almost fifteen years, until 1977, when the Court, in *Abood v. Detroit Board of Education*, began the process of providing guidance in a series of cases.[26] *Abood* was a public employee union security case subject to resolution by application of constitutional principles. Yet the Court held that the precedent under the RLA was controlling. Accordingly, the Court held that it is unconstitutional for a public employer and the union representing its employees to compel the public employees to support financially, over their objections, "ideological causes not germane to [the union's] duties as collective bargaining representative."[27] The Court acknowledged that there will be "difficult problems in drawing lines between collective-bargaining activities, for which contributions may be compelled, and ideological activities unrelated to collective bargaining, for which such compulsion is prohibited, [but added that] we have no occasion in this case . . . to try to define such a dividing line."[28]

The Court undertook to draw "such a dividing line" in *Ellis v. Brotherhood of Railway Clerks*.[29] Here, the Court held:

When employees such as petitioners object to being burdened with particular union expenditures, the test must be whether the challenged expenditures are necessarily or reasonably incurred for the purpose of performing the duties of an exclusive representative of the employees in dealing with the employer on labor-management issues. Under this standard, objecting employees may be compelled to pay their fair share of not only the direct costs of negotiating and administering a collective-bargaining contract and of settling grievances and disputes, but also the expenses of activities or undertakings normally or reasonably employed to implement or effectuate the duties of the union as exclusive representative of the employees in the bargaining unit.[30]

Applying this test, the Court found that unions could not charge for organizing but could charge for their national conventions, social activities, portions of their publications, and certain litigation expenses. In a subsequent case, *Lehnert v. Ferris Faculty Association*, the Court added that (1) employees could be charged a prorated share of costs associated with the activities of state and national union affiliates, even if those activities did not directly benefit the objecting employees' bargaining unit; (2) the union could not charge the objecting employees for expenses of lobbying; and (3) the objecting members could be charged for expenses incidental to preparation for a strike, even though a strike would have been illegal under Michigan law.[31]

The most intricate aspect of the law regulating the rights and obligations of dues objectors entails the complex rules that have developed regarding (1) procedures that objectors must follow to note their objection to the union's use of their agency fee for purposes not germane to representing the bargaining unit employees and then to challenge the union's calculation of the portion of its expenditures that it may charge objectors and (2) procedures that the union must follow to provide notice of nonmembers' right to object and the process for calculating the division between chargeable and nonchargeable expenditures. The specifics of these procedures are beyond the scope of this book. However, two Supreme Court decisions set forth the procedural requirements: *Chicago Teachers Union v. Hudson* and *Air Line Pilots v. Miller*.[32]

By the turn of the twenty-first century, thirty-five years after the start date of this study, the Court's many pre- and post-1965 union security cases seemed to have finally forged a sustainable settlement accommodating unions' claims to be protected from free riders and objectors' claims not to be compelled to financially support political candidates or ideologies with which they disagree. This settlement began to shatter as increasingly more conservative justices joined the Roberts Court, gained influence, and began to question the constitutionality of the settlement as it affected the claims of public employees. Every other term between 2012 and 2018, the Court heard a union security case and increasingly signaled that *any* compelled financial support of unions by state public employees would contravene the free speech and free association principles of the Constitution.

For example, in the 2012 case of *Knox v. Service Employees International Union, Local 1000*, the issue seemed to be narrow.[33] If the union provides an open period for nonmembers to register as dues objectors and after that period ends imposes a special assessment, must the union then provide another open period permitting nonmembers to become dues objectors before lawfully charging nonmembers the assessment? The Court held, five to four, that a new open period must be offered. Then, in a precedent-shattering holding, Justice Alito, writing for the majority, stated that the union was required to "allow members to *opt in* to [paying] the special fee rather than requiring them to opt out."[34] That was a dramatic shift from what had, till this point, been understood to be the constitutional rule that a union could collect dues and fees from a nonmember public employee unless the employee chose to opt out. The majority in *Knox* gratuitously added that the holding in *Abood* was "something of an anomaly," and that there were serious questions about whether an opt-out system "can be [constitutionally] justified during the collection of regular dues on an annual basis."[35]

Two years later, the Court decided *Harris v. Quinn*, another five-to-four decision authored by Justice Alito.[36] In this case, the Court held that an agency fee provision of the Illinois Public Labor Relations Act requiring nonunion Medicaid-funded homecare personal assistants to pay fees to the union representing such assistants was unconstitutional because the provision did not serve a compelling state interest that could not be achieved through means significantly less restrictive of associational freedoms. *Harris* is important, not because of its specific holding with respect to homecare personal assistants but because the five-to-four majority used the decision to question the constitutionality of *Abood*, observing that the analysis in *Abood* was "questionable on several grounds."[37]

The *Abood* decision might well have been reversed two years later, in 2016, in *Friedrichs v. California Teachers Association*, if not for the sudden death of

Justice Scalia.[38] In *Friedrichs*, the Court granted *certiorari* on the question of "whether Abood . . . should be overruled and public-sector 'agency shop' arrangements invalidated under the First Amendment." The Court split four to four, so *Abood* remained the law until 2018, when the Court reversed it in *Janus v. American Federation of State, County, and Municipal Employees, Counsel 31*, another five-to-four decision authored by Justice Alito.[39]

Beginning with the observation that compelling individuals to mouth support for views they find objectionable violates a cardinal constitutional command, the *Janus* majority endorsed what it understood to be a corollary: that "compelling a person to subsidize the speech of other private speakers [with whom they disagree] raises similar First Amendment concerns," even when the subsidized viewpoint is not imputed to the person who is objecting.[40] The majority in *Janus* added that the First Amendment protects not only an objector's right to opt out of paying union fees but also requires that workers affirmatively consent—opt in—before a public employer and a public employees' union may compel any payment of periodic dues and fees.

By articulating an expansive view of freedom of speech that would ban a wide variety of "democratically enacted rules requiring people or corporations to subsidize or transmit messages with which they disagree," *Janus* has created consequences that go far beyond union security.[41] For example, employers argue that requiring an employer to post notices about labor rights, such as the legal right to organize a union, constitutes unconstitutional compelled speech.[42] Likewise, they argue that the NLRB's order that an employer must remedy unfair labor practices by reading a notice declaring that it has committed such practices constitutes unlawful compelled speech because such a public reading is "humiliating and degrading to the employer."[43]

Janus is not directly applicable to NLRA-regulated union security agreements. There is no government action implicating the Constitution when a private sector employer that is not covered by the RLA voluntarily agrees to a union security agreement in a collective bargaining agreement with a private sector union.[44] But *Janus* explicitly left unanswered the question of extending the decision to private sector unions, and it has been argued that courts might conclude that government action is implicated from the exclusive bargaining representation status that the NLRA grants to unions.[45]

The Union Fine Cases

The Court's post-1965 union fine cases represent a remarkable migration in the interpretation of NLRA section 8(b)(1)(A) from a provision that Congress stated was intended to be used to curb certain intimidating organizing conduct and quell violence against persons wishing to cross a union picket line into a legal justification for regulating a broad range of peaceful internal union matters. Added in the 1947 Taft-Hartley amendments, the section provides, in pertinent part, that it shall be an unfair labor practice for a labor organization "to restrain or coerce (A) employees in the exercise of the rights guaranteed in section 7 of [the NLRA]" but adds "provided that this paragraph shall not impair the right of a labor organization to prescribe its own rules with respect to the acquisition or retention of membership."

It is clear that the original intent of section 8(b)(1)(A) was to curb physical violence and intimidation by union agents, not to regulate internal union affairs, as is plain from the unambiguous legislative history of the section.[46] Archibald Cox came to this conclusion in his influential 1947 article "Some Aspects of the Labor Management Relations Act, 1947," and the Court's statements in its pre-1965 union discipline cases confirm it.[47] For example, in *NLRB v. Teamsters, Local 639 (Curtis Brothers)*, the Court concluded that section 8(b)(1)(A) "is a grant of power to the Board limited to authority to proceed against union tactics involving violence, intimidation, and reprisal or threats thereof—conduct involving more than the general pressures upon persons employed by the affected employers implicit in economic strikes."[48] And just days prior to the twentieth anniversary of the section's enactment, the plurality opinion in *NLRB v. Allis-Chalmers Manufacturing Company* concluded that "the repeated refrain throughout the debates on [section] 8(b)(1)(A) and other sections [was] that Congress did not propose any limitations with respect to the internal affairs of unions, aside from barring enforcement of a union's internal regulations to affect a member's employment status."[49] As recently as 1973, the Court reaffirmed that "8(b)(1)(A) was not intended to give the Board power to regulate internal union affairs, including the imposition of disciplinary fines, with their consequent court enforcement, against members who violate the unions' constitutions and bylaws."[50]

Notwithstanding that the legislative history of section 8(b)(1)(A) limits its proscriptions to union acts of violence and intimidation and that the section was not intended by Congress to be used to regulate union internal affairs, the Court has gradually transformed it into a potent weapon to regulate union discipline. This was accomplished in a series of five cases that began with *NLRB v. Industrial Union of Marine and Shipbuilding Workers of America, Local 22*.[51] This was an expulsion, not a fine, case. Limiting its decision in *Allis-Chalmers*, rendered just one year previously, the Court held that the NLRA "assures a union freedom of self-regulation [only] where its legitimate internal affairs are concerned" and agreed with the NLRB that a union may not expel a member for filing an unfair labor practice charge with the board prior to exhausting internal union procedures.[52] The following year, in 1969, the Court decided *Scofield v. NLRB*, a momentous decision that drew the line between permissible and impermissible union action against members: "8(b)(1)(A) leaves a union free to enforce a properly adopted rule which reflects a legitimate union interest, impairs no policy Congress has imbedded in the labor laws, and is reasonably enforced against union members who are free to leave the union and escape the rule."[53] That open-textured test creates many opportunities for judicial intervention and creativity in regulating the relationship between a union and its members. On the facts of *Scofield*, the Court held that the union did not violate the NLRA by imposing fines of $50 and $100 on members for violating a union rule relating to production ceilings. Because they had been imposed on workers who were union members, the fines fell within the ambit of permissible discipline, as set forth in *Allis-Chalmers*. Yet *Scofield* was a gamechanger, transforming section 8(b)(1)(A) from a tool to curb union intimidation during organizing and redress of picket line violence into an invitation for courts to judge when union discipline of members advances a legitimate union interest or, on the contrary, impairs some policy that Congress has imbedded in the labor laws. It did not take long for *Scofield* to take hold and for the NLRB and the courts to review a wide swath of internal union controversies.[54]

NLRB v. Granite State Joint Board, Textile Workers Union of America, Local 1029 inaugurated a series of cases addressing the ability of a union to discipline those who were once union members before resigning and assisting an employer to defeat a strike by crossing a lawful union picket line.[55] In *Granite State*, the Court held that where there were no restraints on resignation from union membership, members were free to resign from the union and return to work during a strike without being subject to fines, even though they had previously participated in a vote to strike and in that vote had agreed to impose fines on any member aiding or abetting the employer. The Court reasoned that Congress has embedded in the NLRA the policy of permitting a person to refrain from union activities. Therefore, "where a member lawfully resigns from a union and thereafter engages in conduct which the union rule proscribes, . . . the union has no more [legal right to] control . . . the former member than it has . . . [to control] the man in the street"[56] In *Granite State*, the Court left open the question of whether it would be lawful for a union to enforce a specific provision in its constitution restricting the right of members to engage in strikebreaking following resignation.

That question was taken up in two subsequent cases. In the year following the decision in *Granite State*, the Court decided *Booster Lodge No. 405, International Association of Machinists and Aerospace Workers v. NLRB*.[57] The case focused on situations in which the union constitution obligates members to abstain from strikebreaking but otherwise the members neither know of nor consent to any limitation on their right to resign from the union and have not been previously informed that the union's constitution forbids strikebreaking. The Court held that, under such conditions, the NLRA authorizes the NLRB to find that a union commits an unfair labor practice in seeking court enforcement of fines imposed for strikebreaking activities on union members who had resigned prior to strikebreaking.[58]

The circuit courts of appeal had split on whether a union may impose explicit restrictions on its members' right to resign. The Court resolved that split in *Pattern Makers League of North America v. NLRB*.[59] In a six-to-three decision along ideological lines, it upheld an NLRB decision that a union violates NLRA section 8(b)(1)(A) by levying fines against members who, in violation of explicit provisions in the union's constitution, resigned during a strike and returned to work. The majority found determinative the provision in section 7 of the NLRA regarding the right to "refrain from" concerted activities.

The dissent in *Pattern Makers* viewed the issue as whether a union may "enforce a worker's promise to his fellow workers not to resign from his union and return to work during a strike, even though the worker freely made the decision to join the union and freely made the promise not to resign at such a time, and even though union members democratically made the decision to strike in full awareness of that promise." The dissent argued that both the language and legislative history of the NLRA fail to support the majority's holding in *Pattern Makers* but added that the holding "traduces the broader aim of federal labor policy . . . to preserve the balance of power between labor and management by guaranteeing workers an effective right to strike."[60] The dissent explained:

To be effective, the decision to strike, like the decision to bargain collectively, must be respected by the minority until democratically revoked. The employees' collective decision to strike is not taken lightly, and entails considerable costs[citing *NLRB v. Mackay Radio*, upholding the employer's right to permanently replace economic strikers]. Before workers undertake such a course, it is reasonable that they have some assurance that collectively they will have the means to withstand the pressures the employer is able lawfully to impose on them. A voluntarily and democratically adopted rule prohibiting resignations during a strike is one such means. By ensuring solidarity during a strike, it enforces the union's "legitimate interest in presenting a united front . . . and in not seeing its strength dissipated and its stature denigrated by subgroups within the unit separately pursuing what they see as separate interests" [citing *Emporium Capwell Company v. Western Addition Community Organization*, 420 U.S. 50 (1975)].

Because of decisions such as *Pattern Makers*, most unions today have no realistic ability to discipline a member who crosses a picket line, rejects a request not to perform certain work, or flouts any other union effort to maintain worker solidarity during economic disputes with employers. By contributing to the loss of worker empowerment, these cases have hastened the decline of the trade union movement. More than that, the union discipline cases reflect a shift in judicial attitude with respect to the role of unions and collective bargaining and the accommodation of collective bargaining to the competing claims of individuals and employers. The majority opinion in *Pattern Makers*, at least implicitly, subscribed to challenges from the right urging rejection of the collectivist underpinnings of our national labor policy—challenges, for example, that describe the NLRA as a "massive 'pro-labor' invention" that needs to be repealed because it grants unions the power to coerce both employees and employers into involuntary associations with unions.[61] This anticollectivist bias may be more evident in the Court's union discipline cases than in many of its other labor cases. But this book has demonstrated that, since 1965, conservative Supreme Court majorities, even up to the present, have exhibited a growing preference for the interests of employers and individuals over the collective interests of worker majorities and the collectivist underpinnings of our national labor policy.

Conclusion

In the preface to this book I wrote:

> [I]n these mostly five-to-four and six-to-three split decisions,
> the Court's majority incrementally dismantled much of the
> NLRA's collectivist foundations through reliance on strained
> and often clumsy renditions of NLRA legislative history and
> congressional intent. Adopting a truncated view of employee
> freedom of collective action, these decisions adopt an ideology
> that prioritizes the interests of individuals, claims for protection
> of management's contractual (or property) rights, and the need
> to afford business greater managerial autonomy. These are serious
> claims that require the careful demonstration contained in the
> following pages.

Readers are like jurors. After being presented with the evidence, they are asked
to render their verdict. I feel confident that the previous chapters have carried
the argument. There is one last stitch that needs to be added, however.

Some have pointed to the 1947 Taft-Hartley amendments to the NLRA
in an attempt to absolve the Supreme Court from claims that it has operated
more like a legislature than a judicial body by effectively amending the Act
and abandoning its collectivist policy underpinnings. The argument is that
by adding the "right to refrain" to section 7 and by adding section 8(b) union
unfair labor practices to the Act, Congress intended to shift national labor
policy away from its NLRA collectivist foundations. Apologists ask, "Why
can't the Court's post–Taft-Hartley Act decisions be understood best as its
conformation to a changed national labor policy, a swing of the pendulum
away from the policies of the Wagner Act?" The answer is that the evidence
will not support a defense of "the Taft-Hartley Act made me do it."

First, Taft-Hartley did not change the NLRA's core collectivist policy
underpinnings. As I have stated several times over the course of this book, the

1947 Taft-Hartley amendments reaffirmed the 1935 Wagner Act commitment that "it is hereby declared to be the policy of the United States [of] encouraging the practice and procedure of collective bargaining and . . . protecting the exercise by workers of full freedom of association, self-organization, and designation of representatives of their own choosing, for the purpose of negotiating the terms and conditions of their employment or other mutual aid or protection." Whatever pendulum swings that the Taft-Hartley amendments may represent, they do not manifest an abandonment of the nation's pledge to American workers to protect their "full freedom" of self-organization.

Second, both before and after Taft-Hartley, a central tenet of our national labor policy has been redressing through law the inequality of bargaining power between management and labor. The Court's post–Taft-Hartley Act cases make clear that the Taft-Hartley amendments did not jettison this foundational Wagner Act goal. For example, in its 1975 *NLRB v. J. Weingarten, Inc.* decision, the Court ruled six to three that our national labor policy

> is designed to eliminate the inequality of bargaining power between employees [and] employers [and that] requiring a lone employee to attend an investigatory interview which he reasonably believes may result in the imposition of discipline perpetuates the inequality the Act was designed to eliminate, and bars recourse to the safeguards the Act provided to redress the perceived imbalance of economic power between labor and management.[1]

Again, in 1984, in *NLRB v. City Disposal Systems, Inc.*, the Court ruled six to three that our national labor policy guarantees the right to engage in concerted activities in order to promote equal bargaining power between labor and management by significantly enhancing workers' ability to assert countervailing power against employers. As the Court stated, "what emerges from the general background of § 7—and what is consistent with the Act's statement of purpose—is a congressional intent to create an equality in bargaining power between the employee and the employer throughout the entire process of labor organizing, collective bargaining, and enforcement of collective-bargaining agreements."[2] But *Weingarten* and *City Disposal* are outlier cases in the sense that overwhelmingly, as the previous chapters have made plain, most of the Court's post-1965 cases have abandoned the nation's pledge to workers to redress through law the inequality of bargaining power between employees and employers. Instead, the Court's cases systematically have enhanced managerial control over the workplace and the workforce and thus its bargaining power. That much is clear. But what also is clear is that the Taft-Hartley amendments have played an insignificant role in causing this enfeebling of American labor law.

Third, for the first twenty-five years or so following the Taft-Hartley amendments, the Court's labor cases (those roughly up to 1970) manifested remarkable fidelity to the Wagner Act's pledge to protect workers' full freedom of self-organization. Throughout those years, the Court perceived nothing in Taft-Hartley requiring a pro-employer shift in labor policy. Indeed, the Court's initial post–Taft-Hartley decisions were largely supportive of workers' right to group action. For example, during the single decade of the 1960s, the Court reinforced the value of concerted activity by affirming nonunion employees' right to walk off the job to protest cold working conditions and protected against employer efforts to chill group action through threats and promised benefits such as granting super-seniority to striker replacements and shutting down part of a business to discourage unionism.[3] Moreover, in the 1960s, the Court bolstered the collective bargaining process by banning employers' unilateral alteration of working conditions without bargaining, by authorizing a Board-enforced bargaining order to remedy serious employer misconduct, and by seeming to require bargaining over most entrepreneurial decisions. And just days prior to the twentieth anniversary of the enactment of Taft-Hartley and the addition of section 8(b)(1)(A) to our national labor policy, the opinion in *NLRB v. Allis-Chalmers Manufacturing Company* concluded that "the repeated refrain throughout the debates on 8(b)(1)(A) and other sections [was] that Congress did not propose any limitations with respect to the internal affairs of unions, aside from barring enforcement of a union's internal regulations to affect a member's employment status."[4] *Lincoln Mills* and the 1960 *Steelworkers Trilogy* seemed to promise meaningful industrial democracy for workers: in those cases, the Court treated collective bargaining as a means to provide a system of industrial self-government. These refreshingly pro-worker attitudes blossomed despite the enactment of the Taft-Hartley amendments, but they did not survive in the Court's post-1970s decisions. The chapters in this book are filled with dozens of examples showing that the Court amended our national labor policy after June 1969, the date when Justice Burger was sworn in as chief justice. For more than four decades, during the eras of the Burger Court, followed by the conservative Rehnquist and Roberts Courts, the Supreme Court's opinions systematically contributed to the loss of worker empowerment and hastened the decline of the trade union movement. Taft-Hartley was in place during the pre-1970s period of the Court's relatively benign labor decisions, and no other legislative changes can explain the post-1970s pattern of the Court's antiworker decisions.[5] What changed was the Court's composition: the enactment of the Taft-Hartley Act did not make them do it.

And now, lurking on the horizon, is the possibility that the Roberts Court's constitutional view of separation of powers will result in the NLRA's becoming unenforceable nationwide. As of November 2024, any employer in Louisiana, Mississippi, and Texas can obtain an injunction barring the NLRB from proceeding against it. This is because of the decision of the Fifth Circuit Court of Appeals in *Jarkesy v. Securities and Exchange Commission*.[6] In *Jarkesy*, the Fifth Circuit interpreted the Roberts Court's separation of powers cases to render unconstitutional the statutory removal protections for the Securities and Exchange Commission's (SEC's) administrative law judges (ALJs) because these judges are insulated by two layers of for-cause removal protection: they can be removed only for cause by SEC members, who themselves can be removed only for cause.[7] This removal protection, according to the Fifth Circuit decision in *Jarkesy*, prevents the president from fully exercising his removal authority under article 2 of the Constitution. NLRB ALJs are afforded the same two layers of for-cause removal protections that the Fifth Circuit found to be unconstitutional with regard to the SEC ALJs. Accordingly, in *Aunt Bertha v. NLRB*, the district court, relying on *Jarkesy* as the rule in the circuit, enjoined the NLRB from proceeding against an employer in an upcoming unfair labor practice administrative proceeding.[8] This portion of the circuit ruling in *Jarkesy* did not go to the Supreme Court when it reviewed the case on other grounds in 2024. While the issue remains unresolved, it may be only a matter of time before the Court hears, and perhaps adopts, the Fifth Circuit's theory in *Jarkesy*, thereby placing the NLRA on life support.[9]

ACKNOWLEDGMENTS

I first taught labor law in the fall of 1972. This class was held at the Columbus School of Law of the Catholic University of America (CUA). I am fortunate that, more than fifty years later, I continue teaching at CUA Law School as a member of its full-time faculty. I thank my former and current students, who have given me a world-class education that informs my thinking about labor-management-relations law and much more. I also thank the many law school deans who have supported my teaching, research, and writing over the years, none more than our current dean, Stephen C. Payne. Without his flexibility in class scheduling and his assistance in gaining me several research leaves of absence, I could not have written this book.

I chose 1965 as the start date for my review of the Supreme Court's labor docket, not entirely arbitrarily. As I mention in the preface, that was the year I graduated from Cornell University's School of Industrial and Labor Relations. Thus, in 1965 I began the first of sixty years spent paying close attention to the Court's labor law work. Over that time, my thinking has been shaped by a trove of research and writing generated by many incisive, talented, and dedicated scholars, to whom I owe a great debt. I dare not surmise who has had the most influence in this regard, for that list would exceed the publisher's page limit. Certainly there are dozens of scholars who have incrementally unearthed important evidence illuminating the Court's abandonment of the collectivist underpinning of our national labor policy. I have benefited from much of this and have attempted in the chapter notes and bibliography to acknowledge their many contributions. The past sixty years may well have been the golden age of American labor law scholarship, which makes all of us a little better at what we try to do.

I have known the labor law scholar Karl Klare so well and so long that I make special reference to him here. Karl's work over the years has had a profound impact on all of us who attempt to navigate among the Court's labor decisions. Certainly much of his insight has worked its way into my own evolution regarding the role of the Court in creating the current crisis in workers' ability to gain collective workplace representation. For his intellectual contributions and for his many years of friendship and support, I want to thank him.

As he has done for each of my last four books, my good friend Bill Osborne, one of this country's premier labor lawyers, has read the entire manuscript and provided many helpful suggestions. He has been a valuable sounding board and provided unremitting encouragement. My brother by choice, Frank McDonald, continues to encourage and keeps me in awe with his broad range of knowledge, which I find helpful in so many ways.

And finally, as always, to Cathy, my scuba diving buddy, pal, copyeditor extraordinaire, and wife, a very special thanks.

APPENDIX

Supreme Court Cases

This list includes not only the one hundred cases that are the book's primary focus but also several pre-1965 cases that are foundational for understanding the post-1965 cases.

ABF Freight System, Inc. v. NLRB (1994)

Abood v. Detroit Board of Education (1977)

Airline Pilots v. Miller (1998)

Allen-Bradley v. Electrical Workers (International Brotherhood of Electrical Workers), Local 3 (1945)

Allen-Bradley, Local No. 1111, v. Wisconsin Employment Relations Board (1942)

Allentown Mack Sales and Service, Inc. v. NLRB (1998)

Allied Chemical and Alkali Workers, Local 1, v. Pittsburgh Plate Glass Company (1971)

Allis-Chalmers Corporation v. Lueck (1985)

American Ship Building Company v. NLRB (1965)

AT&T Mobility, LLC, v. Concepcion (2011)

Auciello Iron Works v. NLRB (1996)

Avco Corporation v. Aero Lodge No. 735 (1968)

Bayside Enterprises, Inc. v. NLRB (1977)

Beasley v. Food Fair of North Carolina, Inc. (1974)

BE & K Construction Company v. NLRB (2002)

Beth Israel Hospital v. NLRB (1978)

Bill Johnson's Restaurants, Inc. v. NLRB (1983)

Boys Market, Inc. v., Retail Clerks, Local 770 (1970)

Buffalo Forge Company v. Steelworkers (1976).

Carpenters, Local 1976, v. NLRB (Sand Door Plywood Company) (1958)

Cary v. Westinghouse (1964)

Caterpillar, Inc. v. Williams (1987)

Cedar Point Nursery v. Hassid (2021)

Central Hardware Company v. NLRB (1972)

Charles D. Bonanno Linen Service, Inc. v. NLRB (1982)

Chicago Teachers Union v. Hudson (1986)

Communication Workers of America v. Beck (1988)

Eastex, Inc. v. NLRB (1978)

Edward J. DeBartolo Corporation v. NLRB (1988)

Electrical Workers (International Union of Electrical Workers), Local 761, v. NLRB (General Electric) (1961)

Ellis v. Brotherhood of Railway, Airline, and Steamship Clerks (1984)

Epic Systems Corporation v. Lewis (2018)

Fall River Dyeing and Finishing Corporation v. NLRB (1987)

Fibreboard Paper Products Corporation v. NLRB (1964)

First National Maintenance Corporation v. NLRB (1981)

Food Employees Local 590, v. Logan Valley Plaza, Inc. (1968)

Friedrichs v. California Teachers Association (2016)

Gateway Coal Company v. United Mine Workers (1974)

Glacier Northwest, Inc. v. International Brotherhood of Teamsters (2024)

Golden State Bottling Company, Inc. v. NLRB (1973)

Harris v. Quinn (2014)

H. K. Porter Company v. NLRB (1970)

Hoffman Plastic Compounds, Inc. v. NLRB (2002)

Holly Farms Corporation v. NLRB (1996)

Houston Insulation Contractors Association v. NLRB (1967)

Howard Johnson Company v. Detroit Local Joint Executive Board (1974)

Hudgens v. NLRB (1976)

International Brotherhood of Electrical Workers v. Hechler (1987)

Janus v. American Federation of State, County, and Municipal Employees, Counsel 31 (2018)

John Wiley and Sons, Inc. v. Livingston (1964)

Knox v. Service Employees International Union, Local 1000 (2012)

Lamps Plus, Inc. v. Varela (2019)

Lechmere, Inc. v. NLRB (1992)

Lehnert v. Ferris Faculty Association (1991)

Linden Lumber Division, Summer and Company v. NLRB (1974)

Lingle v. Norge Division of Magic Chef (1988)

Litton Financial Printing Division v. NLRB (1991)

Livadas v. Bradshaw (1994)

Local 174, Teamsters, v. Lucas Flour Company (1962)

Machinists v. Street (1961)

Mastro Plastics Corporation v. NLRB (1956)

Metropolitan Edison Company v. NLRB (1983)

Mineworkers v. Arkansas Oak Flooring Company (1956)

National Woodwork Manufacturers Association v. NLRB (1967)

NLRB v. Acme Industrial Company (1967)

NLRB v. Babcock and Wilcox Company (1956)

NLRB v. Baptist Hospital, Inc. (1979)

NLRB v. Bell Aerospace Company, Division of Textron, Inc. (1974)

NLRB v. Bildisco and Bildisco (1984)

NLRB v. Brown (1965)

NLRB v. Building and Construction Trades Council (Denver) (1951)

NLRB v. Burns International Secretarial Services, Inc. (1972)

NLRB v. Catholic Bishop of Chicago (1979)

NLRB v. C&C Plywood Corporation (1967)

NLRB v. City Disposal Systems, Inc. (1984)

NLRB v. Curtin Matheson Scientific, Inc. (1990)

NLRB v. Enterprise Association, Pipefitters, Local 638 (1977)

NLRB v. Erie Resistor Corporation (1963)

NLRB v. Fansteel Metallurgical Corporation (1939)

NLRB v. Fleetwood Trailer Company (1939)

NLRB v. Food Store Employees Union, Local 347 (1974)

NLRB v. Fruit and Vegetable Packers and Warehousemen, Local 760 (Tree Fruits)
    (1964)

NLRB v. General Motors Corporation (1963)

NLRB v. Gissel Packing Company (1969)

NLRB v. Great Dane Trailers, Inc. (1967)

NLRB v. Health Care and Retirement Corporation of America (1994)

NLRB v. Hendricks County Rural Electric Membership Corporation (1981)

NLRB v. Insurance Agents International Union (1960)

NLRB v. International Longshoremen's Association I (1980)

NLRB v. International Longshoremen's Association II (1985)

NLRB v. International Rice Milling Company (1951)

NLRB v. International Van Lines (1972)

NLRB v. J. Weingarten, Inc. (1975)

NLRB v. Jones and Laughlin Steel Corporation (1937)

NLRB v. Katz (1962)

NLRB v. Kentucky River Community Care, Inc. (2001)

NLRB v. Local 1229, International Brotherhood of Electrical Workers (Jefferson Broadcasting) (1953)

NLRB v. Local 825, International Union of Operating Engineers (Burns and Roe) (1971)

NLRB v. Local 103, International Association of Bridge, Structural, and Ornamental Iron Workers (1978)

NLRB v. Mackay Radio and Telegraph Company (1938)

NLRB v. Magnavox Company of Tennessee (1974)

NLRB v. Natural Gas Utility District of Hawkins County, Tennessee (1971)

NLRB v. Retail Store Employees Union, Local 1001 (Safeco Title Insurance Co.) (1980)

NLRB v. Rockaway News Supply Company (1953)

NLRB v. Sands Manufacturing Company (1939)

NLRB v. Strong Roofing and Insulating Company (1969)

NLRB v. Town and Country Electric (1995)

NLRB v. Transportation Management Corporation (1983)

NLRB v. Truck Drivers, Local 449 (Buffalo Linen) (1957)

NLRB v. United Insurance Company of America (1968)

NLRB v. United Steelworkers of America (1958)

NLRB v. Wooster Division of Borg-Warner Corporation (1958)

NLRB v. Yeshiva University (1980)

Nolde Brothers v. Bakery and Confectionery Workers, Local 358 (1977)

Radio Officers' Union v. NLRB (1954)

Railway Clerks v. Allen (1963)

Railway Employees v. Hanson (1956)

Republic Aviation Corporation v. NLRB (1945)

Republic Steel Corporation v. Maddox (1964)

Sears, Roebuck, and Company v. San Diego County District Council Carpenters (1992)

Southern Steamship Company v. NLRB (1942)

Starbucks Corporation v. McKinney, Regional Director of Region 15, NLRB (2024)

Steelworkers v. American Manufacturing Company (1960)

Steelworkers v. Enterprise Wheel and Car Corporation (1960)

Steelworkers v. Rawson (1990)

Steelworkers v. Warrior and Gulf Navigation Company (1960)

Sure-Tan, Inc. v. NLRB (1984)

Teamsters, Local 174, v. Lucas Flour Company (1962)

Textile Workers v. Darlington Manufacturing Company (1965)

Textile Workers Union v. Lincoln Mills (1957)

TWA, Inc. v. Flight Attendants (1989)

United Auto Workers, Local 232, v. Wisconsin Employment Relations Board (Briggs-Stratton) (1949)

Woelke and Romero Framing, Inc. v. NLRB (1982)

SELECTED BIBLIOGRAPHY

Adams, Mark L. "Struggling through the Thicket: Section 301 and the Washington Supreme Court." *Berkeley Journal of Employment and Labor Law* 5 (1994).

Albrecht, Sandra L. *The Assault on Labor: The 1986 TWA Strike and the Decline of Workers' Rights in America.* Lanham, MD: Lexington, 2017.

Alleyne, Reginald. "Boycott Ban Prolongs Eastern Strike: Secondary Picketing Could Force Bush or Congress to Act." *Los Angeles Times.* March 24, 1989.

Andrias, Kate. "An American Approach to Social Democracy: The Forgotten Promise of the Fair Labor Standards Act." *Yale Law Journal* 128 (2019).

Andrias, Kate. "Constitutional Clash: Labor, Capital, and Democracy." *Northwestern University Law Review* 118 (2024).

Atleson, James B. *Values and Assumptions in American Labor Law.* Amherst: University of Massachusetts Press, 1983.

Barron, Paul. "A Theory of Protected Employer Rights: A Revisionist Analysis of the Supreme Court's Interpretation of the National Labor Relations Act." *Texas Law Review* 59 (1981).

Bickel, Alexander M., and Harry H. Wellington. "Legislative Purpose and the Judicial Process: The *Lincoln Mills* Case." *Harvard Law Review* 71 (1957).

Bixler, Albert G. "Industrial Democracy and the Managerial Employee Exception to the National Labor Relations Act." *Pennsylvania Law Review* 133 (1985).

Brudney, James J. "Collateral Conflict: Employer Claims of RICO Extortion against Union Comprehensive Campaigns." *Southern California Law Review* 83 (2010).

Brudney, James J. "Reflections on Group Action and the Law of the Workplace." *Texas Law Review* 74 (1996).

Bui, Quoctrung. "50 Years of Shrinking Union Membership, in One Map." *Planet Money.* National Public Radio. February 23, 2015. https://www.npr.org.

Chick, John. "If It Walks Like a Duck: Revisiting the National Labor Relations Board's Political Subdivision Test." *Wisconsin Law Review* (2023).

Collyer, Rosemary M. "Union Access: Developments Since *Jean Country*." *Labor Lawyer* 6 (1990).

Colvin, Alexander J. "The Metastasization of Mandatory Arbitration." *Chicago-Kent Law Review* 94 (2019).

Cooper, Laura J., and Dennis R. Nolan. "The Story of *NLRB v. Gissel Packing*: The Practical Limits of Paternalism." In *Labor Law Stories*, edited by Laura J. Cooper and Catherine L. Fisk. New York: Foundation Press, 2005.

Cox, Archibald. "Some Aspects of the Labor Management Relations Act, 1947." Part 1. *Harvard Law Review* 61 (1947).

Cox, Archibald. "Some Aspects of the Labor Management Relations Act, 1947." Part 2. *Harvard Law Review* 61 (1947).

Dannin, Ellen. "From Dictator Game to Ultimatum Game . . . and Back Again: The Judicial Impasse Amendments." *University of Pennsylvania Journal of Labor and Employment Law* 6 (2004).

Deitsch, Clarence E., and David A. Dilts. "*NLRB v. Yeshiva University*: A Positive Perspective." *Monthly Labor Review* 106 (July 1983).

DiNardo, John, Nicole M. Fortin, and Thomas Lemieux. "Labor Market Institutions and the Distribution of Wages, 1973–1992: A Semiparametric Approach." *Econometrica* 64 (1996): 1001.

Efthimiou, Marcus Paul. "State Legislative Attempts to Mandate Continuation of Collective Bargaining Agreements during Business Change: The Unfulfilled Expectations and the Pre-empted Results." *Cornell Law Review* 77 (1991).

Estlund, Cynthia. "Are Unions a Constitutional Anomaly?" *Michigan Law Review* 114 (2015).

Estlund, Cynthia. "The Black Hole of Mandatory Arbitration." *North Carolina Law Review* 96 (2018).

Estlund, Cynthia L. "Labor, Property, and Sovereignty after *Lechmere*." *Stanford Law Review* 46 (1994).

Estlund, Cynthia L. "The Ossification of American Labor Law." *Columbia Law Review* 102 (2002).

Estlund, Cynthia. "Showdown at Cedar Point: 'Sole and Despotic Dominion' Gains Ground." *Supreme Court Review* 2021 (2022).

Estreicher, Samuel, Michael Heise, and David Sherwyn. "Evaluating Employment Arbitration: A Call for Better Empirical Research." *Rutgers University Law Review* 70 (2018).

Farber, Henry S., et al. "Unions and Inequality over the Twentieth Century: New Evidence from Survey Data." National Bureau of Economic Research working paper 24587. May 2018. https://www.nber.org.

Federal Reserve Bank, St. Louis. "U.S. Wealth Inequality: Gaps Remain Despite Widespread Wealth Gains." February 2024. https://www.stlouisfed.org.

Feldman, George. "Workplace Power and Collective Activity: The Supervisory and Managerial Exclusions in Labor Law." *Arizona Law Review* 37 (1995).

Fortin, Nicole M., Thomas Lemieux, and Neil Lloyd. "Labor Market Institutions and the Distribution of Wages: The Role of Spillover Effects." National Bureau of Economic Research working paper 28375. January 2021. https://www.nber.org.

Foster, Sarah. "Wages Are Finally Rising Faster Than Inflation. Will Americans Ever Feel Like It?" *Bankrate*. September 2023. https://www.bankrate.com.

Freeman, Richard B. "How Much Has De-unionization Contributed to the Rise in Male Earnings Inequality?" In *Uneven Tides: Rising Inequality in America*, edited by Sheldon Danziger and Peter Gottschalk. New York: Russell Sage Foundation, 1993.

Freeman, Richard B., and Joel Rogers. *What Do Workers Want?* Ithaca, NY: Cornell University/ILR Press, 1999.

Galbraith, John Kenneth. *American Capitalism: The Theory of Countervailing Power*. Boston: Houghton Mifflin, 1952.

Getman, Julius G., and Thomas C. Kohler. "The Story of *NLRB v. Mackay Radio & Telegraph Co*: The High Cost of Solidarity." In *Labor Law Stories*, edited by Laura J. Cooper and Catherine L. Fisk. New York: Foundation Press, 2005.

Getman, Julius G. *The Supreme Court on Unions: Why Labor Law Is Failing American Workers*. Ithaca, NY: Cornell University/ILR Press, 2016.

Gillespie, Hal Keith. "The *Mackay* Doctrine and the Myth of Business Necessity." *Texas Law Review* 50 (1972).

Gottesman, Michael H. "Rethinking Labor Law Preemption: State Laws Facilitating Unionization." *Yale Journal on Regulation* 7 (1990).

Gough, Mark. "A Tale of Two Forums: Employment Discrimination Outcomes in Arbitration and Litigation." *ILR Review* 74 (2021).

Gould, William B., IV. *Agenda for Reform: The Future of Employment Relationships and the Law*. Cambridge, MA: MIT Press, 1996.

Gould, William B., IV. "Symposium: The Burger Court and Labor Law: The Beat Goes On." *San Diego Law Review* 24 (1987).

Gross, James A. *Broken Promises: The Subversion of U.S. Labor Relations Policy, 1947–1994*. Philadelphia: Temple University Press, 1995.

Hafiz, Hiba. "Structural Labor Rights." *Michigan Law Review* 119 (2021).

Hamaji, Kate, Rachel Deutsch, Elizabeth Nicolas, Celine McNicholas, Heidi Shierholz, and Margaret Poydock. "Unchecked Corporate Power: Forced Arbitration, the Enforcement Crisis, and How Workers Are Fighting Back." Center for Popular Democracy and Economic Policy Institute. May 2019. https://www.populardemocracy.org.

Hand, Learned. *The Bill of Rights*. Cambridge, MA: Harvard University Press, 1958.

Hartley, Roger C. *Fulfilling the Pledge: Securing Industrial Democracy for American Workers in a Digital Economy*. Cambridge, MA: MIT Press, 2024.

Hartley, Roger C. "Non-Legislative Labor Law Reform and Pre-Recognition Labor Neutrality Agreements: The Newest Civil Rights Movement." *Berkeley Journal of Employment and Labor Law* 22 (2001).

Hartley, Roger C. "Reconceiving the Role of Section 8(B)(1)(A)—1947–1997: An Essay on Collective Empowerment and the Public Good." *Catholic University Law Review* 47 (1998).

Hayes, Michael J. "It's Now Persuasion, Not Coercion: Why Current Law on Labor Protest Violates Twenty-First-Century First Amendment Law." *Hofstra Law Review* 47 (2018).

Hexter, Christopher, Wesley Kennedy, Alexia Kulwiec, Peter Janus, Todd Sarver, and Steven Wheeless. "Twenty-Five Years of Developments in the Law under the National Labor Relations Act." *ABA Journal of Labor and Employment Law* 25 (Spring 2010).

Hiatt, Jonathan. "At Age Seventy, Should the National Labor Relations Act Be Retired." In *Proceedings of the 2005 Annual Meeting, Association of American Law Schools Section on Labor Relations and Employment Law*, edited by Katherine Stone et al. In *Employee Rights and Employment Policy Journal* 9 (2005).

Higgins, John E., ed. *The Developing Labor Law: The Board, the Courts, and the National Labor Relations Act*. 7th ed. Arlington, VA: Bloomberg BNA, 2017.

Jacobs, Simon. "Arbitration and Title VII Pattern-or-Practice Claims after *Epic Systems*." *University of Chicago Law Review* 88 (2021).

Jenkins, Holman W., Jr. "Free Ron Carey! Repeal the Wagner Act!" *Wall Street Journal*. October 14, 1997.

Klare, Karl. "The Bitter and the Sweet: Reflections on the Supreme Court's *Yeshiva* Decision." *Socialist Review* 13 (September–October 1983).

Klare, Karl. "Judicial Deradicalization of the Wagner Act and the Origins of Modern Legal Consciousness, 1937–1941." *Minnesota Law Review* 62 (1978).

Klare, Karl. "Traditional Labor Law Scholarship and the Crisis of Collective Bargaining: A Reply to Professor Finkin." *Maryland Law Review* 44 (1985).

Kochan, Thomas A., Duanyi Yang, and Erin L. Kelly. "Worker Voice in America: Is There a Gap between What Workers Expect and What They Experience?" *Industrial and Labor Relations Review* 73 (2019).

Liang, Amy. "Property versus Antidiscrimination: Examining the Impacts of *Cedar Point Nursery v. Hassid* on the Fair Housing Act." *University of Chicago Law Review* 89 (2022).

Lichtenstein, Nelson. *State of the Union: A Century of American Labor.* Princeton, NJ: Princeton University Press, 2002.

Lieberwitz, Risa L. "Faculty in the Corporate University: Professional Identity, Law, and Collective Action." *Cornell Journal of Law and Public Policy* 16 (2007).

Magner, Brandon R. "The Good Faith Doubt Test and the Revival of *Joy Silk* Bargaining Orders." *University of Michigan Journal of Law Reform* 56 (2022).

Marvit, Moshe Zvi. "On the Greatest Property Transfer That Wasn't: How the National Labor Relations Act Chose Employee Rights and the Supreme Court Chose Property Rights." *Southern University Law Review* 38 (2010).

McCarthy, Justin. "U.S. Approval of Labor Unions at Highest Point Since 1965." *Gallup.* August 30, 2022. https://news.gallup.com.

Mishel, Lawrence, Rhinehart, Lynn, and Lane Windham. "Explaining the Erosion of Private-Sector Unions: How Corporate Practices and Legal Changes Have Undercut the Ability of Workers to Organize and Bargain." Economic Policy Institute. November 18, 2020. https://www.epi.org.

Modjeska, Lee. "The *Tree Fruits* Consumer Picketing Case—A Retrospective Analysis." *University of Cincinnati Law Review* 53 (1984).

More, Paul. "Protections against Retaliatory Employer Lawsuits after *BE & K Construction v. NLRB.*" *Berkeley Journal of Employment and Labor Law* 25 (2004).

Morris, Charles J. "Undercutting *Linden Lumber*: How a Union Can Achieve Majority-Status Bargaining without an Election." *Hofstra Labor and Employment Law Journal* 33 (2017).

National Labor Relations Board. "Case Handling Instructions for Cases Concerning *Bill Johnson's Restaurants* and *BE & K Construction Co.*" Memorandum GC 02–09 September 20, 2002, https://www.nlrb.gov.

Newman, Nathan S. "The Legal Foundations for State Laws Granting Labor Unions Access to Employer Property." *Drake Law Review* 62 (2014).

Note. "Labor Law—Federal Law Controls Construction of Term 'Political Subdivision' in National Labor Relations Act." *Missouri Law Review* 37 (1972).

Note. "The Supreme Court 2022 Term: National Labor Relations Act—Administrative Law—Preemption—Primary Jurisdiction—*Glacier Northwest, Inc. v. International Brotherhood of Teamsters Local Union No. 174.*" *Harvard Law Review* 137 (2023).

Osborne, William W., Jr., ed. *Labor Union Law and Regulation*. 2nd ed. Chicago: American Bar Association, Section of Labor and Employment Law, 2017.

Petruska, Brian J. "Adding *Joy Silk* to Labor's Reform Agenda." *Santa Clara Law Review* 57 (2017).

Pope, James Gray. "How American Workers Lost the Right to Strike, and Other Tales." *Michigan Law Review* 103 (2004).

Presidential Commission on the Supreme Court of the United States. "Final Report." 2021. https://www.whitehouse.gov.

Quach, Michelle. "The Janus Decision and the Future of Private Sector Unionism." *Hastings Business Law Journal* 16 (2020).

Rabin, Robert J. "*Fibreboard* and the Termination of Bargaining Unit Work." *Columbia Law Review* 71 (1971).

Rakoczy, Kate L. Comment. "On Mock Funerals, Banners, and Giant Rat Balloons: Why Current Interpretation of Section 8(b)(4)(ii)(B) of the National Labor Relations Act Unconstitutionality Burdens Union Speech." *American University Law Review* 56 (2007).

Rogers, Brishen. "Passion and Reason in Labor Law." *Harvard Civil Rights–Civil Liberties Law Review* 47 (2012).

Rosenberg, Alicia Gabriela. "Automation and the Work Preservation Doctrine: Accommodating Productivity and Job Security Interests." *UCLA Law Review* 32 (1984).

Roser-Jones, Courtlyn G. "The Roberts Court and the Unraveling of Labor Law." *Minnesota Law Review* 108 (2024).

Saad, Lydia. "More in U.S. See Unions Strengthening and Want It That Way." *Gallup.* August 30, 2023. https://news.gallup.com.

Sachs, Benjamin I. "Labor Law Renewal." *Harvard Law and Policy Review* 1 (2007).

Sayre, Francis Bowes. "Labor and the Courts." *Yale Law Journal* 39 (1930).

Shrider, Emily A., Melissa Kollar, Frances Chen, and Jessica Semega. "Income and Poverty in the United States: 2020." *U.S. Census Bureau.* 2021. https://www.census.gov.

Smith, Hedrick. *Who Stole the American Dream?* New York: Random House, 2012.

Stone, Chad, Danilo Trisi, Arloc Sherman, and Jennifer Beltrán. "A Guide to Statistics on Historical Trends in Income Inequality." *Center on Budget and Policy Priorities.* January 13, 2020. https://www.cbpp.org.

Stone, Katherine Van Wezel. *From Widgets to Digits: Employment Regulation for the Changing Workplace.* New York: Cambridge University Press, 2004.

Stone, Katherine Van Wezel. "Labor and the Corporate Structure: Changing Conceptions and Emerging Possibilities." *University of Chicago Law Review* 55 (1988).

Stone, Katherine Van Wezel. "The Legacy of Industrial Pluralism: The Tension between Individual Employment Rights and the New Deal Collective Bargaining System." *University of Chicago Law Review* 59 (1992).

Stone, Katherine Van Wezel. "The Post-War Paradigm in American Labor Law." *Yale Law Journal* 90 (1981).

Summers, Clyde. "Past Premises, Present Failures, and Future Needs in Labor Legislation." *Buffalo Law Review* 31 (1982).

Taylor, M. Edward. "The Political Subdivision Exemption of the National Labor Relations Act and the Board's Discretionary Authority." *Duke Law Journal* (1982).

Tomlins, Christopher L. *The State and the Unions: Labor Relations, Law, and the Organized Labor Movement in America, 1880–1960.* Cambridge, UK: Cambridge University Press, 1985.

U.S. Bureau of Labor Statistics. "News Release." January 2023. https://www .bls.gov.

Vizy, Nick J. *Corporate Counsel's Guide to Acquisitions and Divestitures.* Eagan, MN: Business Laws, 2023.

Weiler, Paul C. *Governing the Workplace: The Future of Labor and Employment Law*. Cambridge, MA: Harvard University Press, 1990.

Weiler, Paul. "Promises to Keep: Securing Workers' Rights to Self-Organization under the NLRA." *Harvard Law Review* 96 (1983).

Weiler, Paul. "Striking a New Balance: Freedom of Contract and the Prospects for Union Representation." *Harvard Law Review* 98 (1984).

Weiss, Marley S. "*Kentucky River* at the Intersection of Professional and Supervisory Status: Fertile Delta or Bermuda Triangle?" In *Labor Law Stories*, edited by Laura J. Cooper and Catherine L. Fisk. New York: Foundation Press, 2005.

White, Ahmed. "Its Own Dubious Battle: The Impossible Defense of an Effective Right to Strike." *Wisconsin Law Review* (2018).

White House Task Force on Worker Organizing and Empowerment. "Report to the President." February 2022. https://www.whitehouse.gov.

White, Richard. *The Republic for Which It Stands: The United States during Reconstruction and the Gilded Age, 1865–1896*. New York: Oxford University Press, 2017.

Willborn, Steven L. "Workers in Troubled Firms: When Are (Should) They Be Protected?" *University of Pennsylvania Journal of Labor and Employment Law* 7 (2004).

Windham, Lane. *Knocking on Labor's Door: Union Organizing in the 1970s and the Roots of a New Economic Divide*. Chapel Hill: University of North Carolina Press, 2017.

NOTES

Preface

1 Alan Taylor, "50 Years Ago: A Look Back at 1965." *The Atlantic* (March 11, 2015), https://www.theatlantic.com.

2 U.S. Department of Labor, Bureau of Labor Statistics, "News Release," January 19, 2023, https://www.bls.gov. This news release reported that the percent of all wage and salary workers who were members of unions was 10.1 percent in 2022, the lowest on record. The number of union workers employed in the private sector edged down by 0.1 percentage point in 2022 to 6 percent. See Quoctrung Bui, "50 Years Of Shrinking Union Membership, in One Map," *Planet Money*, February 23, 2015, National Public Radio, https://www.npr.org.

3 Arloc Sherman, Danilo Trisi, and Josephine Cureton, "A Guide to Statistics on Historical Trends in Income Inequality," *Center on Budget and Policy Priorities*, January 13, 2020, https://www.cbpp.org.

4 Kate Andrias, "An American Approach to Social Democracy: The Forgotten Promise of the Fair Labor Standards Act," *Yale Law Journal* 128 (2019): 616, 619.

5 Andrias, "An American Approach to Social Democracy," 620, n. 82, citing Estelle Sommeiller, Mark Price, and Ellis Wazeter, "Income Inequality in the U.S. by State, Metropolitan Area, and County," *Economic Policy Institute* 7 (2016), http://www.epi.org.

6 Federal Reserve Bank, St. Louis, "U.S. Wealth Inequality: Gaps Remain Despite Widespread Wealth Gains," February 7, 2024, https://www.stlouisfed.org.

7 Lane Windham, *Knocking on Labor's Door: Union Organizing in the 1970s and the Roots of a New Economic Divide* (Chapel Hill: University of North Carolina Press, 2017), 5. Windham outlines economic data showing a growing income gap.

8 Emily A. Shrider, Melissa Kollar, Frances Chen, and Jessica Semega, "Income and Poverty in the United States: 2020" (Washington, DC: *U.S. Census Bureau*, 2021), fig. 1, tab.A-1, https://www.census.gov. The document reports that median household income decreased 2.9 percent from the 2019 median, the first statistically significant decline in median household income since 2011.

9 Sarah Foster, "Wages Are Finally Rising Faster Than Inflation. Will Americans Ever Feel Like It?," *Bankrate*, September 7, 2023, https://www.bankrate.com.

10 Andrias, "An American Approach to Social Democracy," 620, n. 7, citing Martin Gilens, *Affluence and Influence: Economic Inequality and Political Power in America* (Princeton, NJ: Princeton University Press, 2012), 81.

11 Hedrick Smith, *Who Stole the American Dream?* (New York: Random House, 2012), 73, citing Pew Research Center, January 11, 2012, http://www.pewresearch.org.

12 Henry S. Farber, Daniel Herbst, Ilyana Kuziemko, and Suresh Naidu, "Unions and Inequality over the Twentieth Century: New Evidence from Survey Data," working paper 24587 (Cambridge, MA: National Bureau of Economic Research, 2018), https://www.nber.org.

13 See Farber et al., "Unions and Inequality over the Twentieth Century; Richard Freeman, "How Much Has De-unionization Contributed to the Rise in Male Earnings Inequal-

ity?," in *Uneven Tides: Rising Inequality in America*, ed. Sheldon Danziger and Peter Gottschalk (New York: Russell Sage Foundation, 1993), 133–63; and Nicole M. Fortin, Thomas Lemieux, and Neil Lloyd, "Labor Market Institutions and the Distribution of Wages: The Role of Spillover Effects," working paper 28375 (Cambridge, MA: National Bureau of Economic Research, 2021), 42, https://www.nber.org, citing authority. Accord John DiNardo, Nicole M. Fortin, and Thomas Lemieux, "Labor Market Institutions and the Distribution of Wages, 1973–1992: A Semiparametric Approach," *Econometrica* 64 (1996): 1001–44.

14   See Richard B. Freeman and Joel Rogers, *What Do Workers Want?* (Ithaca, NY: Cornell University/ILR Press, 1999).

15   Thomas A. Kochan, Duanyi Yang, William T. Kimball, and Erin L. Kelly, "Worker Voice in America: Is There a Gap between What Workers Expect and What They Experience?" *Industrial and Labor Relations Review* 73 (2019): 3, 5. Accord Jonathan Hiatt, "At Age Seventy, Should the National Labor Relations Act Be Retired?," in "Proceedings of the 2005 Annual Meeting, Association of American Law Schools Section on Labor Relations and Employment Law," ed. Katherine Stone, *Employee Rights and Employment Policy Journal* 9 (2005): 121, 300, n. 40, citing Peter D. Hart Research Associates, *The Public View of Unions* (2005). According to this report, polling shows that 57 percent of workers would vote for a union if they had the chance to do so. Also see White House Task Force on Worker Organizing and Empowerment, *"Report to the President,"* February 7, 2022, 4,12, www.whitehouse.gov, which states that, as of 2018, 52 percent of nonunion workers (60 million American workers) would vote for a union at their job if given a chance. Moreover, "support for a union in their workplace rises to 74% for workers aged 18 to 24, 75% for Hispanic workers, 80% for Black workers, and 82% for Black women workers." The economists Richard Freeman and Joel Rogers report that 87 percent of workers want some form of representation in the workplace (*What Do Workers Want?*, 147).

16   Kochan et al., "Worker Voice in America," 21.

17   See "Labor Unions," *Gallup*, July 12, 2024, https://news.gallup.com. Accord Lydia Saad, "More in U.S. See Unions Strengthening and Want It That Way," *Gallup*, August 30, 2023, https://news.gallup.com.

18   See Roger Hartley, *Fulfilling the Pledge: Securing Industrial Democracy for American Workers in a Digital Economy* (Cambridge, MA: MIT Press, 2024).

19   For an excellent discussion of these developments and citations to a wealth of background materials, see Nelson Lichtenstein, *State of the Union: A Century of American Labor* (Princeton, NJ: Princeton University Press, 2002), 212–25.

20   See, for example, Cynthia L. Estlund, "The Ossification of American Labor Law," *Columbia Law Review* 102 (2002): 1527, 1529–30; and Katherine V. W. Stone, *From Widgets to Digits: Employment Regulation for the Changing Workplace* (New York: Cambridge University Press, 2004), 260. See also William B. Gould IV, *Agenda for Reform: The Future of Employment Relationships and the Law* (Cambridge, MA: MIT Press, 1996), 18–19. Gould cites the difficulty of organizing recent immigrants from Asia and Central and South America and highly technical workers, stating a "lack of expertise among union organizers to effectively organize high-tech workers."

21   See Hartley, *Fulfilling the Pledge*, 53. Many scholars have documented the role of employer hostility in the decline of the unionized sector. See, for instance, Paul Weiler, "Promises to Keep: Securing Workers' Rights to Self-Organization Under the NLRA," *Harvard Law Review* 96 (1983): 1769, 1769–70, which concludes that employers' coercive tactics are "a major factor" in the decline of the unionized sector. Also see Clyde Summers, "Past Premises, Present Failures, and Future Needs in Labor Legislation," *Buffalo Law Review* 31 (1982): 9, 17, citing employers' "adamant refusal" to accept collective bargaining and the NLRA's legal rules as developed by the NLRB and the courts as "bend[ing] the National Labor Relations Act from its original premises and purposes."

22 National Labor Relations (Wagner) Act, sec. 49, stat. 449, 29 U.S.C., secs. 151–68, hereafter referred to as NLRA. See Hartley, *Fulfilling the Pledge*; and James B. Atleson, *Values and Assumptions in American Labor Law* (Amherst: University of Massachusetts Press, 1983); Karl Klare, "Traditional Labor Law Scholarship and the Crisis of Collective Bargaining: A Reply to Professor Finkin," *Maryland Law Review* 44 (1985): 731, 734, which states that "labor law imposes substantial limitations on unions in organizing employees, in voicing their needs, and in participating with management in making the industrial decisions that affect workers' lives. [M]ost observers sympathetic to collective bargaining are in accord that, at the very least, the legal system has been an important source of labor's present exigencies." Also see Weiler, "Promises to Keep, 1770, which concludes that the legal system "must bear a major share of the blame for providing employers with the opportunity and the incentives to use these [coercive] tactics."

23 In the late 1970s and early 1980s, the depth of the crisis and the difficulties facing unions in the private sector in their efforts to regain momentum and influence became increasingly apparent. In response, some legal scholars during this period provided context by advancing accounts in specific areas of labor law of how the judicial interpretation of the NLRA to that point, especially decisions by the Supreme Court, had subverted the collectivist foundations of the NLRA. See, for example, Julius G. Getman, *The Supreme Court on Unions: Why Labor Law Is Failing American Workers* (Ithaca, NY: Cornell University/ILR Press, 2016); Paul C. Weiler, *Governing the Workplace: The Future of Labor and Employment Law* (Cambridge, MA: Harvard University Press, 1990); Atleson, *Values and Assumptions in American Labor Law*; Katherine van Wezel Stone, "The Post-War Paradigm in American Labor Law," *Yale Law Journal* 90 (1981): 1509; and Karl Klare, "Judicial Deradicalization of the Wagner Act and the Origins of Modern Legal Consciousness, 1937–1941," *Minnesota Law Review* 62 (1978): 265. See also James A. Gross, *Broken Promises: The Subversion of U.S. Labor Relations Policy, 1947–1994* (Philadelphia: Temple University Press, 1995), a thorough study focusing primarily on developments at the NLRB that modified the NLRA into a law favoring management interests over workers' statutory rights.

24 Labor-Management Relations (Taft-Hartley) Act, 61 Stat. 136 (1947), codified as amended in scattered sections of 29 U.S.C. To be clear, my claim is not that national labor policy entails the obligation of government to affirmatively encourage workers to join unions. See Archibald Cox, "Some Aspects of the Labor Management Relations Act, 1947," *Harvard Law Review* 61 (1947): 1, 4. Cox writes: "The [Taft-Hartley] amendments represent an abandonment of the policy of affirmatively encouraging the spread of collective bargaining." In contrast, national labor policy is that the NLRA is to be interpreted in ways that are consistent with its declared policy of "encouraging the practice and procedure of collective bargaining and . . . protecting the exercise by workers of full freedom of association."

25 Klare, "Traditional Labor Law Scholarship," 736–38, citing authority.

26 See Presidential Commission on the Supreme Court of the United States, "Final Report" (2021), https://www.whitehouse.gov, which analyzes arguments for and against limiting the power of the Court.

27 See testimony of Craig Becker before the Presidential Commission on the Supreme Court of the United States, July 16, 2021, https://www.whitehouse.gov, which emphasizes that the Court is unfair to labor but calls for only modest reforms. *See also* Mary Kay Henry, letter to Presidential Commission on the Supreme Court of the United States, October 29, 2021, https://www.whitehouse.gov, stating that the Court has been captured by business interests that are urging various reforms.

28 See Kate Andrias, "Constitutional Clash: Labor, Capital, and Democracy," *Northwestern University Law Review* 118 (2024): 985, 1073–75.

29 Andrias, "Constitutional Clash," 1076.

30   Learned Hand, *The Bill of Rights*, (Cambridge, MA: Harvard University Press, 1958), 14.
31   Nelson Lichtenstein, *State of the Union: A Century of American Labor* (Princeton, NJ: Princeton University Press, 2002),43, 270, 275.
32   For an early effort to isolate the Court's usually unarticulated anti-collectivist policy preferences, see Atleson, *Values and Assumptions in American Labor Law.*

Chapter 1

1   402 U.S. 600 (1971).
2   440 U.S. 490 (1979).
3   467 U.S. 883 (1984).
4   535 U.S. 137 (2002).
5   516 U.S. 85 (1995).
6   429 U.S. 298 (1977).
7   517 U.S. 392 (1996).
8   390 U.S. 254 (1968).
9   416 U.S. 267 (1974).
10   444 U.S. 672 (1980).
11   416 U.S. 653 (1974).
12   511 U.S. 571 (1994).
13   532 U.S. 706 (2001).
14   454 U.S. 170 (1981).
15   NLRA, secs. 1, 3 (29 U.S.C., secs. 152[1)] and152[3]).
16   Kate Andrias, "Constitutional Clash: Labor, Capital, and Democracy," *Northwestern University Law Review* 118 (2024): 985, 1033–34.
17   402 U.S. 600 (1971).
18   *Natural Gas Utility District of Hawkins County, Tennessee*, 167 NLRB 691 (1967).
19   427 F.2d 312 (1970).
20   See *Natural Gas Utility District of Hawkins County, Tennessee*, 167 NLRB 691 (1967), holding that the utility district is not a political subdivision of the state because "in this case it is neither created directly by the State nor administered by State-appointed or elected officials."
21   See John Chick, "If It Walks Like a Duck: Revisiting the National Labor Relations Board's Political Subdivision Test," *Wisconsin Law Review* (2023): 2075, 2089, n. 88, stating that, *sub silentio*, the Court "broadened" the second prong of the Board's test. Though the change may have seemed "subtle," "the Court's articulation of the second prong arguably broadened the scope of the exemption to include entities . . . that were managed by individuals who were neither appointed nor elected officials, but rather merely responsible to them."
22   *NLRB v. Natural Gas Utility Dist. of Hawkins County, Tennessee*, 402 U.S. at 609 (Stewart, J., dissenting). It has been suggested that the change may have resulted from the Court's understanding of language used in the Board's brief (Board11; *NLRB v. Natural Gas Utility District*, 402 U.S. 600 [1971]). *Also see* M. Edward Taylor, "The Political Subdivision Exemption of the National Labor Relations Act and the Board's Discretionary Authority," *Duke Law Journal* (1982): 733, 737–38; and "Labor Law—Federal Law Controls Construction of Term 'Political Subdivision' in National Labor Relations Act," *Missouri Law Review* 37 (1972): 134, 142.
23   See, for example, *Northern Community Mental Health Center*, 241 NLRB 323 (1979) (entity excluded: not administered by public officials but a majority of the Board of directors

appointed by the county Board of supervisors); and *Community Health and Home Care*, 251 NLRB 509 (1980) (entity excluded: not administered by public officials but by the Board of directors appointed by and responsible to local elected officials).

24   440 U.S. 490 (1979).

25   *Catholic Bishop of Chicago v. NLRB*, 559 F.2d 1112 (7th Cir. 1977).

26   *NLRB v. Catholic Bishop of Chicago*, 440 U.S., 507.

27   *NLRB v. Catholic Bishop of Chicago*, 440 U.S. 490, 511, 518 (1979) (Brennan, J., dissenting) concluded that "the interpretation of the National Labor Relations Act announced by the Court today is not fairly possible [and] it is irresponsible [for the Court] to avoid [the constitutional question] by a cavalier exercise in statutory interpretation which succeeds in defying congressional intent."

28   Citing *International Association of Machinists v. Street*, 367 U.S. 740, 749–50 (1961), Brennan explained that, until this case, when a serious doubt of the constitutionality of federal legislation was raised, "it [has been] a cardinal principle that this Court will first ascertain whether a construction of the statute is fairly possible by which the question may be avoided.'" Also see *NLRB v. Catholic Bishop of Chicago*, 440 U.S. 490, 510 (1979) (Brennan, J., dissenting).

29   *NLRB v. Catholic Bishop of Chicago*, 440 U.S. 490, 506 (1979) (Brennan, J., dissenting), citing *Yu Cong Eng v. Trinidad*, 271 U.S. 500, 518 (1926).

30   National Center for Education Statistics, "School Choice in the United States: 2019," https://nces.ed.gov.

31   National Center for Educational Statistics, Table 14: "Number of Private Schools, Students, and Teachers (Headcount), by School Membership in Private School Associations: United States, 2019–20," in "Private School Universe Survey (PSS)," https://nces.ed.gov.

32   See, for example, William B. Gould IV, "Symposium: The Burger Court and Labor Law: The Beat Goes On," 24 *San Diego Law Review* 24 (1987): 51, 56, n. 3, which describes *Catholic Bishop* as a five-to-four decision written by Chief Justice Burger for an "antiunion majority."

33   467 U.S. 883 (1984); 535 U.S. 137 (2002).

34   672 F.2d 592 (7th Cir. 1982).

35   *Sure-Tan, Inc. v. NLRB*, 467 U.S., 891.

36   The Court rejected the employer's argument that it had a First Amendment right to petition the government by informing the Immigration and Naturalization Service for antiunion reasons (467 U.S. 883, 896–97).

37   The facts regarding the employer's knowledge of José Castro's eligibility for employment as of the date that he was hired are far more uncertain than the NLRB and the Court found to be the case. Castro acknowledged on his application form that he was undocumented but subsequently presented false papers. An NLRB attorney who worked on the case later stated that he had assumed that the hiring officer had told Castro to leave and then return with false papers. See Catherine L. Fisk and Michael J. Wishnie, "The Story of *Hoffman Plastic Compounds, Inc. v. NLRB*: Labor Rights without Remedies for Undocumented Immigrants," in *Labor Law Stories*, ed. Laura J. Cooper and Catherine L. Fisk (New York: Foundation Press, 2005), 408–9, 416–17. Moreover, contrary to repeated statements in the majority opinion, at the time the events occurred, the immigration law did not contain any provision making the presentation of false documents illegal. That was added by amendment after Castro's hiring (418).

38   See 535 U.S., 158 (Breyer, J., dissenting).

39   See *Mezonos Maven Bakery, Inc.*, 357 NLRB 376 (2011).

40   In his dissent, Justice Breyer stated: "To deny the Board the power to award backpay . . . might very well increase the strength of th[e] magnetic force [of immigrant labor]" (*Hoffman Plastic Compounds, Inc. v. NLRB*, 535 U.S., 155 [Breyer, J., dissenting]).

41   See *APRA Fuel Oil Buyers Group, Inc.*, 320 NLRB 408, 415, n. 38 (1995): without a potential backpay order, an employer might simply discharge employees who show interest in a union, "secure in the knowledge" that the only penalties would be requirements "to cease and desist and post a notice."

42   *Mezonos Maven Bakery, Inc.*, 357 NLRB 376, 380 (2011) (members Liebman and Pearce, concurring).

43   516 U.S. 85 (1995).

44   The prolabor thrust of *Town and Country* was vitiated by the Bush Board in cases such as *Toering Electric Company*, 351 NLRB 225 (2007) (general counsel has the burden of proving that the "salt" had a genuine interest in the job) and *Oil Capitol Sheet Metal Inc.*, 349 NLRB 1348 (2007) (the usual presumption in calculating backpay is that the discriminatee will remain employed indefinitely, but this does not apply to salting cases; the general counsel must prove the reasonableness of a proposed backpay period and establish that the salt would have remained in employment for that period).

45   Nelson Lichtenstein explains that, in an effort to fight against aligning the South's racial norms with those of the North and the West, "the South's powerful delegation in Congress simply excluded much of the region's people and industry from the scope of New Deal social legislation"—citing as one example the Wagner Act's exclusion of agricultural employees and domestic workers, which at that time employed more than half of all African-Americans (*State of the Union: A Century of American Labor* [Princeton, NJ: Princeton University Press, 2002], 111).

46   *Bayside Enterprises, Inc. v. NLRB*, 429 U.S., 301.

47   *Bayside Enterprises, Inc. v. NLRB*, 429 U.S., 302.

48   *Holly Farms Corporation v. NLRB*, 517 U.S., 401.

49   *Holly Farms Corporation v. NLRB*, 517 U.S. at 412–13 (O'Connor, J., concurring and dissenting).

50   See *Holly Farms Corporation v. NLRB*, 517 U.S. at 409–10 (O'Connor, J., concurring and dissenting), stating that "the Court's conclusion that Holly Farms' chicken catchers and forklift operators do not perform agricultural work runs contrary to common sense and finds no support in the text of the relevant statute."

51   390 U.S. 254 (1968).

52   Lichtenstein, *State of the Union*, 119.

53   Congress also expressed the concern that supervisors might dominate rank and file unions. *See* H.R. Rep. No. 245, 80th Cong., 1st Sess. 14 (1947); S. Rep. No. 105, 80th Cong., 1st Sess. 4 (1947).

54   416 U.S. 267 (1974).

55   444 U.S. 672 (1980).

56   454 U.S. 170 (1981).

57   511 U.S. 571 (1994).

58   532 U.S. 706 (2001).

59   For an excellent development of this thesis, see George Feldman, "Workplace Power and Collective Activity: The Supervisory and Managerial Exclusions in Labor Law," *Arizona Law Review* 37 (1995): 525.

60   *NLRB v. Bell Aerospace Company*, 416 U.S., 276.

61   *NLRB v. Bell Aerospace Company*, 416 U.S., 299 (White, J., concurring in part and dissenting in part).

62   *NLRB v. Bell Aerospace Company*, 416 U.S., 309 (White, J., concurring in part and dissenting in part).

63   *North Arkansas Electric Cooperative, Inc.*, 185 NLRB 550 (1970).

64   *NLRB v. Bell Aerospace Company*, 416 U.S., 298 (White, J., concurring in part and dissenting in part).

65 *Bell Aerospace Company*, 196 NLRB 827, 828 (1972); brief for the National Labor Relations Board, *NLRB v. Bell Aerospace Company*, 416 U.S. 267 (1974), 23 See also discussion in comment, in Albert Bixler, "Industrial Democracy and the Managerial Employee Exception to the National Labor Relations Act," 133 *Pennsylvania Law Review* 133 (1985): 441, 445.

66 Bixler, "Industrial Democracy and the Managerial Employee Exception," 444–45.

67 *General Dynamics Corporation*, 213 NLRB 851, 857–58 (1974).

68 444 U.S. 672 (1980). See, for example, the discussion in Karl Klare, "The Bitter and the Sweet: Reflections on the Supreme Court's *Yeshiva* Decision," *Socialist Review* 13 (September–October 1983): 99, 111, which argues that the *Yeshiva* decision is grounded in the view that "employee status and self-determination in work are incompatible."

69 Reversing a 1951 decision in *Trustees of Columbia University*, 97 NLRB 424 (1951), the NLRB asserted jurisdiction over university faculty in *Cornell University*, 183 NLRB 329, 334 (1970). The next year the Board rejected a university's effort to exclude faculty as managerial employees (*C. W. Post Center*, 189 NLRB 904 [1971]).

70 For a list and a discussion of these 1970s' cases, see Bixler, "Industrial Democracy and the Managerial Employee Exception," 446–47, notes 40–45.

71 See discussion at *NLRB v. Yeshiva University*, 444 U.S., 685–86 as well as brief for the NLRB (36–40).

72 444 U.S., 686.

73 The five-member majority in *Yeshiva* reasoned that "the faculty's professional interests—as applied to governance at a university like Yeshiva—cannot be separated from those of the institution" and that the Board's approach to permitting faculty unionization "would undermine the goal . . . to ensure that employees who exercise discretionary authority on behalf of the employer will not divide their loyalty between employer and union (444 U.S., 687–88). The Court added: "There . . . may be institutions of higher learning unlike Yeshiva where the faculty are entirely or predominantly nonmanagerial, . . . depending upon how a faculty is structured and operates. But we express no opinion on these questions, for it is clear that the unit approved by the Board was far too broad" (444 U.S., 690, n. 31).

74 Clarence E. Deitsch and David A. Dilts, "NLRB v. Yeshiva University: A Positive Perspective," *Monthly Labor Review* 106 (July 1983): 34. For a list of the many highly critical academic assessments of the *Yeshiva* decision, see Bixler, "Industrial Democracy and the Managerial Employee Exception," 449, n. 66.

75 Risa L. Lieberwitz, "Faculty in the Corporate University: Identity, Law and Collective Action," *Cornell Journal of Law and Public Policy* 16 (2007): 263.

76 Lieberwitz, "Faculty in the Corporate University," 274.

77 See discussion in *Yeshiva*, 444 U.S., 699–700 (Brennan, White, Marshall, and Blackmun, JJ., dissenting): "the notion that a faculty member's professional competence could depend on his undivided loyalty to management is antithetical to the whole concept of academic freedom. Faculty members are judged by their employer on the quality of their teaching and scholarship, not on the compatibility of their advice with administration policy."

78 Feldman, "Workplace Power and Collective Activity," 526 (collecting authority), 527: "The Court's reasoning in these cases, even more than the results, approaches a readiness 'to redefine entirely the industrial relations system,' to reject some of the fundamental tenets of American labor law as insufficiently protective of employer control of workplace decisions. While these cases directly question only the limits of legal protection of unionization, their logic is directed at the principle itself." Also see Klare, "The Bitter and the Sweet," 100.

79 *Pacific Lutheran University*, 361 NLRB 1404 (2014), represents the NLRB's most recent analytical framework. It focuses on faculty participation in five areas—academic programs,

enrollment management policies, finances, academic policies, and personnel policies and decision—with the Board giving greater weight to the first three factors. The Board also requires the party asserting managerial status to demonstrate that "faculty actually exercise control or make effective recommendations" relative to the specified areas of consideration.

80   265 NLRB 295 (1982).

81   Accord *Lewis University*, 265 NLRB 1239, 1242 (1982), which finds the faculty not to be managerial employees but expresses willingness to agree with the university regarding the immateriality of the source of the faculty's authority.

82   511 U.S. 571 (1994).

83   532 U.S. 706, 707 (2001).

84   Depriving workers of NLRA protection by expanding the breadth of the section 2(11) supervisor exclusion category is particularly burdensome on those excluded because the states are precluded from providing unionization right for supervisors who have no NLRA protection. See *Beasley v. Food Fair of North Carolina, Inc.*, 416 U.S. 653 (1974).

85   NLRA, sec. 2(11), 29 U.S.C. 152(11).

86   *NLRB v. Health Care and Retirement Corporation*, 511 U.S. 571, 576 (1994).

87   *NLRB v. Health Care and Retirement Corporation*, 511 U.S., 589–90 (Ginsburg, Blackmun, Stevens, and Souter, JJ., dissenting).

88   *NLRB v. Health Care and Retirement Corporation*, 511 U.S., 598 (Ginsburg, Blackmun, Stevens, and Souter, JJ., dissenting).

89   See *NLRB v. Kentucky River Community Care, Inc.*, 532 U.S., 708.

90   348 NLRB 686 (2006).

91   See *Integrated Health Services of Mich., at Riverbend, Inc. v. NLRB*, 191 F.3d 703, 713 (6th Cir. 1999) (Jones, J., concurring); and Julius G. Getman, *The Supreme Court on Unions: Why Labor Law Is Failing American Workers* (Ithaca, NY: Cornell University/ILR Press, 2016), 143, which comments on the "barrier to unionization" created by the Court's two nurse cases.

92   Marley S. Weiss, "*Kentucky River* at the Intersection of Professional and Supervisory Status: Fertile Delta or Bermuda Triangle?," in Cooper and Fisk, *Labor Law Stories*, 353, 394–95, n. 71 (collecting cases).

93   Weiss, "*Kentucky River* at the Intersection of Professional and Supervisory Status," 398.

94   *NLRB v. Hendricks County Rural Electric Membership Corporation*, 454 U.S., 194 (Powell, J., dissenting).

95   *NLRB v. Hendricks County Rural Electric Membership Corporation*, 454 U.S., 200 (Powell, J., dissenting).

96   Lichtenstein, *State of the Union*, 118.

97   Lichtenstein, *State of the Union*, 118–21, 129, 176–77.

Chapter 2

1   395 U.S. 575 (1969).

2   419 U.S. 301 (1974).

3   324 U.S. 793 (1945).

4   357 U.S. 357 (1958).

5   415 U.S. 322 (1974).

6   437 U.S. 483 (1978).

7   437 U.S. 556 (1978).

8   442 U.S. 773 (1979).

9   391 U.S. 308 (1968).
10   407 U.S. 539 (1972).
11   424 U.S. 507 (1976).
12   436 U.S. 180 (1978).
13   502 U.S. 527 (1992); also see *NLRB v. Babcock and Wilcox Co*mpany, 351 U.S. 105 (1956).
14   594 U.S. 139 (2021).
15   See Roger C. Hartley, "Non-Legislative Labor Law Reform and Pre-Recognition Labor Neutrality Agreements: The Newest Civil Rights Movement," *Berkeley Journal of Employment and Labor Law* 22 (2001): 369, 387–96, which summarizes various ways in which organizing agreements are reached, including a union leveraging state and local political power.
16   Benjamin I. Sachs, "Labor Law Renewal," *Harvard Law and Policy Review* 1 (2007): 375, 378.
17   Pre-recognition neutrality agreements are lawful, insofar as they are in accordance with the framework set out in *Dana Corporation*, 356 N.L.R.B. 256 (2010), *affirmed sub nom.* See *Montague v. NLRB*, 698 F.3d 307 (6th Cir. 2012).
18   Charles J. Morris, "Undercutting *Linden Lumber*: How a Union Can Achieve Majority-Status Bargaining without an Election," *Hofstra Labor and Employment Law Journal* 33 (2017): 1, 15.
19   National Labor Relations Act, 29 U.S.C., sec. 159(a).
20   351 U.S. 62 (1956); *United Mine Workers v. Arkansas Oak Flooring Company*, 351 U.S., 71–72, n. 8.
21   *Joy Silk Mills, Inc.*, 85 NLRB 1263, 1264 (1949); *modified and enforced, Joy Silk Mills, Inc. v. NLRB*, 185 F.2d 732 (D.C. Cir. 1950).
22   395 U.S. 575 (1969).
23   Brief for the NLRB, 21–24, 26, in *NLRB v. Gissel Packing Company*. 395 U.S. 575 (1969). See discussion in Laura J. Cooper and Dennis R. Nolan, "The Story of *NLRB v. Gissel Packing*: The Practical Limits of Paternalism," in *Labor Law Stories*, ed. Laura J. Cooper and Catherine L. Fisk (New York: Foundation Press, 2005), 207: one of the authors of the NLRB's *Gissel* brief acknowledged to his father in a letter that the NLRB had "blur[ed] the difference between [employer bad faith being determined by an evaluation of subjective motivation and being determined by the presence of employer unfair labor practices]").
24   See, for instance, *Aaron Bros.*, 158 NLRB 1077, 1079 (1966), holding that the burden is on the NLRB general counsel to show the employer's bad faith "in the light of all of the relevant facts of the case[, which might include] substantial unfair labor practices [or] a course of conduct which does not constitute an unfair labor practice."
25   Brief for the NLRB, 21–24, 26, in *NLRB v. Gissel Packing Company*, 395 U.S. 575 (1969).
26   Cooper and Nolan, "The Story of *NLRB v. Gissel Packing*," 190.
27   *NLRB v. Gissel Packing Company*, 395 U.S., 594.
28   The Court explained that, to support a bargaining order, the unfair labor practices must have a tendency to undermine majority strength and be of such severity that the NLRB "finds that the possibility of erasing the effects of past practices and of ensuring a fair election (or a fair rerun) by the use of traditional remedies, though present, is slight and that employee sentiment once expressed through cards would, on balance, be better protected" (*NLRB v. Gissel Packing Company*, 395 U.S., 614–15). In dicta, the Court also indicated the possibility of a bargaining order without the union having ever established its majority status in "extraordinary" cases to remedy "pervasive" and "outrageous" unfair labor practice conduct. In *Gourmet Foods*, 270 NLRB 578 (1984), the NLRB indicated that it would issue bargaining orders only to unions that had established majority support.
29   Under the doctrine announced in *Cumberland Shoe Corporation*, 144 NLRB 1268 (1963), and reaffirmed in *Levi Strauss and Company*, 172 NLRB no. 57, 68 LRRM 1338 (1968),

authorization cards can support a showing of union majority support "if the card itself is unambiguous (i.e., states on its face that the signer authorizes the Union to represent the employee for collective bargaining purposes and not to seek an election), . . . [and] the employee was told that the card was to be used solely for the purpose of obtaining an election [and were obtained without] misrepresentation." See *NLRB v. Gissel Packing Company*, 395 U.S., 584.

30   John Kenneth Galbraith, *American Capitalism: The Theory of Countervailing Power* (Boston: Houghton Mifflin, 1952), 114.

31   *NLRB v. Gissel Packing Company*, 395 U.S., 595.

32   419 U.S. 301 (1974).

33   Chairman Edward B. Miller and members Howard Jenkins Jr. and Ralph E. Kennedy concluded: "We decline, . . . to reenter the "good-faith" thicket of Joy Silk. . . . [An employer] should not be found guilty of a violation of Section 8(a)(5) solely upon the basis of its refusal to accept evidence of majority status other than the results of a Board election (*Linden Lumber*, 190 NLRB, 720–21). See discussion in Morris, "Undercutting *Linden Lumber*," 1–2.

34   *Linden Lumber*, 190 NLRB, 722 (members Fanning and Brown dissenting).

35   *Truck Drivers Union, Local No. 413, v. NLRB*, 487 F.2d 1099 (D.C. Cir. 1973).

36   *Truck Drivers Union, Local No. 413, v. NLRB*, 487 F.2d, 240–41.

37   *Linden Lumber Division, Summer and Company, v. NLRB*, 419 U.S., 309–10.

38   *Linden Lumber Division, Summer and Company, v. NLRB*, 419 U.S., 312 (Stewart, J., dissenting).

39   *Linden Lumber Division, Summer and Company, v. NLRB*, 419 U.S., 313 (Stewart, J., dissenting).

40   *Truck Drivers Union, Local No. 413, v. NLRB*, 487 F.2d, 241, n. 48, citing evidence from previous NLRB decisions and from the experience of NLRB regional directors that when employers are willing to go to an election or agree to a consent election, the election is held more expeditiously than is the case when either party has to be forced to an election.

41   See, for example, Brandon R. Magner, "The Good Faith Doubt Test and the Revival of *Joy Silk* Bargaining Orders," *University of Michigan Journal of Labor Reform* 56 (2022): 151, showing that "the last fifty-two years have borne witness to the swift degradation and virtual irrelevance of the bargaining order. By the end of the twentieth century even pro-enforcement officials in the NLRB were acknowledging the difficulty of obtaining an enforceable bargaining order, and the remedy rarely appears these days in the agency's published decisions."

42   Brian J. Petruska, "Adding *Joy Silk* to Labor's Reform Agenda," *Santa Clara Law Review* 57 (2017): 97, 112.

43   Petruska, "Adding *Joy Silk* to Labor's Reform Agenda," 115. *Accord* Magner, "The Good Faith Doubt Test and the Revival of *Joy Silk* Bargaining Orders," 188: "Within two years of the *Gissel* decision, a majority of the circuits had rejected enforcement of such bargaining orders and criticized the Labor Board's failure to heed the heavy evidentiary burden required to sustain the 'extraordinary' remedy."

44   See discussion of hallmark violations that will support the issuance of a bargaining order in most cases, in *NLRB v. Jamaica Towing Company*, 632 F.2d 208, 212 (2d Cir. 1980).

45   Petruska, "Adding *Joy Silk* to Labor's Reform Agenda," 112.

46   See Cooper and Nolan, "The Story of *NLRB v. Gissel Packing*," 230–31, n. 76, which also reports that, by the turn of the twenty-first century, the circuit courts were enforcing only 50 percent of bargaining order cases.

47   Cooper and Nolan, "The Story of *NLRB v. Gissel Packing*," 231–32, providing statistics of the decline in the number of bargaining orders issued by the NLRB.

48   Cooper and Nolan, "The Story of *NLRB v. Gissel Packing*," 234. See also Julius Getman, *The Supreme Court on Unions: Why Labor Law Is Failing American Workers* (Ithaca, NY:

Cornell University/ILR Press, 2016), 33, n. 55, discussing studies showing the unlikelihood that bargaining orders will result in the creation of productive bargaining relationships.

49 Morris, "Undercutting *Linden Lumber*," 3–4.

50 372 NLRB no. 130 (2023).

51 See *Mike O'Connor Chevrolet Buick-GMC Company*, 209 NLRB 701, 703 (1974), enforcement denied on other grounds, 512 F.2d 684 (8th Cir. 1975). By mid-2024, the NLRB had begun issuing *Cemex* bargaining orders. See NLRB, "Region 28–Phoenix Wins *Cemex* Board Order Requiring Las Vegas Casino Bargain with Union," June 21, 2024, https://www.nlrb.gov.

52 Beverly Banks, "NLRB Election Petitions Jump 35% in 1st Half of FY 2024," *LexisNexis, Law 360*, April 9, 2024, https://www.law360.com.

53 Robert Iafolla, "Employer Bids for Union Elections Boom in Wake of *Cemex* Ruling," *Bloomberg Law*, February 27, 2024, https://news.bloomberglaw.com: "The number of employer-filed election requests, known as 'RM petitions,' following *Cemex* represents a more than 2,700% increase over the nine petitions filed in the six months before the decision was issued."

54 Cynthia L. Estlund, "Labor, Property, and Sovereignty after *Lechmere*," *Stanford Law Review* 46 (1994): 305, 307, n. 6 (collecting authority).

55 Estlund, "Labor, Property, and Sovereignty after *Lechmere*," 307.

56 306 U.S. 240 (1939).

57 324 U.S. 793 (1945).

58 See *Republic Aviation Corporation v. NLRB*, 324 U.S., 803, n. 10.

59 Paul Barron, "A Theory of Protected Employer Rights: A Revisionist Analysis of the Supreme Court's Interpretation of the National Labor Relations Act," *Texas Law Review* 59 (1981): 421, 432, citing *May Department Stores Company*, 59 NLRB 976 (1944), enforced 154 F.2d 533 (8th Cir. 1946).

60 442 U.S. 773 (1979)

61 The court of appeals opinion, whose reasoning the Court rejected, would have granted the hospital an even broader right to ban union solicitation at the hospital during employees' nonworking time (*NLRB v. Baptist Hospital, Inc.*, 442 U.S., 777).

62 357 U.S. 357, 361–62 (1958).

63 373 NLRB no. 136 (November 13, 2024). The Board provided a "safe harbor" for conducting voluntary meetings, in the workplace on work time to express its views on unionization if, reasonably in advance of the meeting, it informs employees that the Employees will not be subject to discipline, discharge or other adverse consequences for failing to attend the meeting or for leaving the meeting and the employer will not keep records of which employees attend, fail to attend or leave the meeting.

64 437 U.S. 483 (1978).

65 Four members of the Court wrote or joined concurring opinions (Chief Justice Burger and Justices Rehnquist, Blackmun, and Powell).

66 *Beth Israel Hospital v. NLRB*, 437 U.S., 509 (Blackmun, J., Chief Justice Burger, and Rehnquist, J., concurring).

67 *Beth Israel Hospital v. NLRB*, 437 U.S., 510, 516 (Powell, J., Chief Justice Burger, and Rehnquist, J., concurring). In 1978, the Court decided another *Republic Aviation*–like case favorably for workers, *Eastex, Inc. v. NLRB*, 437 U.S. 556 (1978), holding that the right to engage in activities for mutual aid and protection includes urging employees to write their legislators to oppose incorporation of a state's right-to-work statute into a revised state constitution and criticizing the presidential veto of an increase in the federal minimum wage. Another access case that promotes the dissemination of organizational communication at the workplace is *NLRB v. Magnavox Company of Tennessee*, 415 U.S. 322 (1974), upholding a Board rule that a union may not agree to a collective bargaining provision that waives bargaining unit members' rights of solicitation and distribution at the workplace.

68 *NLRB v. Babcock and Wilcox Company*, 351 U.S. 105, 113 (1956).

69 See, for instance, *Caesar's Entertainment*, 368 NLRB, no. 143, 9, n. 56 (2019). Reversing precedent and based on the bare property interest of corporate ownership of its IT equipment, the Trump NLRB held that, without requiring proof of any need to maintain production or discipline or to preserve the efficiency of the IT system itself, and even though the employer grants employees access to its email system for personal use, employers have no legal duty "to permit access to their IT systems for Section 7 purposes [except] in those atypical and rare situations in which employees otherwise would be deprived of 'adequate avenues for communication' necessary for the exercise of their Section 7 rights."

70 351 U.S. 105 (1956).

71 *NLRB v. Babcock and Wilcox Company*, 351 U.S., 113: "When the inaccessibility of employees makes ineffective the reasonable attempts by nonemployees to communicate with them through the usual channels, the right to exclude from property has been required to yield to the extent needed to permit communication of information on the right to organize."

72 *NLRB v. Babcock and Wilcox Company*, 351 U.S., 113: "The plants are close to small well-settled communities where a large percentage of the employees live. The usual methods of imparting information are available. . . . The various instruments of publicity are at hand. Though the quarters of the employees are scattered they are in reasonable reach."

73 See discussion in Estlund, "Labor, Property, and Sovereignty after *Lechmere*," 316.

74 391 U.S. 308 (1968), overruled by *Hudgens v. NLRB*, 424 U.S. 507 (1976), and extending the principle of *Marsh v. Alabama*, 326 U.S. 501 (1946), by equating a shopping center to a company town whose operation served as a public function and thus constituted government action regulated by the Constitution.

75 407 U.S. 539 (1972). In *Lloyd Corporation v. Tanner*, 407 U.S. 551 (1972), a case involving antiwar activists who were barred from distributing leaflets at a shopping center, the Court distinguished *Logan Valley* on the grounds that, in *Tanner*, the speech did not relate to the shopping center's operations.

76 424 U.S. 507 (1976).

77 *Hudgens v. NLRB*, 424 U.S., 511.

78 *Hudgens v. NLRB*, 424 U.S., 522.

79 Brief for the NLRB, 23, in *Lechmere, Inc. v. NLRB*, 502 U.S. 527 (1992) (no. 90–970).

80 436 U.S. 180 (1978).

81 *Sears, Roebuck, and Company v. San Diego County District Council of Carpenters*, 436 U.S., 205–6, n. 41, citing *NLRB v. S. and H. Grossinger's, Inc.*, 372 F.2d 26 (CA2 1967), a remote resort case, and *NLRB v. Lake Superior Lumber Corporation*, 167 F.2d 147 (CA6 1948), a remote lumber camp case.

82 291 NLRB 11 (1988).

83 Estlund, "Labor, Property, and Sovereignty after *Lechmere*," 318–19, quoting *Jean Country*, 291 NLRB, 19, and citing Rosemary M. Collyer, "Union Access: Developments Since *Jean Country*," 6 *Labor Lawyer* 6 (1990): 839, 844, 856–57, for commentary on the mechanics of the *Jean Country* balancing test.

84 502 U.S. 527 (1992).

85 *Lechmere, Inc. v. NLRB*, 502 U.S., 848.

86 *Lechmere, Inc. v. NLRB*, 502 U.S., 849–50.

87 Estlund, "Labor, Property, and Sovereignty after *Lechmere*," 325–43.

88 Estlund, "Labor, Property, and Sovereignty after *Lechmere*," 336–37, 343–44.

89 436 U.S. 180 (1978).

90 Nathan S. Newman, "The Legal Foundations for State Laws Granting Labor Unions Access to Employer Property," *Drake Law Review* 62 (2014): 689.

91 See Newman, "The Legal Foundations for State Laws Granting Labor Unions Access to Employer Property," 691–93.

92 See, for example, *Sears, Roebuck, and Company v. San Diego County District Council of Carpenters*, 599 P.2d 676, 680, 682–83 (1979), holding that employer has no federally protected right to enjoin peaceful picketing on property it has opened to public use and that California's Moscone Act deprives the trial court of jurisdiction to enjoin peaceful labor picketing.

93 See Estlund, "Labor, Property, and Sovereignty after *Lechmere*," 337–38.

94 592 P.2d 341 (1979), affirmed 447 U.S. 74 (1980).

95 See Estlund, "Labor, Property, and Sovereignty after *Lechmere*," 338, n. 199 (collecting cases).

96 510 U.S. 200, 217, n. 21 (1994). Accord *NLRB v. Calkins*, 187 F.3d 1080, 1094–95 (9th Cir. 1999), holding that "state trespass law that does not guarantee the right to exclude causes no conflict [with federal law], in that it does not prohibit federally protected conduct; instead, such law grants broader accommodation of protected conduct than is required by the federal labor law." Compare *Rum Creek Coal Sales, Inc. v. Caperton*, 926 F.2d 353, 365–66 (4th Cir. 1991), in which West Virginia law was preempted: the law intended to influence the outcome of a labor dispute because it suspended enforcement of the state's criminal trespass laws only during strikes.

97 311 NLRB 437 (1993).

98 594 U.S. 139 (2021).

99 *Cedar Point Nursery v. Hassid*, 594 U.S., 140. These appropriations are summarized in Cynthia Estlund, "Showdown at Cedar Point: 'Sole and Despotic Dominion' Gains Ground," *Supreme Court Review* 2021 (2022): 125, 17.

100 Estlund, "Showdown at Cedar Point," 125, 137: "The decision may signal a new willingness on the part of the newly fortified conservative majority of the Court to constitutionalize restrictions on the regulatory state through takings law." See also Amy Liang, "Property versus Antidiscrimination: Examining the Impacts of *Cedar Point Nursery v. Hassid* on the Fair Housing Act," *University of Chicago Law Review* 89 (2022): 1793, 1803–05, explaining two ways in which the *Cedar Point* decision altered the definition of per se takings.

101 Kate Andrias, "Constitutional Clash: Labor, Capital, and Democracy," *Northwestern University Law Review* 118 (2024): 985, 1050: "Though such claims are unlikely to prevail in the short term, *Cedar Point* further entrenches business's [property interests] over labor's."

102 *Cedar Point Nursery v. Hassid*, 594 U.S., 141.

Chapter 3

1 376 U.S. 543 (1964).

2 406 U.S. 272 (1972).

3 414 U.S. 168 (1973).

4 417 U.S. 249 (1974).

5 482 U.S. 27 (1987).

6 379 U.S. 203 (1964).

7 452 U.S. 666 (1981).

8 465 U.S. 513 (1984).

9 *John Wiley and Sons, Inc. v. Livingston*, 376 U.S. 543 (1964); *NLRB v. Burns International Secretarial Services, Inc.*, 406 U.S. 272 (1972); *Golden State Bottling Company, Inc. v. NLRB*, 414 U.S. 168 (1973); *Howard Johnson Company v. Detroit Local Joint Executive Board*, 417 U.S. 249 (1974); *Fall River Dyeing and Finishing Corporation v. NLRB*, 482 U.S. 27 (1987).

10 See discussion in Katherine Van Wezel Stone, "Labor and the Corporate Structure:

Changing Conceptions and Emerging Possibilities," *University of Chicago Law Review* 55 (1988): 73, 102.

11   376 U.S. 543 (1964); 406 U.S. 272 (1972); 417 U.S. 249 (1974).

12   *John Wiley and Sons, Inc. v. Livingston*, 376 U.S., 549

13   *John Wiley and Sons, Inc. v. Livingston*, 376 U.S., 549.

14   See "John M. Harlan II," *Oyez*, https://www.oyez.org.

15   *NLRB v. Burns International Security Services, Inc.*, 406 U.S., 287–88.

16   *NLRB v. Burns International Security Services, Inc.*, 406 U.S., 285, paraphrasing the rejected NLRB position in *Burns*.

17   *NLRB v. Burns International Security Services, Inc.*, 406 U.S., 286, (also distinguishing that *Wiley* was a merger case in which local New York law provided that surviving entities assume the obligations of the merged entity).

18   While the successor employer is free to hire its own workforce, it may not refuse to hire the predecessor's employees by a motivation to avoid the duty to recognize the predecessor union. See, for example, *NLRB v. Staten Island Hotel Ltd. Partnership*, 101 F.3d 858 (2d Cir. 1996).

19   Stone, "Labor and the Corporate Structure," 103–4, citing Sarah Siskind, "Employer Instability and Union Decline," in *Proceedings of the N.Y.U. 39th Annual Conference on Labor*, ed. R. Adelman (1986), 8–1, 8–9, comparing an employer's ability to evade its labor obligations in a successor situation by initiating a Chapter 11 bankruptcy proceeding.

20   417 U.S. 249 (1974).

21   482 U.S. 27 (1987).

22   See *Fall River Dyeing and Finishing Corporation v. NLRB*, 482 U.S., 46, n. 12, rejecting the reference found in *Howard Johnson* that the yardstick is whether the new employer has hired a majority of the predecessor's employees.

23   See discussion in John E. Higgins, ed., *The Developing Labor Law: The Board, the Courts, and the National Labor Relations Act*, 7th ed. (Arlington, VA: Bloomberg BNA, 2017), 15-26-15-27.

24   Confirming dicta first stated in *Burns*, the Court in *Fall River* stated that the duty to bargain could arise when a demand for bargaining was made when it was "perfectly clear" that a majority of the new employer's workforce would be drawn from the predecessor's employees (482 U.S., 47 n. 14).

25   See the discussion at *NLRB v. Burns International Security Services, Inc.*, 406 U.S., 292–94.

26   Higgins, *The Developing Labor Law*, 15–21.

27   See *Howard Johnson Company v. Detroit Local Joint Executive Board*, 417 U.S., 268–69 (Douglas, J., dissenting), pointing out that the Court's successorship cases permit any new employer "to determine for himself whether he will be bound [to bargain] by the simple expedient of arranging for the termination of all of the prior employer's personnel." The academic literature contains similar criticisms. See Stone, "Labor and the Corporate Structure,"149 (collecting authority).

28   See *United Mine Workers (Lone Star Steel Company)*, 262 NLRB 368 (1982).

29   414 U.S. 168 (1973).

30   The development of the rule upheld in *Golden State* was uneven, with many NLRB reversals of position, until the Board, in *Perma Vinyl*, 164 NLRB 968 (1967), finally settled on the rule that the Supreme Court upheld in *Golden State*. See discussion in Higgins, *The Developing Labor Law*, 15-126-15-127.

31   See *Fitzsimmons v. Western Airlines, Inc.*, 290 A.2d 682, (Del. Ch. 1972), holding that the obligation of a corporation under a collective bargaining agreement passed to the surviving corporation by operation of a state merger statute. See generally discussion of

state merger statutes in Marcus Paul Efthimiou, "State Legislative Attempts to Mandate Continuation of Collective Bargaining Agreements during Business Change: The Unfulfilled Expectations and the Pre-empted Results," *Cornell Law Review* 77 (1991): 47, 65–66, notes 140, 141.

32 Delaware Code Annotated, title 19, sec. 706(a). Massachusetts, Pennsylvania, and Rhode Island have similar laws, while other states have adopted narrower legislation requiring, for example, that the predecessor's collective bargaining agreement have a successor and assigns clause. See Nick J. Vizy, *Corporate Counsels' Guide to Acquisitions and Divestures*, 2nd ed. (Eagan, MN: Business Laws, 2023), sec. 24:23.

33 *United Steelworkers of America v. Saint Gabriel's Hospital*, 871 F. Supp. 335 (D. Minn. 1994), holding that because it is an impermissible intrusion by state into collective bargaining process to compel a new employer to honor, against its will, the terms of a collective bargaining agreement negotiated by a predecessor, the legislation is preempted under both *Garmon* and *Machinists* preemption doctrines.

34 See *California Grocers Association v. City of Los Angeles*, 54 P.3d 1019, 1037 (2011) (collecting cases). Accord *Washington Service Contractors v. District of Columbia*, 54 F.3d 811(D.C. Cir. 1995); *Rhode Island Hospitality Association v. City of Providence*, 775 F.Supp.2d 416 (DRI 2011); and *Alcantara v. Allied Properties, LLC*, 334 F.Supp.2d 336 (EDNY 2004).

35 *Rhode Island Hospitality Association v. City of Providence*, 775 F.Supp.2d, 431–32.

36 *Fibreboard Paper Products Corporation v. NLRB*, 379 U.S. 203 (1964); *First National Maintenance Corporation v. NLRB*, 452 U.S. 666 (1981). Also see James J. Brudney, "Reflections on Group Action and the Law of the Workplace," *Texas Law Review* 75 (1996): 1563, 1573, showing that, between 1940 and 1994, "while the union-aligned position [at the Supreme Court] prevailed nearly eighty percent of the time between 1940 and 1969, unions' success rate [fell] to fifty percent [from 1970 to 1994]."

37 See listing of cases in Brudney, "Reflections," 1574–75, notes 45–52. Also see *NLRB v. Washington Aluminum Company*, 370 U.S. 9, 14, 16 (1962).

38 *NLRB v. Gissel Packing Company*, 395 U.S. 575, 587–89, 616–20 (1969); *NLRB v. Exchange Parts Company*, 375 U.S. 405 (1964); *NLRB v. Erie Resistor Corporation*, 373 U.S. 221 (1963); *Textile Workers Union v. Darlington Manufacturing Company*, 380 U.S. 263 (1965).

39 *NLRB v. Katz*, 369 U.S. 736 (1962); *NLRB v. Gissel Packing Company*, 395 U.S. 575, 595–616 (1969); *Fibreboard Paper Products Corporation v. NLRB*, 379 U.S. 203 (1964).

40 502 U.S. 527 (1992).

41 444 U.S. 672 (1980); 511 U.S. 571 (1994); 532 U.S. 706 (2001).

42 452 U.S. 666 (1981).

43 356 U.S. 342 (1958).

44 *NLRB v. Wooster Division of Borg-Warner Corporation*, 356 U.S., 349.

45 Paul Barron, "A Theory of Protected Employer Rights: A Revisionist Analysis of the Supreme Court's Interpretation of the National Labor Relations Act," *Texas Law Review* 59 (1981): 421, 436–37.

46 379 U.S. 203 (1964).

47 *Fibreboard Paper Products Corporation v. NLRB*, 379 U.S., 211, 213.

48 *Fibreboard Paper Products Corporation v. NLRB*, 379 U.S., 223 (Stewart, J., concurring): "Many decisions made by management affect the job security of employees. Decisions concerning the volume and kind of advertising expenditures, product design, the manner of financing, and sales, all may bear upon the security of the workers' jobs. Yet it is hardly conceivable that such decisions so involve 'conditions of employment' that they must be negotiated with the employees' bargaining representative."

49 Stone, "Labor and the Corporate Structure," 73, 88.

50 See discussion in Stone, "Labor and the Corporate Structure," 90, notes 61–67.

51   Robert J. Rabin, "*Fibreboard* and the Termination of Bargaining Unit Work," *Columbia Law Review* 71 (1971): 803, 804.

52   Michael H. Gottesman, "Rethinking Labor Law Preemption: State Laws Facilitating Unionization," *Yale Journal on Regulation* 7 (1990): 355, 401.

53   *First National Maintenance Corporation v. NLRB*, 452 U.S., 667, also explaining that the employer has a duty to bargain over the effects of the management decision.

54   *First National Maintenance Corporation v. NLRB*, 452 U.S., 689 (Brennan, J., dissenting).

55   See *Gunderson Rail Service, D/B/A Greenbrier Rail Services*, 364 NLRB 279 (2016), which resulted in a bargaining order because "labor costs were a primary factor in the . . . assessment of whether various facilities . . . should be . . . "closed." The NLRB has devised a complex three-part test to determine the duty to bargain in production relocation cases. See *Dubuque Packing Company*, 303 NLRB 386 (1991). The Board and the courts of appeal typically find no duty to bargain in relocation cases. See Higgins, *The Developing Labor Law*, 16-104-16-108 (discussing cases).

56   Stone, "Labor and the Corporate Structure," 96.

57   Christopher Hexter et al., "Twenty-Five Years of Developments in the Law under the National Labor Relations Act," 25 *ABA Journal of Labor and Employment Law* 25 (Spring 2010): 4.

58   Nelson Lichtenstein, *State of the Union: A Century of American Labor* (Princeton, NJ: Princeton University Press, 2002), 124, 176–77.

59   Brudney, "Reflections," 1579.

60   James B. Atleson, *Values and Assumptions in American Labor Law* (Amherst: University of Massachusetts Press, 1983), 134.

61   465 U.S. 513 (1984); William B. Gould IV, *Agenda for Reform: The Future of Employment Relationships and the Law* (Cambridge, MA: MIT Press, 1993), 20–22.

62   Lawrence Mishel, Lynn Rhinehart, and Lane Windham, "Explaining the Erosion of Private-Sector Unions: How Corporate Practices and Legal Changes Have Undercut the Ability of Workers to Organize and Bargain," November 18, 2020, https://www.epi.org.

63   Rhinehart et al., "Explaining the Erosion of Private-Sector Unions," citing observation by Babette Ceccotti, "Lost in Transformation: The Disappearance of Labor Policies in Applying Section 1113 of the Bankruptcy Code," *American Bankruptcy Institute Law Review* 15 (2007): 415. Accord Steven L. Willborn, "Workers in Troubled Firms: When Are (Should) They Be Protected?," *University of Pennsylvania Journal of Labor and Employment Law* 7: (2004): 35, 42: "Th[e] ability to reduce [labor contract] wage rates is sometimes a major reason firms enter bankruptcy."

64   Willborn, "Workers in Troubled Firms," 41; Gould, *Agenda for Reform*, 22, n. 33.

Chapter 4

1   420 U.S. 251 (1975).
2   465 U.S. 822 (1984).
3   336 U.S. 245 (1949).
4   361 U.S. 477 (1960).
5   306 U.S. 240 (1939).
6   316 U.S. 31 (1942).
7   598 U.S. 771 (2023).
8   306 U.S. 332 (1939).
9   345 U.S. 71 (1953).
10   460 U.S. 693 (1983).
11   350 U.S. 270 (1956).
12   369 U.S. 95 (1962).

13   346 U.S. 464 (1953).

14   356 U.S. 342 (1958).

15   404 U.S. 157 (1971).

16   452 U.S. 666 (1981).

17   Katherine Van Wezel Stone, "Labor and the Corporate Structure: Changing Conceptions and Emerging Possibilities," *University of Chicago Law Review* 55 (1988): 73, 85.

18   Stone, "Labor and the Corporate Structure," 73, 85.

19   Hiba Hafiz, "Structural Labor Rights," *Michigan Law Review* 119 (2021): 651, 664–665, 680. Accord Ahmed White, "Its Own Dubious Battle: The Impossible Defense of an Effective Right to Strike," *Wisconsin Law Review* (2018): 1065.

20   *Eastex, Inc. v. NLRB*, 437 U.S. 556, 567 (1978): "§ 7 . . . protect[s] concerted activities for the somewhat broader purpose of 'mutual aid or protection' as well as for the narrower purposes of 'self-organization' and 'collective bargaining,.'"

21   420 U.S. 251 (1975); 465 U.S. 822 (1984).

22   See NLRA, sec. 1, which identifies workers' inequality of bargaining power compared to their employers as an obstruction to the free flow of commerce and states that it is the policy of the United States to "eliminate the causes of [these] obstructions."

23   *NLRB v. J. Weingarten, Inc.*, 420 U.S., 261–62.

24   *NLRB v. J. Weingarten, Inc.*, 420 U.S., 262.

25   *NLRB v. J. Weingarten, Inc.*, 420 U.S., 274–75 (Powell, J., dissenting). Chief Justice Burger dissented for a different reason: because, in its *Weingarten* opinion, the NLRB had not adequately justified its interpretation of the NLRA.

26   This holding followed the court of appeal's prior decision in *ARO, Inc. v. NLRB*, 596 F.2d 713, 718 (CA6 1979), in which the court had held: "For an individual claim or complaint to amount to concerted action under the Act it must . . . be made on behalf of other employees or at least be made with the object of inducing or preparing for group action."

27   City Disposal, 465 U.S. at 832.

28   *NLRB v. Jones and Laughlin Steel Corporation*, 301 U.S. (1937), 45–46.

29   See the discussion in Moshe Zvi Marvit, "On the Greatest Property Transfer That Wasn't: How the National Labor Relations Act Chose Employee Rights and the Supreme Court Chose Property Rights," *Southern University Law Review* 38 (2010): 79, 94.

30   *United Auto Workers, Local 232, v. Wisconsin Employment Relations Board (Briggs-Stratton)*, 336 U.S. 245 (1949); 9 NLRB 676, 686 (1938).

31   *United Auto Workers, Local 232, v. Wisconsin Employment Relations Board (Briggs-Stratton)*, 336 U.S., 256.

32   *United Auto Workers, Local 232, v. Wisconsin Employment Relations Board (Briggs-Stratton)*, 336 U.S., 264.

33   Through similar *ipse dixit* reasoning, the Court in *NLRB v. Insurance Agents International Union*, 361 U.S. 477 (1960), held that a concerted slowdown is unprotected.

34   Archibald Cox, whose views on labor law interpretation have been criticized as lacking "inquiry into inequality of power or issues of substantive fairness" (Karl Klare, "Traditional Labor Law Scholarship and the Crisis of Collective Bargaining: A Reply to Professor Finkin," *Maryland Law Review* 44 [1985]: 731, 768), argued in 1951 that slowdowns and similar tactics "cost the employees nothing and, if they were protected activities, management would be helpless to resist. Hence such weapons are too effective to permit them to be part of the employees' arsenal" ("The Right to Engage in Concerted Activities," 26 *Indiana Law Journal* 26 [1951]: 319, 338).

35   See, for instance, *Allen-Bradley, Local No. 1111, v. Wisconsin Employment Relations Board*, 315 U.S. 740 (1942). (mass picketing); *Southern Steamship Company v. NLRB*, 316 U.S. 31 (1942) (strike contravening federal maritime law); and *NLRB v. Fansteel Metallurgical Corporation*, 306 U.S. 240 (1939) (sitdown strikes in violation of state trespass law).

36   White, "Its Own Dubious Battle," 1126.

37   White, "Its Own Dubious Battle," 1127.

38   598 U.S. 771 (2023).

39   *Glacier Northwest, Inc. v. International Brotherhood of Teamsters*, 598 U.S., 782–83.

40   *Glacier Northwest, Inc. v. International Brotherhood of Teamsters*, 598 U.S., 814 (Jackson, J., dissenting), citing *Leprino Cheese Company*,170 NLRB 601, 605 (1968), and explaining that the majority's expansion of the reasonable-precautions principle "shifts the duty of protecting an employer's property from damage or loss incident to a strike onto the striking workers, beyond what the Board has already permitted via the reasonable-precautions principle."

41   Order denying respondent's motion for postponement of hearing at 7, *Glacier Northwest, Inc. v. International Brotherhood of Teamsters*, no. 19-CA-203068, January 11, 2023. For a discussion of the administrative law judge's view that the union's conduct was at least "arguably protected," see the note in "The Supreme Court 2022 Term: National Labor Relations Act—Administrative Law—Preemption—Primary Jurisdiction—*Glacier Northwest, Inc. v. International Brotherhood of Teamsters Local Union No. 174*," *Harvard Law Review* 137 (2023): 450, 452.

42   *Glacier Northwest, Inc. v. International Brotherhood of Teamsters*, 598 U.S., 791, 796–98 (Jackson, J., dissenting): "The General Counsel's complaint asserts that the Union's claim that its strike conduct was protected 'appears to have merit.'" See note 3 in the majority opinion dismissing the fact of the general counsel's complaint, refusing to consider the legal significance of the complaint because it had been issued after the state court rulings and because "the lower courts ha[d] not addressed the significance, if any, of the Board's complaint with respect to *Garmon* preemption."

43   *Glacier Northwest, Inc. v. International Brotherhood of Teamsters*, 598 U.S., 796–99 (Jackson, J., dissenting).

44   594 U.S. 139 (2021).

45   Brief for petitioner at 2, *Glacier Northwest, Inc. v. International Brotherhood of Teamsters*, 598 U.S. 771 (no. 21–1449).

46   See the discussion in Courtlyn G. Roser-Jones, "The Roberts Court and the Unraveling of Labor Law," *Minnesota Law Review* 108 (2024): 1407, 1480.

47   *Glacier Northwest, Inc. v. International Brotherhood of Teamsters*, 598 U.S. (Thomas, J., concurring), advocating that the Court "reexamine" *Garmon's* arguably protected wing of labor preemption.

48   Roser-Jones, "The Roberts Court and the Unraveling of Labor Law," 1414.

49   Kate Andrias, "Constitutional Clash: Labor, Capital, and Democracy," *Northwestern University Law Review* 118 (2024): 985, 991–92, 1059, stating that in its *Glacier Northwest* decision, by concluding in the first instance that the workers' activity was unprotected, "the Court evinced a . . . hostility to the NLRB's authority [by] arrogat[ing] the Board's authority to determine what strike activity was 'arguably protected' by the NLRA."

50   Roser-Jones, "The Roberts Court and the Unraveling of Labor Law," 1484–86.

51   306 U.S. 332 (1939).

52   *NLRB v. Sands Manufacturing Company*, 306 U.S., 344, citing *Fansteel*, decided on the same day.

53   345 U.S. 71 (1953).

54   *Redwing Carriers*, 137 NLRB 1545 (1962).

55   *NLRB v. Rockaway News Supply Company*, 345 U.S., 80. In *Metropolitan Edison Company v. NLRB*, 460 U.S. 693 (1983), the Court agreed with the NLRB that the imposition of more severe discipline on union officials for participating in an unlawful work stoppage violates section 8(a)(3). While a union may waive this protection by clearly imposing contractual duties on its officials to ensure the integrity of no-strike clauses, in *Metropolitan Edison* there was no waiver.

56   415 U.S. 322 (1974).

57 Paul Barron, "A Theory of Protected Employer Rights: A Revisionist Analysis of the Supreme Court's Interpretation of the National Labor Relations Act," *Texas Law Review* 59 (1981): 421, 429: "The Supreme Court has enforced no-strike clauses in contracts since the Taft-Hartley Act added § 301 to the NLRA" (citing *Boys Markets, Inc. v. Retail Clerks, Local 770*, 398 U.S. 235 [1970], and *Gateway Coal Company v. United Mine Workers*, 414 U.S. 368 [1974]).

58 Barron, "A Theory of Protected Employer Rights," 429. In *Mastro Plastics Corporation v. NLRB*, 350 U.S. 270 (1956), the Court held that a general no-strike clause does not waive the employees' right to strike in response to employer unfair labor practices. In *Teamsters, Local 174, v. Lucas Flour Company*, 369 U.S. 95 (1962), the Court held that even when the contract is silent with respect to the waiver of the right to strike, a no-strike obligation will be inferred as a matter of law with respect to all disputes that the parties have agreed to resolve through arbitration. See also *Gateway Coal Company v. United Mine Workers*, 414 U.S., finding that courts may enjoin as in breach of contract strikes over disputes that the parties have agreed to arbitrate.

59 346 U.S. 464 (1953).

60 *NLRB v. Local 1229, International Brotherhood of Electrical Workers (Jefferson Standard Broadcasting)*, 346 U.S., 468–69. Apparently the union's strategy was to place economic pressure on the company through a loss, or threatened loss, of advertising in an effort to secure a favorable outcome of its bargaining dispute with the company. The strategy began to work to the extent, as the NLRB found, that the leaflets "caused [the company] to apprehend a loss of advertising revenue due to dissatisfaction with its television broadcasting service" (471).

61 *NLRB v. Local 1229, International Brotherhood of Electrical Workers (Jefferson Standard Broadcasting)*, 346 U.S.. 468.

62 *NLRB v. Local 1229, International Brotherhood of Electrical Workers (Jefferson Standard Broadcasting)*, 346 U.S., 471.

63 *NLRB v. Local 1229, International Brotherhood of Electrical Workers (Jefferson Standard Broadcasting)*, 346 U.S., 472.

64 *NLRB v. Local 1229, International Brotherhood of Electrical Workers (Jefferson Standard Broadcasting)*, 346 U.S., 472.

65 *NLRB v. Local 1229, International Brotherhood of Electrical Workers (Jefferson Standard Broadcasting)*, 346 U.S., 476.

66 *NLRB v. Local 1229, International Brotherhood of Electrical Workers (Jefferson Standard Broadcasting)*, 346 U.S., 480–81 (Frankfurter, J., dissenting).

67 See John E. Higgins, ed., *The Developing Labor Law: The Board, the Courts, and the National Labor Relations Act*, 7th ed. (Arlington, VA: Bloomberg BNA, 2017), 6-185-6-191, stating that even when criticism is shown to be related to a labor dispute, some courts adopt a "more restricted reading of section 7" and deem criticism unprotected if considered by the court to be "egregious" or "constitute a disparagement or vilification of the employer's product or reputation," while other courts adopt a "narrow definition of disloyalty" permitting disparagement of the employer's product if the disparagement is related to an ongoing labor dispute.

68 See the discussion of these employer options in chaps. 5 and 6.

69 *NLRB v. Local 1229, International Brotherhood of Electrical Workers (Jefferson Standard Broadcasting)*, 346 U.S., 479–80 (Frankfurter, J., dissenting).

70 *NLRB v. Local 1229, International Brotherhood of Electrical Workers (Jefferson Standard Broadcasting)*, 346 U.S., 480 (Frankfurter, J., dissenting).

71 *FibreBoard Paper Products Corporation v. NLRB*, 379 U.S. 203, 219, n. 2 (1964) (Stewart, J., concurring).

72 See, for instance, *Singer Manufacturing Company*, 24 NLRB 444 (1940).

73   See Barron, "A Theory of Protected Employer Rights," 434–35.

74   *NLRB v. Wooster Division of Borg-Warner Corporation*, 452 U.S. 666 (1981).

75   See the discussion in Barron, "A Theory of Protected Employer Rights," 435–36. See generally *Professional Medical Transport, Inc.*, 362 NLRB 534 (2015), insisting on a non-mandatory subject of bargaining described as an "illegal demand."

76   404 U.S. 157 (1971).

77   In *Mastro Plastics Corporation v. NLRB*, 350 U.S. 270 (1956), the Court held that a general no-strike clause is to be interpreted to ban economic strikes and not unfair labor practice strikes.

78   452 U.S. 666 (1981).

79   *First National Maintenance Corporation v. NLRB*, 452 U.S., 667.

80   Stone, "Labor and the Corporate Structure," 96.

Chapter 5

1   304 U.S. 333 (1938).

2   347 U.S. 17 (1954).

3   409 U.S. 48 (1972).

4   350 U.S. 270 (1956).

5   373 U.S. 221 (1963).

6   388 U.S. 26 (1967).

7   389 U.S. 375 (1967).

8   489 U.S. 426 (1989).

9   353 U.S. 87 (1957).

10   380 U.S. 278 (1965).

11   Paul Barron, "A Theory of Protected Employer Rights: A Revisionist Analysis of the Supreme Court's Interpretation of the National Labor Relations Act," *Texas Law Review* 59 (1981): 421, 439–40, discussing the value of viewing judicially created rules that permit adverse employer responses to employees' protected concerted activity as creating employer rights.

12   304 U.S. 333 (1938).

13   See the discussion in Julius G. Getman and Thomas C. Kohler, "The Story of *NLRB v. Mackay Radio & Telegraph Co*: The High Cost of Solidarity," in *Labor Law Stories*, ed. Laura J Cooper and Catherine L. Fisk. (New York: Foundation Press, 2005), 14, 43.

14   Ahmed White, "Its Own Dubious Battle: The Impossible Defense of an Effective Right to Strike," *Wisconsin Law Review* (2018): 1065, 1126.

15   These deficiencies are summarized in James Gray Pope, "How American Workers Lost the Right to Strike, and Other Tales," 103 *Michigan Law Review* 103 (2004): 518, 528–29. Unless otherwise indicated, this is the source of interlineated quotes in the text.

16   See Getman and Kohler, "The Story of *NLRB v. Mackay Radio & Telegraph Co.*," 49: "The *Mackay* doctrine gives employers a powerful argument against unionization" and that the decision "provides employers with an incentive seek a strike as a union-avoidance technique."

17   Cynthia L. Estlund, "The Ossification of American Labor Law," *Columbia Law Review* 102 (2002): 1527, 1538.

18   Kate Andrias, "Constitutional Clash: Labor, Capital, and Democracy" *Northwestern University Law Review* 118 (2024): 985, 1019–22, 1025–26: "Since 2018, and especially in 2023 . . . workers have walked off the job at rates not seen since the 1980s."

19   For example, in 2021, the Labor Department reported that there were only eight major

work stoppages that began in 2020. This was the third lowest number of major work stoppages since 1947, when the department began keeping track of such strikes. See U.S. Bureau of Labor Statistics, "Major Work Stoppages (Annual) News Release," February 19, 2021, https://www.bls.gov.

20   See Hal Keith Gillespie, "The *Mackay* Doctrine and the Myth of Business Necessity," *Texas Law Review* 50 (1972): 782, 788–95; and Paul Weiler, "Striking a New Balance: Freedom of Contract and the Prospects for Union Representation," *Harvard Law Review* 98 (1984): 351, 391. Citation to these authorities appears in Pope, "How American Workers Lost the Right to Strike," n. 63.

21   347 U.S. 17 (1954).

22   373 U.S. 221, 231 (1963).

23   388 U.S. 26 (1967), holding that employer grant of vacation benefits to striker replacements but not to strikers is unlawful notwithstanding absence of motive to punish strikers because the disparate treatment was inherently destructive of the worker's NLRA rights; 389 U.S. 375, 380 (1967), holding that, absent substantial business justification, the employer must rehire former strikers before hiring new employees where "employees continued to make known their availability and desire for reinstatement, and that at all times respondent intended to resume full production to reactivate the jobs and to fill them."

24   *NLRB v. Erie Resistor Corporation*, 373 U.S., 231.

25   White, "Its Own Dubious Battle," 1126.

26   See Getman and Kohler, "The Story of NLRB v. Mackay Radio & Telegraph Co.," 49, n. 79, citing a proposal by Samuel Estreicher.

27   350 U.S. 270 (1956); 409 U.S. 48 (1972).

28   White, "Its Own Dubious Battle," 1093.

29   Julius G. Getman, *The Supreme Court on Unions: Why Labor Law Is Failing American Workers* (Ithaca, NY: Cornell University/ILR Press, 2016), 56, 66, 194; Jonathan Hiatt, "At Age Seventy, Should the National Labor Relations Act Be Retired?," in *Proceedings of the 2005 Annual Meeting, Association of American Law Schools Section on Labor Relations and Employment Law*, ed. Katherine Stone., in *Employee Rights and Employment Policy Journal* 9 (2005): 121, 139: the "major destigmatizing of the use of permanent replacements [following the PATCO strike] that led private sector employers to start making use of this tactic much more than before").

30   The report of the Senate Committee on Labor and Human Resources on the striker replacement bill makes this case most fully. See Workplace Fairness Act, S. Rep. no. 102–111, 102d Cong., 1st sess. 6–16 (1991) (employers only began to hire permanent replacements routinely in the 1980s); and testimony before Congress by William B. Gould IV, in William B. Gould IV, *Agenda for Reform: The Future of Employment Relationships and the Law* (Cambridge, MA.: MIT Press, 1993), 186.

31   489 U.S. 426 (1989).

32   See Sandra L. Albrecht, *The Assault on Labor: The 1986 TWA Strike and the Decline of Workers' Rights in America* (Lanham, MD: Lexington, 2017), discussing internal conflicts after the conclusion of the strike.

33   353 U.S. 87 (1957); 380 U.S. 278 (1965).

34   *NLRB v. Truck Drivers, Local 449 (Buffalo Linen)*, 353 U.S., 93.

35   *NLRB v. Truck Drivers, Local 449 (Buffalo Linen)*, 353 U.S., 96.

36   380 U.S. 278 (1965).

37   *NLRB v. Brown*, 380 U.S., 282.

38   This appraisal of the majority opinion is primarily informed by the reasoning of Justice White in his dissent in *Brown* (380 U.S., 294–99).

39   *Brown Food Store, Inc.*, 137 NLRB 73, 77 (1962).

40   *NLRB v. Brown*, 380 U.S., 297–98 (White, J., dissenting). Justice White also argued

that, more fundamentally, when unionized employees lose their jobs because they are unionized and those jobs are taken by nonunionized workers, even temporarily, the employer has displaced union members with nonunion members solely on account of union membership; this is the prototype of discrimination proscribed by section 8(a)(3). Justice White rejected "the Court's justification for this invasion of employee rights by a member of a multiemployer unit [of] the employer's right to burden the union strike fund with all its members to bring economic pressure to bear on the union."

Chapter 6

1   380 U.S. 263 (1965).
2   395 U.S. 575 (1969).
3   380 U.S. 300 (1965).
4   369 U.S. 736 (1962).
5   461 U.S. 731 (1983).
6   536 U.S. 516 (2002).
7   454 U.S. 404 (1982).
8   494 U.S. 775 (1990).
9   517 U.S. 781 (1996).
10   522 U.S. 359 (1998).
11   I am indebted to Paul Barron, who first brought this distinction to my attention in his groundbreaking evaluation of how the Supreme Court creates employer rights. See his "A Theory of Protected Employer Rights: A Revisionist Analysis of the Supreme Court's Interpretation of the National Labor Relations Act," 59 *Texas Law Review* 59 (1981): 421, 445–52.
12   380 U.S. 263 (1965); 395 U.S. 575 (1969).
13   See James B. Atleson, *Values and Assumption s in American Labor Law* (Amherst: University of Massachusetts Press, 1983), 139, emphasis in the original.
14   *Textile Workers v. Darlington Manufacturing Company*, 380 U.S., 270.
15   But "we had always supposed that the purpose of the statute was affirmatively to protect employees in the exercise of their rights, not merely to preclude employers from profiting from destruction of those rights" (Atleson, *Values and Assumptions in American Labor Law*, 140).
16   *Textile Workers v. Darlington Manufacturing Company*, 380 U.S., 275.
17   *Textile Workers v. Darlington Manufacturing Company*, 380 U.S., 275, n. 20 : "Nothing . . . in this opinion [precludes an employer] from announcing [in advance of a union election] a decision to close already reached by the board of directors or other management authority empowered to make such a decision." See also Barron, "A Theory of Protected Employer Rights," 448, arguing that it was naïve for the Court recognize "the possibility that [permitting an employer to announce an intent to close the company if the employees choose unionization] may result in some deterrent effect on organizational activities independent of that arising from the closing itself [because] an employer may be encouraged to make a definitive decision to close on the theory that its mere announcement before a representation election will discourage the employees from voting for the union, and thus his decision may not have to be implemented [but then to conclude that] [s]uch a possibility is not likely to occur [because] a solidly successful employer is not apt to hazard the possibility that the employees will call his bluff by voting to organize."
18   *Textile Workers v. Darlington Manufacturing Company*, 380 U.S., 276. See discussion in Atleson, *Values and Assumptions in American Labor Law*, 140.
19   *NLRB v. Gissel Packing Company*, 395 U.S., 618, citing *Textile Workers v. Darlington*

Manufacturing Company, 380 U.S., 263, 274, n. 20.

20   380 U.S. 300 (1965).

21   Julius G. Getman. *The Supreme Court on Unions: Why Labor law Is Failing American Workers* (Ithaca, NY: Cornell University/ILR Press, 2016), 83–84.

22   369 U.S. 736 (1962).

23   Ellen Dannin, "From Dictator Game to Ultimatum Game . . . and Back Again: The Judicial Impasse Amendments," *University of Pennsylvania Journal of Labor and Employment Law* 6 (2004): 241, 255.

24   See *Darling and Company*, 171 NLRB 801 (1968), finding the pre-impasse offensive lockout lawful, assuming that there was no proven motive to discourage union activity or to evade bargaining obligation.

25   *Harter Equipment*, 280 NLRB 597 (1986). The NLRB views the hiring of permanent replacements for locked-out employees as a violation of the NLRA. See *Ancor Concepts*, 323 NLRB 742 (1997).

26   See *Ancor Concepts*, 323 NLRB 742 (1997), holding that lawful lockout was initiated when the employer adequately communicated to striking workers that it would refuse to offer reinstatement until a new agreement was reached.

27   *NLRB v. Mackay Radio and Telegraph Company*, 304 U.S. 333 (1938). Following an economic striker's unconditional offer to return to work, permanently replaced economic strikers are entitled only to be placed on a preferential hiring list. Full reinstatement is available only upon the departure of the replacement, which could be years after the strike occurred, and then only if the striker has not acquired regular and substantially equivalent employment and the employer is unable to show a legitimate and substantial business reason for failing to reinstate. See *Laidlow Corporation*, 171 NLRB 1366 (1968).

28   Paul More, "Protections against Retaliatory Employer Lawsuits after *BE & K Construction v. NLRB*," *Berkeley Journal of Employment and Labor Law* 25 (2004): 205, 209, 212–14.

29   See, for instance, James J. Brudney, "Collateral Conflict: Employer Claims of RICO Extortion against Union Comprehensive Campaigns," *Southern California Law Review* 83 (2010): 731.

30   More, "Protections against Retaliatory Employer Lawsuits," 211.

31   461 U.S. 731 (1983); 536 U.S. 516 (2002).

32   For a summary of the NLRB general counsel's view of the holdings in *Bill Johnson's Restaurants, Inc. v. NLRB* and *BE & K Construction Company v. NLRB*, see NLRB, "Case Handling Instructions for Cases Concerning *Bill Johnson's Restaurants* and *BE & K Construction Co.*" memo GC 02–09, September 20, 2002, https://www.nlrb.gov.

33   *Bill Johnson's Restaurants, Inc. v. NLRB*, 461 U.S., 742–43, 747, 749.

34   See *Beverly Health and Rehabilitation Services, Inc.*, 331 NLRB 960 (2000), which directs that the unfair labor practice charge be held in abeyance pending the conclusion of the suit because the evidence in the case raised questions of the proper inferences to be drawn from undisputed facts.

35   329 N.L.R.B. 717, 722–23, 726–27 (1999).

36   *BE & K Construction Company v. NLRB*, 536 U.S., 530–32.

37   *BE & K Construction Company v. NLRB*, 536 U.S., 534.

38   *BE & K Construction Company v. NLRB*, 536 U.S., 536–37.

39   The *Bill Johnson's/BE & K Construction* calculus for deciding when a retaliatory lawsuit violates the NLRA does not apply to suits brought in state court that are preempted by the NLRA. In a note in *Bill Johnson's*, the Supreme Court carved out an exception by placing preempted lawsuits outside of its First Amendment analysis (461 U.S., 737, n. 5): "The Board has consistently declined to apply the *Bill Johnson's* analysis to lawsuits that were preempted by the Act." See *Can-Am Plumbing, Inc. v. NLRB*, 321 F.3d 145, 151 (D.C. Cir. 2003).

40   454 U.S. 404 (1982); 494 U.S. 775 (1990); 517 U.S. 781 (1996); 522 U.S. 359 (1998).

41 *Retail Associates*, 120 NLRB 388 (1958).

42 *Hi-Way Billboards*, 206 NLRB 22 (1973), is considered to contain the authoritative state-
    ment of the rules regarding withdrawal due to unusual circumstances. See the discussion
    of cases in John E. Higgins, ed., *The Developing Labor Law: The Board, the Courts, and the
    National Labor Relations Act*, 7th ed. (Arlington, VA: Bloomberg BNA, 2017), 11-87-11-88.

43 *Charles D. Bonanno Linen Service, Inc. v. NLRB*, 454 U.S., 414–15.

44 In *Levitz Furniture Company of the Pacific, Inc.*, 333 NLRB 717 (2001), the NLRB modified
    these rules by providing that the employer could unilaterally withdraw recognition only
    if the employer can demonstrate that the union has in fact lost majority support.

Chapter 7

1   400 U.S. 297 (1971).

2   456 U.S. 212 (1982).

3   386 U.S. 612 (1967).

4   386 U.S. 664 (1967).

5   429 U.S. 507 (1977). Full disclosure: in private practice, I worked on this case, prior to
    the Supreme Court granting *certiorari*.

6   447 U.S. 490 (1980).

7   473 U.S. 61 (1985).

8   456 U.S. 645 (1982).

9   434 U.S. 335 (1978).

10 377 U.S. 58 (1964).

11 447 U.S. 607 (1980).

12 485 U.S. 568 (1988).

13 Section 8(b)(4) provides in pertinent part: "It shall be an unfair labor practice for a labor
    organization or its agents . . . (4)(ii) to threaten, coerce, or restrain any person engaged
    in commerce or in an industry affecting commerce, where . . . an object thereof is . . .
    (B) forcing or requiring any person to cease using, selling, handling, transporting, or
    otherwise dealing in the products of any other producer, processor, or manufacturer, or
    to cease doing business with any other person . . . *Provided*, That nothing contained in
    this clause (B) shall be construed to make unlawful . . . any primary strike or primary
    picketing."

14 *Carpenters, Local 1976 v. NLRB (Sand Door Plywood Company)*, 357 U.S. 93 (1958).

15 See, for instance, *NLRB v. International Rice Milling Company*, 341 U.S. 665 (1951). This
    right to assert a cease-doing-business object at the site of the primary employer is more
    limited when the primary employer's facility is a "common situs" having neutral employers
    also located there. See *International Union of Electrical Workers (IUE), Local 761, v. NLRB*,
    366 U.S. 667 (1961).

16 *Electrical Workers (IUE), Local 761, v. NLRB (General Electric)*, 366 U.S. 667, 674 (1961);
    NLRB v. Building and Construction Trades Council (Denver), 341 U.S. 675, 692 (1951).

17 400 U.S. 297 (1971).

18 In *Burns and Roe*, the Operating Engineers union sought exclusive authority to start
    and stop electric welders, but one of the subcontractors on the job assigned that work to
    another union. The Operating Engineers asked the general contractor to agree to enter
    into subcontracts only with contractors who would assign the electric welder work to
    the Operating Engineers. When the general contractor refused, the Operating Engineers
    struck with the goal of shutting down the entire job. The Operating Engineers defended
    the charge of a secondary boycott by arguing that it was not asking the neutral general

contractor to completely cease doing business with the subcontractor who would not assign the disputed work to the Operating Engineers but to use its influence to persuade the subcontractor to assign the work to the Operating Engineers. The court of appeals agreed with the union, but the Supreme Court had no difficulty rejecting the defense, reasoning that as long as the subcontractor refused to assign the work to the Operating Engineers, the only resolution of the dispute was for the general contractor to remove the subcontractor from the job: that is, to cease doing business with the subcontractor.

19 Nelson Lichtenstein, *State of the Union: A Century of American Labor* (Princeton, NJ: Princeton University Press, 2002), 118–20.

20 Lichtenstein, *State of the Union*, 118.

21 Christopher L. Tomlins, *The State and the Unions: Labor Relations, Law, and the Organized Labor Movement in America, 1880–1960* (Cambridge, UK: Cambridge University Press, 1985), 299–300.

22 456 U.S. 212 (1982).

23 See James Gray Pope, "How American Workers Lost the Right to Strike, and Other Tales," *Michigan Law Review* 103 (2004): 518, 545, n. 14, discussing the judicial reluctance of American courts to hold strikes lawful except when motivated by the prospect of immediate economic gain for the strikers themselves.

24 Richard White, *The Republic for Which It Stands: The United States during Reconstruction and the Gilded Age, 1865–1896* (New York: Oxford University Press, 2017), 818–19; Francis Bowes Sayre, "Labor and the Courts," *Yale Law Journal* 39 (1930): 682.

25 See the discussion in John E. Higgins, ed., *The Developing Labor Law: The Board, the Courts, and the National Labor Relations Act*, 7th ed. (Arlington, VA: Bloomberg BNA, 2017), 22-29-15-27.

26 Lee Modjeska, "The *Tree Fruits* Consumer Picketing Case—A Retrospective Analysis," *University of Cincinnati Law Review* 53 (1984): 1005, 1025.

27 *Burlington Northern v. Brotherhood of Maintenance Employees*, 481 U.S. 430, 446–47 (1987): "The RLA [Railway Labor Act] does not contain an express mandate limiting the scope of self-help available to a union once the RLA's major dispute resolution procedures have been exhausted"; therefore, secondary activity is permitted after exhaustion of the proper dispute resolution procedures.

28 Reginald Alleyne, "Boycott Ban Prolongs Eastern Strike: Secondary Picketing Could Force Bush or Congress to Act," *Los Angeles Times*, March 24, 1989.

29 357 U.S. 93 (1958).

30 Section 8(e) provides in pertinent part: "It shall be an unfair labor practice for any labor organization and any employer to enter into any contract or agreement, express or implied, whereby such employer ceases or refrains or agrees to cease or refrain from handling, using, selling, transporting or otherwise dealing in any of the products of any other employer, or to cease doing business with any other person."

31 See, for instance, Alicia Gabriela Rosenberg, "Automation and the Work Preservation Doctrine: Accommodating Productivity and Job Security Interests," *UCLA Law Review* 32 (1984): 135, 135–36.

32 See *National Woodwork Manufacturing v. NLRB*, 386 U.S. 612 (1967).

33 See *Houston Insulation Contractors Association v. NLRB*, 386 U.S. 664 (1967).

34 See *NLRB v. Enterprise Association, Pipefitters, Local 638*, 429 U.S. 507 (1977).

35 386 U.S. 612 (1967).

36 *National Woodwork Manufacturing v. NLRB*, 386 U.S., 645. Accord *Houston Insulation Contractors Association v. NLRB*, 386 U.S., a companion case to *National Woodwork*. Here, the Court agreed that a contract provision that reserved the cutting of stainless steel bands at the jobsite for unit employees had a primary work preservation object. The majority in *National Woodwork* distinguished an earlier antitrust case, *Allen-Bradley v.*

Electrical Workers (International Brotherhood of Electrical Workers), Local 3, 25 U.S. 797 (1945), in which a union and employer group used a collective bargaining agreement as a sword to monopolize jobs for union members. In contrast, the agreement in *National Woodwork* was used as a shield to protect or preserve work customarily performed within the bargaining unit.

37   *National Woodwork Manufacturing v. NLRB*, 386 U.S., 650 (Stewart, J., dissenting).

38   429 U.S. 507 (1977). Full disclosure: as a young lawyer, I worked on this case, prior to the Supreme Court's granting of *certiorari*.

39   *National Woodwork Manufacturing v. NLRB*, 386 U.S., 632.

40   *Enterprise Association of Steam Pipefitters*, 204 NLRB 760, 760 (1973).

41   *NLRB v. Enterprise Association, Pipefitters, Local 638*, 429 U.S., 535–36 (Brennan, J., dissenting).

42   *NLRB v. Enterprise Association, Pipefitters, Local 638*, 429 U.S., 543–44-(Stewart, J., dissenting).

43   See, for instance, *Electrical Workers (International Brotherhood of Electrical Workers), Local 501 (Atlas Construction Company)*, 216 NLRB 417 (1975).

44   447 U.S. 490 (1980).

45   473 U.S. 61 (1985).

46   *NLRB v. International Longshoremen's Association (Dolphin's Forwarding)*, 447 U.S, 508 (quoting 613 F.2d, 909).

47   *International Longshoremen's Association*, 266 NLRB 230 (1983).

48   *International Longshoremen's Association*, 266 NLRB, 237.

49   *NLRB v. International Longshoremen's Association (New York Shipping Association)*, 473 U.S., 81–82.

50   *Woelke and Romero Framing, Inc. v. NLRB*, 456 U.S. 645 (1982).

51   434 U.S. 335 (1978).

52   *NLRB v. Local Union No. 103, International Association of Bridge, Structural, and Ornamental Iron Workers (Higdon Construction Company)*, 444 U.S., 353 (Stewart, J., dissenting).

53   The NLRA's section 8(b)(7), the dissent argued, does not bar picketing to enforce a pre-hire agreement; for as interpreted by the NLRB, it was intended to proscribe only "picketing having as its target forcing or requiring an employer's *initial acceptance* of the union as the bargaining representative of his employees" (citing *Building and Construction Trades Council of Santa Barbara County (Sullivan Electric Company)*, 146 NLRB 1086, 1087, emphasis in the original). Also see *NLRB v. Local Union No. 103, International Association of Bridge, Structural, and Ornamental Iron Workers (Higdon Construction Company)*, 444 U.S., 354 (Stewart, J., dissenting).

54   377 U.S. 58 (1964).

55   Modjeska, "The *Tree Fruits* Consumer Picketing Case," 1006.

56   The majority opinion was joined by Chief Justice Warren and Justices Clark, White, and Goldberg, with a concurring opinion by Justice Black. Justice Harlan dissented, joined by Justice Stewart, and Justice Douglas did not participate.

57   *NLRB v. Fruit and Vegetable Packers and Warehousemen, Local 760 (Tree Fruits)*, 377 U.S., 63.

58   *NLRB v. Fruit and Vegetable Packers and Warehousemen, Local 760 (Tree Fruits)*, 377 U.S., 63.

59   *NLRB v. Fruit and Vegetable Packers and Warehousemen, Local 760 (Tree Fruits)*, 377 U.S., 70.

60   *NLRB v. Fruit and Vegetable Packers and Warehousemen, Local 760 (Tree Fruits)*, 377 U.S., 76–80 (Black, J., concurring). Justice Harlan, joined by Justice Stewart, dissented, arguing that Congress's intent to ban all secondary consumer picketing is made manifest from statutory language and legislative history. The dissent also reasoned that the picketing

by Local 760 threatened to create a complete cessation of business between Safeway and Tree Fruits because some of the customers would boycott Safeway entirely, either from a desire to avoid the picket line or because of confusion regarding the limited object of the picketing. Or Safeway might have suspended business dealings with Tree Fruits to avoid having its stores subject to picketing. Justice Harlan added that the risk of coercing the neutral to cease doing business altogether with the primary employer increases as the picketed entity's sales of the struck product represent an increasingly larger percentage of the picketed entity's total sales (80–94 [Harlan, J., dissenting]).

61 *NLRB v. Fruit and Vegetable Packers and Warehousemen, Local 760 (Tree Fruits)*, 377 U.S., 79 (Black, J., concurring).

62 *NLRB v. Fruit and Vegetable Packers and Warehousemen, Local 760 (Tree Fruits)*, 377 U.S., 79 (Black, J., concurring).

63 447 U.S. 607 (1980).

64 In one of the more unusual Supreme Court concurring opinions, Justice Blackmun recognized that banning peaceful labor picketing but not functionally similar nonlabor picketing constituted content discrimination but concurred in the Safeco decision "only because I am reluctant to hold unconstitutional Congress' striking of the delicate balance between union freedom of expression and the ability of neutral employers, employees, and consumers to remain free from coerced participation in industrial strife. *NLRB v. Retail Store Employees Union, Local 1001 (Safeco Title Insurance Company)*, 447 U.S., 617–18 (Blackmun, J,, concurring). Justice Stevens, too, concluded that the *Safeco* case was "another situation in which regulation of the means of expression is predicated squarely on its content." Yet he agreed that this content-based restriction was permissible because "picketing is a mixture of conduct and communication. In the labor context, it is the conduct element rather than the particular idea being expressed that often provides the most persuasive deterrent to third persons about to enter a business establishment. [The content discrimination in this case is constitutional because] the statutory ban in this case affects only that aspect of the union's efforts to communicate its views that calls for an automatic response to a signal, rather than a reasoned response to an idea" (618–19 [Stevens, J., concurring]).

65 *NLRB v. Retail Store Employees Union, Local 1001 (Safeco Title Insurance Company)*, 447 U.S., 622 (Brennan, J., dissenting).

66 Modjeska, "The *Tree Fruits* Consumer Picketing Case," 1005.

67 Modjeska, "The *Tree Fruits* Consumer Picketing Case," 1024, 1032: "The legislative history indicates that the President, proponents and opponents of the bills, and the members of the Conference Committee which compromised the differences between the Senate and House bills, all gave specific consideration to the question whether to prohibit all secondary consumer picketing, and that in the end, with full understanding of the import of their action, determined to do so."

68 310 U.S. 88, 101–2 (1940).

69 *Teamsters, Local 695, v. Vogt, Inc.*, 354 U.S. 284, 293 (1957).

70 *Electrical Workers, Local 501, v. NLRB (Langer)*, 341 U.S. 694, 705 (1951), rejecting a constitutional challenge to the NLRA's ban on peaceful picketing that violates the Act's secondary boycott provisions.

71 See *Fruit and Vegetable Packers and Warehousemen, Local 760, v. NLRB*, 308 F.2d 311, 316 (D.C. Cir. 1962).

72 In this section, I track the reasoning in Modjeska, "The *Tree Fruits* Consumer Picketing Case," 1036–38.

73 *Bakery and Pastry Drivers and Helpers Local, etc., v. Wohl*, 315 U.S. 769, 776–77 (1942) (Douglas, J., concurring). See also *Giboney v. Empire Storage and Ice Company*, 336 U.S. 490, 499 (1949): the signal to act must yield to the states' power "to set the limits of

permissible contest open to industrial combatants."

74   *Fruit and Vegetable Packers and Warehousemen, Local 760, v. NLRB*, 308 F.2d, 316, citing
Archibald Cox, "Strikes, Picketing and the Constitution," *Vanderbilt Law Review* 4 (1951):
574, 594.

75   *Fruit and Vegetable Packers and Warehousemen, Local 760, v. NLRB*, 308 F.2d, 316.

76   Modjeska, "The *Tree Fruits* Consumer Picketing Case," 1040.

77   *NLRB v. Fruit and Vegetable Packers and Warehousemen, Local 760 (Tree Fruits)*, 377 U.S.,
79 (Black, J., concurring).

78   485 U.S. 568 (1988).

79   485 U.S., 578.

80   182 F.3d 948 (D.C. Cir. 1999).

81   *Warshawsky and Company v. NLRB* 182 F.3d, 961 (Wald, J., dissenting).

82   *H. K. Porter Company v. NLRB*, 397 U.S. 99, 110 (1970) (Douglas, J, dissenting).

83   See, for instance, *Southwest Regional Council of Carpenters, Local 184 (New Star)*, 356 NLRB
613, 616–18 (2011) (member Hays, dissenting and relying on *Warshawsky* in support of a
broad ban on all union communication with neutral employees, notwithstanding that
no neutral employee ceased work).

84   See the discussion in Michael J. Hayes, "It's Now Persuasion, Not Coercion: Why Current
Law on Labor Protest Violates Twenty-First Century First Amendment Law," *Hofstra
Law Review* 47 (2018): 563: "The D.C. Circuit's position [regarding] the LMRA, is especially important because the D.C. Circuit is the only federal appellate court to which all
decisions of the NLRB can be appealed, and thus the only such court to which any and
all parties 'aggrieved' by a Board decision can appeal."

85   See the discussion in Kate Andrias, "Constitutional Clash: Labor, Capital, and Democracy," *Northwestern University Law Review* 118 (2024): 985, 1074, n. 440 (citing authority).

86   See Brishen Rogers, "Passion and Reason in Labor Law," *Harvard Civil Rights–Civil
Liberties Law Review* 47 (2012): 313, 328–29. Indeed, as James Gray Pope has shown, the
Supreme Court accords labor picketing less First Amendment protection than hate speech
and "fighting words" ("The First Amendment, the Thirteenth Amendment, and the Right
to Organize in the Twenty-First Century," *Rutgers Law Review* 51 [1999]: 941, 951–52). For
an example of the broad First Amendment protection provided to social protest other than
in the context of labor picketing, see *NAACP v. Claiborne Hardware Company*, 458 U.S.
886 (1982), which distinguishes broad constitutional protection accorded to civil rights
boycotts from the more constricted protection accorded to labor protest on the grounds
that the "delicate balance" of Congress justified existing prohibitions on the latter. See
the discussion of *Claiborne Hardware* in Hayes, "It's Now Persuasion, Not Coercion,"
630–31. Also see *NLRB v. Retail Store Employees Union, Local 1001 (Safeco Title Insurance
Company)*, 447 U.S., 618–19 (Stevens, J., concurring).

87   *Fruit and Vegetable Packers and Warehousemen, Local 760, v. NLRB*, 308 F.2d 311(D.C.
Cir. 1962), citing Cox, "Strikes, Picketing and the Constitution," 574, 594.

88   *Granite State Joint Board, Textile Workers Union, Local 1029*, 409 U.S. 213, 217 (1972).

89   Cynthia Estlund, "Are Unions a Constitutional Anomaly?," *Michigan Law Review* 114
(2015): 169, 225–28.

90   For a discussion of the leading case, *Lumber and Sawmill Workers, Local Union No. 2797
(Stoltze Land and Lumber)*, 156 NLRB 388 (1965), and of the continuing reliance on the
Stoltze Lumber view, see Hayes, "It's Now Persuasion, Not Coercion," 584–88. See also
Kate L. Rakoczy's comment in "On Mock Funerals, Banners, and Giant Rat Balloons:
Why Current Interpretation of Section 8(b)(4)(ii)(B) of the National Labor Relations Act
Unconstitutionality Burdens Union Speech," *American University Law Review* 56 (2007):
1621, which summarizes judicial decisions that find the use of symbols as a form of union
protest unlawful.

Chapter 8

1   397 U.S. 99 (1970).
2   417 U.S. 1 (1974).
3   462 U.S. 963 (1983).
4   510 U.S. 317 (1994).
5   602 U.S. 339 (2024).
6   353 U.S. 448 (1957).
7   *Steelworkers of America v. American Manufacturing Company*, 363 U.S. 564 (1960); *Steelworkers of America v. Warrior and Gulf Navigation Company*, 363 U.S. 574 (1960); *Steelworkers of America v. Enterprise Wheel and Car Corporation*, 363 U.S. 593 (1960).
8   375 U.S. 261 (1964).
9   379 U.S. 650 (1964).
10 385 U.S. 421 (1967).
11 385 U.S. 432 (1967).
12 393 U.S. 357 (1969).
13 398 U.S. 235 (1970).
14 414 U.S. 368 (1974).
15 428 U.S. 397 (1976).
16 430 U.S. 243 (1977).
17 501 U.S. 190 (1991).
18 563 U.S. 333 (2011).
19 584 U.S. 49 (2018).
20 587 U.S. 176 (2019).
21 369 U.S. 95 (1962).
22 390 U.S. 557 (1968).
23 471 U.S. 202 (1985).
24 482 U.S. 386 (1987).
25 481 U.S. 851 (1987).
26 486 U.S. 399 (1988).
27 495 U.S. 362 (1990).
28 512 U.S. 107 (1994).
29 *H. K. Porter Co. v. NLRB*, 397 U.S. 99 (1970); *NLRB v. Food Store Employees Union, Local 347*, 417 U.S. 1 (1974); *NLRB v. Transportation Management Corporation*, 462 U.S. 963 (1983); and *ABF Freight System, Inc. v. NLRB*, 510 U.S. 317 (1994).
30 NLRA, sec. 10(c).
31 The Supreme Court described the employer's bargaining strategy as designed "solely to frustrate the making of any collective-bargaining agreement" (*H. K. Porter Co. v. NLRB*, 397 U.S., 101).
32 William B. Gould IV, *Agenda for Reform: The Future of Employment Relationships and the Law* (Cambridge, MA: MIT Press, 1996), 220.
33 *H. K. Porter Co. v. NLRB*, 397 U.S., 102.
34 *H. K. Porter Co. v. NLRB*, 397 U.S., 100.
35 *H. K. Porter Co. v. NLRB*, 397 U.S., 110 (Harlan J., concurring).
36 *NLRB v. Food Store Employees Union, Local 347*, 417 U.S. 1 (1974).
37 194 NLRB 1234 (1972).
38 See the discussion in John E. Higgins, ed., *The Developing Labor Law: The Board, the Courts, and the National Labor Relations Act*, 7th ed. (Arlington, VA: Bloomberg BNA, 2017), 32–87, 32–88. See also *Thryv, Inc.*, 372 NLRB, no. 22, December 13, 2022: the NLRB

expanded remedies under the NLRA to include "all direct or foreseeable pecuniary harms suffered as a result of the respondent's unfair labor practice."

39 823 F.3d 668, 678–81 (D.C. Cir. 2016).

40 *HTH Corporation v. NLRB*, 823 F.3d, 676–79.

41 See *Camelot Terrace, Inc. v. NLRB*, 824 F.3d 1085, 1094–95 (D.C. Cir. 2016). Accord *NLRB v. Ampersand Publishing, LLC*, 43 F.4th 1233 (9th Cir. 2022), upholding the award of attorney fees generated in representing the union in collective bargaining, as distinguished from attorney fees generated in litigation.

42 372 NLRB, no. 22, slip op., 13, December 13, 2022, enforcement denied on other grounds; *Thryv, Inc. v. NLRB*, 102 F.4th 727 (5th Cir. 2024).

43 S.Ct., no. 22–859, June 27, 2024.

44 See NLRB, "Case Search Results," https://www.nlrb.gov.

45 462 U.S. 963 (1983); 510 U.S. 317 (1994).

46 *Starbucks Corporation v. McKinney, Regional Director of Region 15, NLRB*, S.Ct., no. 23–367.

47 *Miller v. California Pacific Medical Center*, 19 F. 3d 449, 460 (9th Cir. 1994), en banc.

48 *Starbucks Corp. v. McKinney, Regional Director of Region 15, NLRB*, S.Ct., no. 23–367 (Jackson, J., dissenting), citing *Boys Markets, Inc. v. Retail Clerks*, 398 U. S. 235, 250 (1970).

49 See case list at the beginning of this chapter.

50 363 U.S. 564 (1960); 363 U.S. 574 (1960); 363 U.S. 593 (1960).

51 See the discussion of the asserted advantages of labor arbitration over the judicial resolution of labor disputes in Alexander M. Bickel and Harry H. Wellington, "Legislative Purpose and the Judicial Process: The *Lincoln Mills* Case," *Harvard Law Review* 71 (1957): 1, 24–25, emphasizing arbitrators' special expertise and the informality, efficiency, and flexibility of the arbitration procedure.

52 Katherine Van Wezel Stone, "The Post-War Paradigm in American Labor Law," *Yale Law Journal* 90 (1981): 1509.

53 Stone, "The Post-War Paradigm," 1525–26.

54 Stone, "The Post-War Paradigm," 1528.

55 *Steelworkers v. Warrior and Gulf Navigation Company*, 363 U.S. 574, 580 (1960).

56 See, for example, Archibald Cox, "Reflections upon Labor Arbitration," *Harvard Law Review* 72 (1959): 1482, 1498–99, referring to the "governmental nature of the collective bargaining process" and the collective agreement as incorporating "a common law of the shop."

57 *Textile Workers Union v. Lincoln Mills*, 353 U.S. 448, 456 (1957).

58 *Steelworkers v. American Manufacturing Company*, 363 U.S. 564 (1960).

59 *Steelworkers v. Warrior and Gulf Navigation Company*, 363 U.S. 574, 582–83 (1960). See *Nolde Brothers v. Bakery and Confectionery Workers, Local 358*, 430 U.S. 243 (1977), holding that the presumption of arbitrability is so strong that the obligation to arbitrate contractual grievances may survive contract expiration.

60 *Steelworkers v. Enterprise Wheel and Car Corporation*, 363 U.S. 593, 597 (1960).

61 Stone, "The Post-War Paradigm," 1529.

62 375 U.S. 261, 270 (1964).

63 See *Collyer Insulated Wire*, 192 NLRB 837 (1971); and *Spielberg Manufacturing Company*, 112 NLRB 1080 (1955).

64 Cementing the primacy of arbitration over judicial enforcement of collective bargaining agreements required precluding individuals from circumventing the grievance-arbitration procedure by enforcing judicially claims that an employer had deprived an employee of a right secured by the collective bargaining agreement. This was accomplished in *Republic Steel Corporation v. Maddox*, 379 U.S. 650, 656 (1964).

65 385 U.S. 421 (1967).

66 *NLRB v. C & C Plywood Corporation*, 385 U.S., 428.

67 385 U.S. 432 (1967); 393 U.S. 357 (1969).

68 *NLRB v. Acme Industrial Company*, 385 U.S., 437.

69 501 U.S. 190 (1991).

70 Higgins, *The Developing Labor Law*, 8–12.

71 See *Gateway Coal Company v. United Mine Workers*, 414 U.S. 368, 380–84 (1974): "implied a no-strike obligation found in contracts containing duty to arbitrate; and *Local 174, Teamsters, v. Lucas Flour Company*, 369 U.S. 95, 104–06 (1962): a strike over a dispute covered by a contract's arbitration provision violates an agreement even in the absence of no-strike clause.

72 29 U.S.C., sec. 104 (1998).

73 See *New Negro Alliance v. Sanitary Grocery Company*, 303 U. S. 552, 561–62 (1938), explaining that Congress "deprive[d] the courts of jurisdiction to issue an injunction in any case involving or growing out of a labor dispute, except [under specified circumstances and with particular procedural checks]." See also *Marine Cooks v. Panama Steamship Company*, 362 U. S. 365, 369 (1960): "The language [of the Norris-LaGuardia Act] is broad because Congress was intent upon taking the federal courts out of the labor injunction business except in very limited circumstances."

74 See *Sinclair Refining Company v. Atkinson*, 370 U.S. 195 (1962), holding that collective bargaining agreements' no-strike clauses are not specifically enforceable in federal court. See also *Avco Corporation v. Aero Lodge 735*, 90 U.S. 557 (1968): a 301 suit brought in state court is removable to federal court. The combination of *Sinclair* and *Avco* severely truncated the availability of injunctions to remedy breaches of a no-strike clause. Such injunction actions would be dismissed if initially brought in federal court; if brought in state court, they could be removed to federal court where no injunction could be issued.

75 398 U.S. 235 (1970).

76 The Court in *Boys Market* reversed *Sinclair Refining Company v. Atkinson*, 370 U.S. 195 (1962).

77 428 U.S. 397 (1976).

78 *Buffalo Forge Company v. Steelworkers*, 428 U.S., 408.

79 See, for instance, Kate Hamaji, Rachel Deutsch, Elizabeth Nicolas, Celine McNicholas, Heidi Shierholz, and Margaret Poydock, "Unchecked Corporate Power: Forced Arbitration, the Enforcement Crisis, and How Workers Are Fighting Back" (May 2019), Center for Popular Democracy and Economic Policy Institute, https://www.populardemocracy.org.

80 See, for instance, Alexander J. Colvin, "The Metastasization of Mandatory Arbitration," *Chicago-Kent Law Review* 94 (2019): 3, 9–10, reporting results of a 2017 study finding that more than half of private sector, nonunion workers were subject to mandatory arbitration clauses.

81 Hamaji et al., "Unchecked Corporate Power," 1.

82 Simon Jacobs, "Arbitration and Title VII Pattern-or-Practice Claims after *Epic Systems*," *University of Chicago Law Review* 88 (2021): 1157, 1161–62.

83 Hamaji et al., "Unchecked Corporate Power," 3.

84 See, e.g., *Murphy Oil, USA, Inc.*, 361 NLRB 774 (2014): FLSA litigation initiated on behalf of an employee and other similarly situated employees alleged that the employer failed to compensate the plaintiffs for overtime and for various required work-related activities.

85 See the discussion in Jacobs, "Arbitration and Title VII Pattern-or-Practice Claims," 1165–68.

86 Jacobs, "Arbitration and Title VII Pattern-or-Practice Claims," 1160.

87 563 U.S. 333, 352 (2011).

88 *Lamps Plus, Inc. v. Varela*, 587 U.S. 176 (2019).

89 *Lamps Plus, Inc. v. Varela*, 587 U.S. 176, 185, citing *Stolt-Nielsen S.A. v. Animal Feeds International Corporation*, 559 U.S. 662, 687 (2010).

90 *Epic Systems v. Lewis*, 584 U.S. 497 (2018).

91   *Murphy Oil, USA, Inc.*, 361 N.L.R.B. 774 (2014).

92   *Epic Systems v. Lewis*, 138 S. Ct., 1625, quoting *NLRB v. Alternative Entertainment, Inc.*, 858 F.3d 393, 414–415 (6th Cir. 2017) (Sutton, J., concurring in part and dissenting in part).

93   Hamaji et al., "Unchecked Corporate Power," 2.

94   *McDonald v. City of West Branch*, Michigan, 466 U.S. 284, 291 (1984), quoting *Gardner-Denver*, 415 U.S., 57–58.

95   See Cynthia Estlund, "The Black Hole of Mandatory Arbitration," *North Carolina Law Review* 96 (2018): 679, 688, 696. Compare Samuel Estreicher, Michael Heise, and David S. Sherwyn, "Evaluating Employment Arbitration: A Call for Better Empirical Research," *Rutgers University Law Review* 70 (2018): 375, challenging Estlund's methodology and conclusions. See also Mark Gough, "A Tale of Two Forums: Employment Discrimination Outcomes in Arbitration and Litigation," *ILR Review* 74 (2021): 875, discussing studies showing that employee win rates and monetary awards are lower in arbitration than in litigation.

96   David Steele, "Law Profs Throw Flag on NFL's 'Unconscionable' Arbitration," *Law 360*, July 19, 2024, https://www.law360.com; Michael McCann, "Goodell's Role in Flores Case Sets 'Egregious' Precedent, Law Profs Warn," *Sportico*, March 22, 2023, https://www.sportico.com.

97   Public law 117–90, 135 Stat. 26 (codified at 9 U.S.C., secs. 401–2), effective March 3, 2022. The federal Pregnant Workers Fairness Act, enacted in 2022 (42 U.S.C., sec. 2000gg-1[1]), bans discrimination based on pregnancy. Because pregnancy discrimination is a form of sex discrimination, see 42 U.S.C., sec. 2000e(k) of the Ending Forced Arbitration of Sexual Assault and Sexual Harassment Act, which should prevent enforcement of forced arbitration agreements of sexual harassment claims based on pregnancy.

98   See, for instance, *Michael v. Bravo-Brio Restaurants, LLC*, no. 23–3691 (DNJ, June 10, 2024), unpublished, in which federal law barring forced arbitration of workplace sexual harassment claims covers a restaurant server's case against a supervisor over homophobic comments.

99   Restoring Justice for Workers Act, H.R. 2749 and S. 1491, 116th Congress (2019–20), prohibiting forced arbitration and class- and collective-action waivers in labor and employment disputes; Forced Arbitration Repeal Act, H.R. 1423, 116th Congress, (2019–20), eliminating forced arbitration clauses in employment, consumer, and civil rights cases.

100   Katherine Van Wezel Stone, "The Legacy of Industrial Pluralism: The Tension between Individual Employment Rights and the New Deal Collective Bargaining System," *University of Chicago Law Review* 59 (1992): 575, 635–36.

101   *Allis-Chalmers Corporation v. Lueck*, 471 U.S. 202, 220 (1985).

102   See *Textile Workers Union v. Lincoln Mills*, 353 U.S. 448 (1957).

103   369 U.S. 95 (1962).

104   390 U.S. 557 (1968).

105   471 U.S. 202 (1985).

106   471 U.S., 218.

107   In *Republic Steel Corporation v. Maddox*, 379 U.S. 650, 656 (1964), the Court had held that the national labor policy giving primacy to the arbitration process required that employees use the contract's grievance-arbitration procedure rather than seek redress judicially to resolve claims that an employer had deprived an employee of a right secured by a collective bargaining agreement.

108   482 U.S. 386 (1987).

109   *Caterpillar, Inc. v. Williams*, 482 U.S., 394–95 (citing *Lueck*).

110   481 U.S. 851 (1987).

111   *Steelworkers v. Rawson*, 495 U.S. 362 (1990), also involved a suit against a union. The case demonstrates how important the location of a duty of care is in 301 preemption

cases. In *Rawson*, survivors of miners killed in an underground fire brought a state-law wrongful-death action against the miners' union, alleging negligence in conducting safety inspections. The lower courts and the dissent located the union's agreement to inspect the mine as a gratuitous act, with the standard of care determined by common law tort principles not requiring any reference to the collective bargaining agreement. The Court's majority found 301 preemption by locating the union's authority to inspect, and thus the care owed in inspecting, in the collective bargaining agreement whose terms would be integral in adjudicating the dispute.

112   486 U.S. 399 (1988).
113   *Lingle v. Norge Division of Magic Chef,* 486 U.S., 410.
114   512 U.S. 107 (1994).
115   See Stone, "The Legacy of Industrial Pluralism," 606–7, listing cases typically preempted.
116   Mark L. Adams, "Struggling through the Thicket: Section 301 and the Washington Supreme Court," *Berkeley Journal of Employment and Labor Law* 5 (1994): 106, 110–11.

Chapter 9

1   *Railway Employees v. Hanson,* 51 U.S. 225 (1956); *Machinists v. Street,* 367 U.S. 740 (1961); *Railway Clerks v. Allen,* 373 U.S. 113 (1963); *NLRB v. General Motors Corporation,* 373 U.S. 734 (1963).
2   431 U.S. 209 (1977).
3   466 U.S. 435 (1984).
4   475 U.S. 292 (1986).
5   487 U.S. 735 (1988).
6   500 U.S. 507 (1991).
7   523 U.S. 866 (1998).
8   567 U.S. 298 (2012).
9   573 U.S. 616 (2014).
10 578 U.S. 1 (2016).
11 585 U.S. 878 (2018).
12 388 U.S. 175 (1967).
13 391 U.S. 418 (1968).
14 394 U.S. 423 (1969).
15 409 U.S. 213 (1972).
16 412 U.S. 67 (1973).
17 412 U.S. 84 (1973).
18 473 U.S. 95 (1985).
19 481 U.S. 573 (1987).
20 *Railway Employees v. Hanson,* 51 U.S. 225, 232 (1956), reasoning that the negotiation and enforcement of union security agreements authorized by the RLA constitutes government action on which the Constitution operates because that act preempts all state laws banning union-security agreements and therefore is the source of authority by which private rights are compromised.
21 487 U.S. 735 (1988).
22 *Communication Workers of America v. Beck,* 487 U.S. 735, 761 (1988).
23 367 U.S. 740 (1961); 373 U.S. 113 (1963); 373 U.S. 734 (1963).
24 *Communication Workers v. Beck,* 487 U.S., at 751, citing *Machinists v. Street,* 367 U.S., 764.
25 *Machinists v. Street,* 367 U.S., 774.
26 431 U.S. 209 (1977).

27   *Abood v. Detroit Board of Education*, 431 U.S., 235.

28   *Abood v. Detroit Board of Education*, 431 U.S., 236.

29   *Ellis v. Brotherhood of Railway Clerks*, 466 U.S. 435 (1984).

30   *Ellis v. Brotherhood of Railway Clerks*, 466 U.S., 448. Later in the decision, the Court reformulated the test as a three-part evaluation required by the Constitution, but the reformulation did not affect which union expenditures the Court found were legally chargeable to objectors. See also *Lehnert v. Ferris Faculty Association*, 500 U.S. 507, 519 (1991), also restating this three-part test.

31   *Lehnert v. Ferris Faculty Association*, 500 U.S. 507, 527–32 (1991). For an extensive analysis of categories of union expenditures that courts have found to be chargeable or nonchargeable to dues objectors, see the discussion in William W. Osborne, Jr., ed., *Labor Union Law and Regulation*, 2nd ed. (Chicago: American Bar Association, Section of Labor and Employment Law, 2017), 5-78-5-97.

32   *Chicago Teachers Union v. Hudson*, 475 U.S. 292 (1986); *Airline Pilots v. Miller*, 523 U.S. 866 (1998). For an excellent review and discussion of those procedures, see Osborne, *Labor Union Law and Regulation*, 5-35-5-78.

33   *Knox v. Service Employees International Union, Local 1000*, 567 U.S. 298 (2012).

34   *Knox v. Service Employees International Union, Local 1000*, 567 U.S., 317.

35   *Knox v. Service Employees International Union, Local 1000*, 567 U.S., 311, 317.

36   *Harris v. Quinn*, 573 U.S. 616 (2014).

37   *Harris v. Quinn*, 573 U.S. at 635.

38   *Friedrichs v. California Teachers Association*, 578 U.S. 1 (2016).

39   *Janus v. American Federation of State, County, and Municipal Employees, Counsel 31*, 585 U.S. 878 (2018).

40   *Janus v. American Federation of State, County, and Municipal Employees, Counsel 31*, 585 U.S., 893.

41   See the discussion in Kate Andrias, "Constitutional Clash: Labor, Capital, and Democracy," *Northwestern University Law Review* 118 (2024): 985, 1047–49.

42   See *National Association of Manufacturers v. NLRB*, 717 F.3d 947, 959 (D.C. Cir. 2013), finding that the required posted notices constitute unconstitutional compelled speech. It was overruled by *American Meat Institute v. U.S. Department of Agriculture*, 760 F.3d 18 (D.C. Cir. 2014).

43   *Denton County Electrical Cooperative, Inc. v. NLRB*, 962 F.3d 161, 174 (5th Cir. 2020). See the discussion in Andrias, "Constitutional Clash," 1047–48.

44   The Court has held that union-security agreements in the RLA sector are imbued with governmental action to the extent that the RLA preempts local right-to-work laws. See *Railway Employees Department v. Hanson*, 351 U.S. 225 (1956).

45   See Michelle Quach, "The *Janus* Decision and the Future of Private Sector Unionism," 16 *Hastings Business Law Journal* 16 (2020): 119, 129–30.

46   See Roger C. Hartley, "Reconceiving the Role of Section 8(B)(1)(A)—1947–1997: An Essay on Collective Empowerment and the Public Good," *Catholic University Law Review* 47 (1998): 825, 870–74, app. A, summarizing the legislative history of section 8(b)(1)(A).

47   See Archibald Cox, "Some Aspects of the Labor Management Relations Act, 1947," part 1, *Harvard Law Review* 61 (1947): 1; and Archibald Cox, "Some Aspects Of the Labor Management Relations Act, 1947," part 2, *Harvard Law Review* 61 (1947): 274.

48   362 U.S. 274 (1960).

49   *NLRB v. Allis-Chalmers Manufacturing Company*, 388 U.S. 175, 185 (1967), holding that court enforcement of fines against a union member for crossing picket lines did not "restrain or coerce" employees within the meaning of the NLRA.

50   *NLRB v. Boeing Company*, 412 U.S. 67, 71 (1973): the reasonableness of a union fine for a member is not justiciable.

51   391 U.S. 418 (1968).

52   *NLRB v. Industrial Union of Marine and Shipbuilding Workers*, 391 U.S., 421, 424–26.
     By 1968, relying on neither the text of the NLRA nor its legislative history but without
     abandoning any of its previous holdings or rationalizations, the NLRB simply held that
     the freedom of self-regulation assured to unions by section 8(b)(1)(A) is trumped if dis-
     cipline "run[s] counter to other recognized public policies." See *Local 138, International
     Union of Operating Engineers*, 148 NLRB 679, 682 (1964).

53   394 U.S. 423, 429–30 (1969).

54   See Hartley, "Reconceiving the Role of Section 8(B)(1)(A)," 873–76, app. B, collecting
     section 8(b)(1)(A) union discipline cases; and Osborne, *Labor Union Law and Regulation*,
     1-91-1-94, discussing, for example, use of section 8(b)1)(A) to prohibit union discipline
     of members who solicited authorization cards for another union, crossed a lawful union
     picket line, or refused to join other members in engaging in lawful concerted activity
     that section 7 does not protect.

55   *NLRB v. Granite State Joint Board, Textile Workers Union of America, Local 1029*, 409
     U.S. 213 (1972).

56   *NLRB v. Granite State Joint Board, Textile Workers Union of America, Local 1029*, 409
     U.S., 217.

57   *Booster Lodge No. 405, Intern. Association of Machinists and Aerospace Workers v. NLRB*,
     412 U.S. 84 (1973).

58   In a companion case, *NLRB v. Boeing Company*, 412 U.S. 67 (1973), the Court held that
     the reasonableness of a union fine against a member was not subject to judicial review.

59   *Pattern Makers League of North America v. NLRB*, 473 U.S. 95 (1985).

60   *Pattern Makers League of North America v. NLRB*, 473 U.S, 117 (Blackmun, J., dissenting).

61   Holman W. Jenkins, Jr., "Free Ron Carey! Repeal the Wagner Act!," *Wall Street Journal*,
     October 14, 1997.

Conclusion

1   *NLRB v. J. Weingarten, Inc.*, 420 U.S. 251, 262 (1975).

2   *NLRB v. City Disposal Systems, Inc.*, 465 U.S. 822, 835 (1984). The Court added that the
     Board's *Interboro* doctrine—applying section 7 protection to the actions of individual
     employees who are invoking their rights under a collective bargaining agreement—is
     "based on a recognition that the potential inequality in the relationship between the
     employee and the employer continues beyond the point at which a collective-bargaining
     agreement is signed, mitigates that inequality throughout the duration of the employment
     relationship, and is, therefore, fully consistent with congressional intent" (836).

3   See chapter 3 for these cases and citations.

4   *NLRB v. Allis-Chalmers Manufacturing Company*, 388 U.S. 175, 185 (1967), holding that
     court enforcement of fines against a union member for crossing picket lines did not
     "restrain or coerce" employees within the meaning of the Act.

5   The Labor-Management Reporting and Disclosure Act, 29 U.S.C., chap. 11. secs. 401–531,
     was enacted in 1959, and it added some substantive changes to the NLRA, but none are
     implicated in the post-1970s Supreme Court labor cases discussed in this book.

6   *Jarkesy v. Security and Exchange Commission*, 34 F.4th 446 (5th Cir. 2022), affirmed on
     other grounds, U.S., 144 S. Ct. 2117 (2024).

7   *Jarkesy v. Security and Exchange Commission*, 34 F.4th, 465.

8   2024 WL 4202383 (N.D. TX, September 16, 2024). Accord *Space Exploration Technologies
     Corporation v. NLRB*, 41 F.Supp.3d 630 (W.D. TX 2024). The NLRB was enjoined from

proceeding against an employer because of the substantial likelihood that both the NLRB members and the ALJs were unconstitutionally insulated from removal.

9   If the Supreme Court agrees to review *Humphrey's Executor v. United States*, 295 U.S. 602 (1935), and reverse this ninety-year-old precedent, Congress will not be able to limit the president's ability to remove members of administrative commissions such as the NLRB. This change in the relations between Congress and the executive branch may then preserve the constitutionality of the NLRA and permit the NLRB to continue to function but will result in the specter of a wholesale replacement of NLRB members following each change of presidential administration.

United Mine Workers v. Arkansas Oak Flooring Company (1956), 30
United States v. Hutcheson (1940), 19
United Steelworkers of America v. Saint Gabriel's Hospital (1994), 193n33
university faculty, 15, 18–21, 57

Wald, Patricia, 126
Warren, Earl, 204n56
Warren Court (1953–1969): on access to employer property, 41–42; on secondary strikes, 111–12; on statutory coverage, 13–14; on successor liability, 50–53. *See also specific cases*

Warshawsky and Company v. NLRB (1999), 125–26
wealth gap, ix–xii
Weiler, Paul C., 181nn21–2
whipsaw strikes, 89–93, 97, 102–3
White, Ahmed, 71, 85, 86–87
White, Byron, 36, 118, 200n40, 204n56
Woelke and Romero Framing, Inc. v. NLRB (1982), 117–18
worker solidarity, 107–10, 158
work preservation doctrine, 110–17

Yeshiva University, 15, 18–21, 57

www.ingramcontent.com/pod-product-compliance
Lightning Source LLC
Chambersburg PA
CBHW030733280326
41926CB00086B/1339